Trials of the Heart

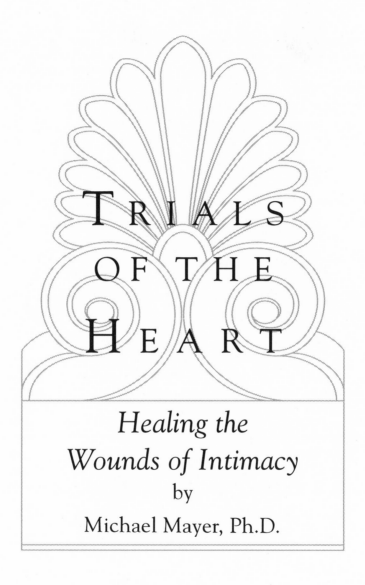

TRIALS OF THE HEART

Healing the
Wounds of Intimacy

by

Michael Mayer, Ph.D.

Celestial Arts
Berkeley, California

Cover design by Fifth Street Design

Text design by Victor Ichioka

First Celestial Arts Printing 1993

Library of Congress Cataloging-in-Publication Data

Mayer, Michael, 1947–
    Trials of the heart: healing the wounds of intimacy / by Michael Mayer.
        p. cm.
    Includes bibliographical references and index.
    ISBN 0-89087-700-9
    1. Intimacy (Psychology) 2. Conflict (Psychology)
3. Interpersonal relations. 4. Mythology—Psychological aspects.
5. Initiation rites—Mythology. I. Title
BF575.I5M284   1993
158'.2—dc20   93-30267 CIP

1 2 3 4 5 6 7 / 99 98 97 96 95 94 93

The excerpt on page 172 from *The Road Less Traveled*, ©1978 by M. Scott Peck, M.D. is reprinted with permission by Simon and Schuster, Inc.

The poem by Rumi on page 203 is excerpted from *Open Secret* and appears by permission of Threshold Books, RD 4, Box 600, Putney VT 05346.

Dedication

This book is dedicated to fellow journeyers on the path of love. May you keep this book in mind while you sit in coffeehouses, lounge at beaches, ride in subways, take breaks at work, or relax at home with your partners. May it attract into your lives deep sharing about the Trials of the Heart— may it help you to become initiates in the Temple of Love.

For in every place there is a potential to meet Ariadne who may help us find the thread to go down into our depths, and in every moment our psyches have an opportunity to discover Eros, who may compassionately wipe away the sleep from our eyes, opening us to the deeper mysteries of love.

TABLE OF CONTENTS

SECTION 3: FINDING OUR OWN PERSONAL MYTH

PREFACE

So long as human beings change and make history, so long as children are born and old people die, there will be tales to explain why sorrow darkens the day and stars fill the night. We invent stories about the origin and conclusion of life because they help us find our way, our place at the heart of the mystery.

SAM KEEN

Healing Stories

Stories have always been close to my heart. When I was very young my father would tell me one at bedtime each night. It was one of my first bonds with him. Later, stories took on another purpose in our home; they were used to control me. I was told stories of children who did their homework and became successful in life, and I was expected to do the same. I soon realized that if I could find an image, example, or story that contradicted theirs, I could release my parents' control of me. "What about the Beatles?" I asked. "They became successful without being bookworms."

Gradually I became like Scheherazade in the *Arabian Nights*. To stay alive, Scheherazade was to tell the King a new story every night; if not, she would be beheaded. My quest, like hers, was to save myself. I searched for tales from distant cultures to contradict my parents' stories.

For instance, one of the battles revolved around my tendency to daydream for hours. My parents told me a story which ended with "Life is with people. " On my Scheherazadian quest to save myself, I discovered that centuries ago there were people called shamans who retreated to the woods and learned healing secrets. They discovered these secrets from self-reflection, being with nature, and opening themselves to Wakantanka, the Great Mystery. Their solitary connection with nature and the universe was highly valued by their culture. From people like them, though they came from a distant world, I realized the value of my aloneness. My parents listened.

Long before I understood the use of stories in psychotherapy, I had developed a deep appreciation for the power and value of cross-cultural storytelling. Stories had been central to my survival and healing.

In earlier times, myths and stories explained the world to people bewildered by natural phenomena, assisted them through life's passages, and enabled them to participate in the mysteries of the cosmos. When people felt lost, they would go to a spiritual leader of the village or tribe who would comfort and heal them with a story. These early healers of the psyche were masters of the symbolic process. Their ability to translate the symbolic language of nature and dreams soothed and transformed the soul.[1] Their words transported the person from the mundane to the wider universe of meaning. Like Scheherazade gathered stories from diverse traditions to heal the wounds of love, so shall we cast our net wide to gather the myths, fairy tales, and initiatory practices of ancient cultures. These ancient sacred wisdom traditions will be woven together with current psychological knowledge and stories of modern lovers to heal the wounds of our love lives. We will bring them back to the King in us who, at the same time that he is on the verge of killing love, asks for the vitality of new stories from a wider kingdom to heal his troubled relationship with the potential Queen of his life.

Maybe the King in us unconsciously knows that symbols from the inner world have the power to break impasses to love when all else seems to fail. Just as a dream sends us messages from our psyches, so do these ancient tales give us a message from the collective psyche. Hearing the right story is similar to a healing dream—it lifts us out of the problem and brings a new and fresh perspective.

For example, having breathing room in my relationships is very important to me. When I'm in a creative mood, another person's presence in my space sometimes unnerves me. Then I remember a wonderful story about a rabbi. A man like myself who got married came to him because he had a hard time adjusting to close quarters. As a bachelor he could do whatever he wanted to in his house.

The rabbi replied that each day of the week he should bring one of the animals from his yard into the house. "Add one animal every day," said the rabbi, "except on the Sabbath, when, of course, you should just rest." On the first day, the man brought in the dog, next the goat, then a chicken, until finally he had six animals (including the cow) in the house. According to plan, on the day after the Sabbath he reported back to the rabbi. He was angry with the rabbi and said that this plan did not work. It was worse than ever; now he had no space. Then the rabbi told him to take one animal out of the house each day. By the end of the week, the man felt so happy to be alone with his wife, appreciating all the room he had![2]

Stories do have the capacity to change our perspective. Regardless of the form—whether told to us in our dreams, by the light of day, or by a campfire at night, they can bring us healing awareness.

This book contains personal stories of my clients and students who have struggled, like all of us, to find their own mythic solutions to relationship issues. I owe the greatest of thanks to these storytellers, for they have found images that speak to the very heart of the human predicament. For confidentiality purposes, their names and other particulars have been altered without distorting their experiences. Their journeys have helped my own, and what is presented here is what we have learned together. Each example, like all of our lives, is a story still in the making, a mythic journey in process.

By not including a psychomythological perspective into our understanding of love, we commit a crime analogous to our culture's trampling over the Native Americans; we got to occupy the land, but lost the sacred knowledge of how to be with its treasures. This book is an exploration of the treasure-house of ancient psychomythological perspectives on our psyche's initiation through the trials of love.

---

[1] Joseph Campbell's television interviews with Bill Moyers helped to acquaint people with his life's work, *Hero with a Thousand Faces*. World Publishing Co., 1949; *The Masks of God* series. Penguin Books 1959-1969 etc.; Robert Bly is a key figure in the men's movement and is known for his poetry including his translation of Rilke and the books, *Iron John: A Book for Men, A Little Book on the Human Shadow*; James Hillman is known for spearheading the movement in Archetypal Psychology and his writings such as *Revisioning Psychology*. Harper and Row, 1975.

[2] Retold from a story in *Counseling in the Hassidic Tradition*.

Acknowledgements

For assistance in developing the heart of this book and serving as Ariadne by giving me the threads to find the way to work on my inner Minotaur: Deborah Knighton, Donna Matera, Jean Hayek, Sonia Hernandez, Deborah Gallo, Nancy Sharfstein and those many others with whom I have danced the dance in the labyrinth of love.

Those authors whose intellectual seeds and perennial wisdom helped this book to sprout: Robert Bly, Joseph Campbell, Edward Edinger, Helen Fisher, Eugene Gendlin, Marija Gimbutas, Robert Graves, James Hillman, Jean Houston, Robert Johnson, Carl Jung, Sam Keen, Stanley Krippner, John Welwood and numerous significant others.

My parents, Abraham and Freda Mayer, whose love still remains strong well into its fourth decade. My thanks for having a model for love's ability to sustain through a lifetime, and to be able to be part of the heartfelt, intense and stimulating communication that happened through it all.

My friends, colleagues, and support system who gave me emotional, intellectual and spiritual sustenance, guidance, and feedback during the course of working on *Trials of the Heart*: Paul Baum, Mark Fromm, Michael Gach, Demetra George, Cynthia Yaguda Gould, Alena Hutchinson, Sandy Rosenberg, Yannis Toussulis, Katie Wesdorf, Bryan Wittine, and David Yulansey.

Sifu Fong Ha and my other Tai Chi and Chi Gung teachers, Ken Cohen, Cai Sang Fang, Al Huang, and Han Sing Yuen, who have taught me to simply stand, move as a meditation, dance with life, and not so simply, be.

Deborah Grandinetti, Rona Spalten, and Sherry Weinstein for creative editorial input and believing in the vision of this book. My deep appreciation for your clearing the ventricles of *Trials of the Heart*, making it beat with a more harmonious rhythm. Special thanks to Veronica Randall, Managing Editor, who carried the weight of hard decisions, put in the extra effort needed, and streamlined the book for publication.

My agent Peter Beren for opening the pathway to Celestial Arts.

Celestial Arts for giving the seeds in this book a ground from which they can grow.

SECTION 1:

THE HEART'S

JOURNEY

CHAPTER 1
RELATIONSHIP AS A
RITE OF INITIATION

---

*For one human being to love
another: that is perhaps the
most difficult task of all...,
the work for which all other
work is but preparation.
It is a high inducement to the
individual to ripen...a great
exacting claim upon us, something that chooses us out and
calls us to vast things.*

RAINER MARIA RILKE

Picture a Native American warrior one hundred years ago, attached to a rope by an eagle's claw that rips into the muscles around his heart as he swirls around a sacred wooden pole. While this Sioux, Arapaho, or Blackfoot initiate blew on an eagle's wing-bone whistle, he prayed to the sun and Wakantanka (the *Great Mystery* that pervades all things) for strength and wisdom.[1] This image captures the feeling of many relationships today.

If you think the analogy is stretched, look in a therapist's office and witness the pain and anguish on a jilted spouse's face, called upon to change a pattern that contributed to the dissolution of a thirty-year marriage. This spouse, left dangling and suffering, becomes like the Native American Sun Dance initiate, looking to the sun in the heavens above and to the Great Mystery, to shed light on the situation.

Our culture is now undergoing such an initiatory experience. But it's not the solid tree of the sacred Sun Dance Lodge from which we hang, it's the shaky center beam of our culture's house of relationship. We were raised on "Father Knows Best" and "Leave It to Beaver." We believed that relationships lasted forever and if we met the right person, we'd live "happily ever after" like Cinderella and Prince Charming.

Today, the divorce rate is climbing. Recent statistics report forty to fifty percent of marriages in the United States end in divorce.[2] Seventy percent of Americans engage in an affair sometime during their marital life.[3] Even the royal couple Prince Charles and Princess Diana have separated. Here in the emotionally charged atmosphere of the '90s, battered women's shelters abound. Sexuality is undergoing vast changes in many other ways, too. Life in the '80s and '90s seems like a horror movie produced by a cosmic trickster. First herpes arrived on the scene, giving the free love culture of the '60s a need for caution. Then, with the AIDS crisis, the unconscious fear that men and women have always had about relationships became literalized— "being with him or her could kill me." Relationships are not what we thought they would be.

When suffering enters our lives, it's natural to wonder why, for the desire to understand our suffering is basic to being human. Is there some grand design at play, some wider meaning, or are we living in a meaningless cosmos, spun around by the chaotic forces of fate? The most mundane person becomes a philosopher in a moment of pain, and enters into relationship with the Great Mystery, by whatever name it's called.

The following folk story gives a Buddhist perspective on suffering in relationships:

> *In the olden days, there was a time when the Demons of Sickness were very powerful.... It got so bad the people complained to Lord Buddha, "Where is your compassion?" they cried. "We are grievously afflicted with the Sickness Demons, and they are rampaging freely over the land. You must save us." So the Buddha called the Chief of the Sickness Demons (Mahakola Sanniyaksaya), who came before him.*
>
> *"You must stop afflicting my people," said the Buddha. "But, Lord Buddha," said the Great Sickness Demon, for he was wise and crafty, "the people are lazy and given to self-gratification.... It is we who keep the people humble and pious. When they are well, they strut around and fatten their egos. When they are sick, their eyes roll heavenward, they begin to think of what they have done wrong, and meditate upon spiritual things and the nature of their attachment to the chain of suffering."[4]*

If we asked Mahakola Sanniyaksaya today about suffering in relationships, we might hear the same answer that Buddha did: "Suffering exists to make our eyes roll heavenward." As we look upward to the heavens, we may become aware of the connection between our lives and the wider whole of which we are a small but integral part.

This idea is expressed in the Hermetic axiom, "As above so below." This ancient message, taught by Thoth, the greatest Egyptian high priest, is that there is an order to the universe whereby the lower level of reality reflects the higher order of things. For example, to refer to the stomach, one must refer to the next higher order—the body—to understand its state of being; and the body reflects our state of mind, the next higher order, and so on.

Changing Relationship Patterns: A Socio-cultural Point of View

Marshall McLuhan's often quoted phrase "the medium is the message"[5] is a contemporary way of stating the Hermetic axiom— our relationships reflect the realties of our wider socio-cultural

5

environment. Living in a high-tech world, we spend our days in "over-choice," shifting quickly from one product to another, always searching for the latest and the best. At the local supermarket our heads spin as we choose from many different brands of tuna fish, spaghetti sauce, and cat food. If you're "health conscious," there are innumerable exercise programs and diets from which to choose. (Enough to make you sick with worry.)

Alvin Toffler, in his book *Future Shock*,[6] predicted that this world of over-choice would produce a supermarket mentality in terms of re-lationships. And now we do inhabit a world where many people dis-card relationships like they throw away products with built-in obsolescence.

Our childhood memories, or at least those of our parents or grand-parents, recall a simpler world where we might live in one town for a lifetime. Not long ago, choice was not an option in the arena of rela-tionship; arranged marriages were common. For Catholics, divorce was impossible; and prevailing cultural norms and social stigma compelled couples to stay in stifling marriages.

In this era of high divorce rate and the death of permanence in relationships, traditional guidelines have dissolved. The modern person is married to a sea of endless possibility—with both positive and nega-tive results.

The issue of over-choice is reflected in a public speaker's dream: *I am about to give a speech and have gathered so much information from so many different sources that as I begin, I realize that I've forgotten the purpose of the speech.*

The problem can also be seen in the rise of the latest psychological category: borderline personality organization. As we read the Diagnostic and Statistical Manual of The American Psychiatric Association, we see the parallels to our fast-paced society: unstable and intense interper-sonal relationships, identity disturbance manifested by uncertainty about several issues relating to identity, affective instability, chronic feel-ings of emptiness or boredom. The borderline syndrome is an extreme manifestation of the loss of a cohesive sense of self and center.

Manifestations of this loss of self in a world of expanding possi-bilities are: not knowing what to do when the television is turned off, feeling hypnotized by idealized images of men and women and forget-ting the purpose of relationship, or getting so trapped in varied role ex-pectations that we "burn out" (i.e. the superwoman-housewife).

Telephone lines and other mechanical mediums have become the stage for the enactment of mythic dramas, as much as the bedroom was in the past. One lover is anxiously on hold while another enters the sanctum of "call waiting." Returning home from a tedious day, a tired husband turns on cable TV and compulsively changes channels by remote control as he carries on a half-hearted conversation with his partner. People play "phone tag" with answering machines, deciding whether or not to answer incoming calls from loved ones. Sometimes significant love affairs are ended on tape. Hearts hang in electronic space as more and more people seem to be members of the Non-Phone Callers Society of the Modern World. (If you're forlorn and want to join to be closer to your "intimate connections," don't bother, the society doesn't return phone calls.) Love is undergoing the difficult process of trying to have intercourse in a mechanical world!

The world increasingly seems like the one depicted in the film *Koyaanisqatsi*, which means "world in chaos" in the Hopi language. In this film, through advanced time-lapse photography, one gets a sense of just how fast-paced is modern life. The film overlays an image of a rush-hour subway with a meat processing plant depicting "the meat market" life in the fast lane. The film juxtaposes grid-locked traffic jams with beautiful high-speed photography of freeways at night, where headlights merge and transform traffic into moving strands of pearls. Both a blessing and a curse, the beauty and horror of modern technology leave the viewer of this film ambivalent about its effect, wondering whether moving at this pace will destroy us or lead us to a super-world.

Certainly, moving at this pace as a society whose nervous system has not been programmed to cope with such rapid change does inevitably cause death for some, nervous breakdown for others, and a wide variety of stress reactions for most of us. We who were raised in an automobile age are now being asked to operate at light speed. But beyond the apparent negative effects, the visionary can see a purpose in the change. The same technology that brings stress to us has unlimited potential to expand the capacities of the human mind, body, and spirit.

For generations, a major purpose of relationship was biological procreation—now we have sperm banks. For generations, people stayed together for security needs—now we have social security.[7] Although basic needs like procreation and security still play a part in our relationships, we now inhabit a world of greater personal choice. And it is this "choice" that's the blessing and curse, the gift from heaven and the dragon of the underworld.

There is an endless variety of relationships, unimaginable even a generation ago. Computer dating, serial monogamy, the sexual identity revolution, and single parents surround us and contradict our concepts of what it means to have "a normal relationship." Interracial marriage is relatively commonplace, and homosexuality is more widely accepted than ever before.

With more choices, the individual can find his or her unique meanings to the trials of intimate relationship. Though it is difficult adapting to all the new forms at light speed, each person has the opportunity to stretch his or her evolutionary capacities to find the pearls on the freeway of modern relationship.

A Cosmocentric View

Before the Copernican revolution, we believed that the universe revolved around a single center. Relationships also revolved around a single significant other. Our belief now in an expanding universe parallels the range of relationship possibilities.

We can explore the symbolic meanings of celestial bodies to find answers about the changing tide of relationships. Whether we believe astrology is a science or not, we can approach it like a psychologist who studies the responses of people to Rorschach cards . . . aspects of our inner universe are revealed.[8]

Some people believe a direct relationship exists between the planets and our lives. An essential belief of the ancient sacred wisdom traditions was that events of this world were reflections of a wider whole; and, as Mahakola Sanniyaksaya taught the Buddha, the meaning of our suffering is illuminated by looking to the heavens above.

Carl Jung brought this idea into modern psychology with his discussion of "synchronicity," the coincidences that we experience in life derive from a mysterious non-causal connecting principle of the universe. For instance, when we dream about someone that we haven't seen for years, and that person telephones the next morning, the coincidence fills our life with meaning and leads us to consider underlying unity in the universe. A sense of sacredness, wonder, and awe may be born. According to the doctrine of synchronicity, "whatever is born or done in this moment of time has the quality of this moment of time," like a wine made in a particular year has the qualities of the rainfall, weather, and soil conditions of that year.

From the point of view of astrological synchronicity, there is purpose to the changes we are undergoing in the realm of relationship. The 1960s and 1970s marked the movement of the Trans-saturnian planets into the zodiacal signs of relationship (which start with Libra). These are the planets past Saturn: Uranus, Neptune, and Pluto. Since these planets are beyond what the naked eye can see, they are said to represent spiritual realities or aspects of our collective unconscious.

The astrological signs beginning with Libra symbolize relationships with others, while those preceding Libra are related to individual unfoldment. Libra is situated at the time of the fall equinox, when the balance of light and darkness shift so that the nights are longer than the days, i. e. the realm of the collective begins to overshadow the realm of the individual. Perhaps Libra's symbolic meaning derives from the fact that winter was the time when our ancestors depended upon the community and relationships for warmth and sustenance during the cold times ahead. Libra, the autumn equinox, signaled the beginning of these shared times.

In November 1983, Pluto completed a 245-year cycle and returned to its home sign, Scorpio, and will not move into Sagittarius until January of 1995. A fixed water sign (water relates to feelings), Scorpio symbolizes the intense feelings that arise in intimate relationship. Like acid, the energy of Scorpio deeply penetrates whatever it contacts. It has been called the sign of death, rebirth, and transformation; for the Scorpion's sting kills, but has the power to transform through the pain it brings—if one survives.

Synchronistically, death does seem to be visiting the area of relationship in our culture, and perhaps this has a positive meaning along with pain. Though the AIDS crisis epitomizes the darkest fears about relationship, this deadly disease also has transformative potential. Both herpes and AIDS have caused people to more consciously choose their sexual partners.[9]

Astrological symbologists point out that when Pluto, the planet farthest away in the deep reaches of space, entered Libra in October 1971, deep and far-reaching changes came in the way we related to others. Following the free love era of the 1960s, the early 1970s signaled a new consciousness and deeper dimension of sexual intimacy. And when Pluto entered Scorpio (the sign of sexuality) in 1984, AIDS changed the way we related to others sexually. It was determined that AIDS was a sexually transmitted disease, and cases were doubling every six months in the United States—another cosmic synchronicity that makes us "look to the heavens" and wonder about the mystical order of things and the meaning of suffering.

It may seem that when Pluto entered the signs of relationship our culture entered into a consciousness that dwelt on the dark side of love. The last twenty years have seen an explosion of sensational stories in the media. Vicious incidents of wife battering, horrifying cases of child abuse, date rape, and murderous "crimes of passion" have become commonplace. Dating and family life have become dangerous occupations.

However, it would be erroneous to think that only because of Pluto's presence in Scorpio men and women have begun to struggle with deep emotional conflicts and murderous impulses. Twenty-five hundred years ago Socrates understood the pain of a difficult relationship: "By all means marry, if you have a good one you'll be happy; if you have a bad one you'll become a philosopher." What, then, is the significance of Pluto in the signs of relationship?

The scorpion is a hunter whose tail whips up and over it's head while holding its prey in its pincers. The venomous sting can kill its prey, but sometimes it misses and kills itself. The return of Pluto to the sign of Scorpio from 1984 to 1995 heralds a time when we must come to a painful realization—that when we lash out at each other, we end up stinging and killing ourselves.

A higher evolution of Scorpio is the Eagle. So perhaps we are being called upon to evolve to a higher vision of the emotional conflicts between the sexes. When one member of a couple attacks their partner for "not being feeling enough" or "not contributing enough to the household," a higher "eagle" vision enables us to see the issues that we are confronting as part of broad cultural themes that the sexes have been struggling with in their dance through time. Such a perspective invites us to find a way to present our emotional issues with the outstretched hands of partnership rather than the grabbing pincers of our emotional attachment.

Our task, in this era of Pluto in Scorpio, is to follow wherever our relationships take us on the journey to meet the demons of our underworld. Through reflection upon our emotional suffering, it is possible to see how our feelings and myths can function like the blood of the

Hydra: they can heal or kill. For example, the biblical myth of Eve's creation from Adam's rib has been used to demean women. And the argument that male power is inherently associated with violence is experienced by men as a scorpion's sting.

A Mythological and Initiatory Perspective

A mythological analysis of Pluto in Libra and Scorpio adds understanding to the meaning of suffering visiting the house of relationship in our culture. In Greek mythology, Pluto was the God of Death and the Underworld. He abducted Persephone, a naive maiden, from the land of innocence, and initiated her into the deeper knowledge of relationship. Though her worried mother, Demeter, would have argued that nothing positive could result from her daughter's pain, Persephone was transformed into a mature adult and Queen of the Underworld.

Like Persephone, we have been abducted by Pluto and are being forced to mature. It is a time of death for many myths—particularly our hero myths. Our cultural heroes have been exposed by the mass media in ways that almost instantly destroy our ideals. The sexual exploits of politicians, of gurus, and of fundamentalist preachers have shattered their images. Yet this destruction is of value—it encourages us to understand the multifaceted nature of human beings.

Carl Jung said that the greater the light, the darker the shadow. He believed that the integration of our darker side, the shadow, was a fundamental part of the individuation process. Our culture is now visiting the dark side of love.

Our youthful ideals—the myths of permanent and stable relationships, of happily-ever-after marriages, of clear-cut roles between masculine and feminine, of another person fulfilling our ideals—are undergoing a process of transformation.[10] Each person swims in the sea of over-choice and of shattered expectations and must find his or her own shore in a rapidly changing world.

In the premodern era, when a person or tribe lost its centeredness, initiation rites took place. A Native American who felt unbalanced might seek a vision in the woods; the ancient Greek might go to the Temple of Aesculapius to incubate a dream. The power of the inner world and its stories, images, and visions were greatly valued in ancient cultures. Is there an equivalent in the modern world?

Mircea Eliade, one of the modern masters of mythology, says:

*One of the characteristics of the modern world is the disap-
pearance of any meaningful rites of initiation. Of primary
importance in traditional societies, in the modern Western
world significant initiation is practically nonexistent.*[11]

Through the initiation rite, a person came to know himself or
herself. The term initiation denotes a body of rites and oral teachings
whose purpose is to produce a decisive alteration in the religious and
social status of the initiate. According to Eliade:

*In philosophical terms initiation is equivalent to a basic change
in existential condition; the novice emerges from his ordeal
endowed with a totally different being from that which he
possessed before his initiation; he has become* another.[12]

Eliade claims that there is practically no initiation in the modern
world—yet if you look around, relationships today have become an
arena where initiation takes place and we enter into the process of
"becoming" *another.*

Trials occur in intimate relationships as they do in initiatory
ordeals. When we're abandoned by a long-term lover, we're left dangling on an initiatory pole, our heart muscles pulled by the strings of
a higher force while we look up and wonder why. When we are
subjected to a partner's rage, it may seem that we are dealing with a
demon, and we wonder what trials we are asked to endure. We wonder
what magical implements may exist to help us change our heavy hearts
into a golden treasure.

It is interesting that in ancient Greece, initiation into the "lesser
mysteries" took place during the spring equinox, while the initiation
into the greater mysteries of Demeter/ Persephone took place in the
city of Eleusis during the autumn equinox.[13] As noted, Libra (the
autumn equinox) is a symbol for the process of entering into relationship, which suggests that relationships provide an entry into "The
Great Initiation."

Unfortunately, what went on in these initiation ceremonies is,
to this day, enshrouded in mystery. We have only bits of symbols and
pieces of images to connect us to the lost wisdom of the past. An image
of Heracles' initiation into the mysteries appears on a sarcophagus; his
head is covered, his eyes are shut and his hand is before his mouth as
if, perhaps, to say, "*shhh*, don't talk about this."

The word "to initiate" developed from the Greek word *uvelv*
meaning "to close the eyes or mouth." According to Kerenyi, the

Mystery Celebration may have begun when the initiate closed his eyes and fell back into his or her own darkness. These celebrations were enacted at night and included a mysterious process of engendering light. According to legend, light emanated from the place where the Mystery Celebration took place, and could be seen miles away from Eleusis, far beyond the boundary of where it seemed possible to see anything. A numinous event took place where light was born out of darkness and a drama was enacted depicting the rebirth of Persephone after her abduction by Pluto.[14]

Just as the participant journeyed from darkness to light, so does the modern-day person in the great initiatory drama of intimate relationship. We are each Persephone abducted into the dark mysteries every time we have a naive belief challenged and are disillusioned, each time we let go of an old way of being and try another for the sake of love. And we, too, are blessed by the wisdom and light gained from our soul's journey into the underworld of love.

How do we find the way through the dark caverns of this mysterious underworld? Like Heracles, we close our eyes and our mouth and enter into the darkness. Just as we can see farther out into the universe in the night sky than during the day, so can one see farther into the inner universe by closing our eyes and mouth and looking and listening within.

From the terrain of the inner world, stories grow. Just as Heracles and other initiates were healed by the story enacted during this sacred time of the year, so are we healed by stories. Whether a story is told by an elder, appears as a dream, or is found in the pages of an age-old mythological text, it has the power to transform us as it transformed our ancestors.

---

[1] Mails, T. *The Mystic Warriors of the Plains*. Doubleday, 1972.

[2] *APA Monitor*. November 1985, 16:11, p. 13 Turkington, Carol. These statistics were reported at the annual American Psychological Association's convention by Ayala Pines, Ph.D.

[3] According to the June 1, 1987 issue of *Marriage and Divorce Today*, "The Hidden Meaning: An analysis of different types of affairs." The statistics on adultery are variable depending upon the source cited and the time frame. In *Psychology Today*, February 1986, Laurel Richardson's article "The New Other Woman" quotes research by Ira Reiss and Anthony Thompson who say that forty to fifty percent of all married men report

having affairs. In *Cosmopolitan* magazine in the early 1980s fifty-four percent of married women had participated in at least one affair according to Wolfe L., "Women & Sex in the 80's: The Cosmo Report," Arbor House 1981; and in a poll of 7000 men, seventy-two percent of those married over two years had been adulterous according to Hite, S. *The Hite Report on Male Sexuality*, Ballantine Books, 1981.

[4] Larsen, S. & R. *Parabola* magazine. "The Healing Mask," Vol VI, No. 3.

[5] McLuhan, Marshall. *Understanding Media*. McGraw-Hill, 1965.

[6] Toffler, A. *Future Shock*. Random House, 1970, p. 234.

[7] In societies where spouses are dependent on each other to make ends meet, divorce rates are much lower. In preindustrial Europe, and all other societies that use the plow for agriculture, such as India and China, couples need each other to survive. A woman depends on her husband to move rocks, fell trees, and plow the land. Her husband needs her to sow, weed, pick, prepare, and store the vegetables. The industrial revolution changed this economic relationship. Between 1960 and 1983, the number of working women doubled, and between 1966 and 1976, the divorce rate doubled. For a more complete discussion of this issue, see Dupaquier J. *Marriage and Remarriage in Populations of the Past*, Academic Press, 1981; Fisher, H. *The Anatomy of Love*. W.W. Norton, 1992.

[8] For a further discussion of the questions of astrological validity, see Mayer M. *The Mystery of Personal Identity*. ACS Publications: San Diego, 1985.The point of view expressed is that regardless of whether there is an actual correspondence between cosmos and personality, looking into celestial patterns can allow unconscious symbolic processes to be activated that can bring meaning to one's life.

[9] Leonard, George. *The End of Sex*. J.P. Tarcher, 1983.

[10] For a broader discussion of marital myths see Lazarus, A. Ph.D. *Marital Myths*. Impact Publishers: San Luis Obispo, 1985.

[11] Eliade, Mircea. *Rites and Symbols of Initiation*, Harper and Row, 1958 p. ix.

[12] Ibid.

[13] Article by Campbell, Joseph. *The Mysteries: Papers from the Eranos Yearbooks*. Bollingen Series XXX, 1978. Schmitt, Paul "Ancient Mysteries and Their Transformation," p. 99.

[14] Kerenyi, K. "The Mysteries of the Kabeiroi," from Campbell, J. *The Mysteries*. Bollingen, 1955.

CHAPTER 2
NAMING OUR GRAIL:
FINDING THE GODS AND
GODDESSES THAT RULE
OUR RELATIONSHIPS

---

*Our complexes are not only
wounds that hurt and mouths
that tell our myths, but also
eyes that see what the normal
and healthy parts cannot
envision. . . . Afflictions
point to gods, gods reach us
through afflictions.*

JAMES HILLMAN

Symbols, myths, and stories have been, throughout history, initiators, companions, and guides to the soul's quest for meaning. From the Bible to fairy tales like those of the Grimm brothers, wisdom can be found. When we hear the legend of Parcival questing after the Grail to restore Arthur's barren and war-torn kingdom, we resonate with the similar themes in our own lives. When we feel barren or war-torn in the realm of love, we send the young naive knight within us on a quest to heal the kingdom. The Grail is a symbol for that which will quench our thirst.

The Quest for the Grail of Love

"Who does the quest for the Grail serve?" Parcival could have asked this question early in his search, but didn't do so because his mother taught him not to ask too many questions. As a result, the Grail Castle's entrance was closed to him. After many years of searching and self-development, Parcival freed himself from his mother's spell and learned to ask the right questions. He finally asked about the higher purpose of his quest. This signaled a shift from an egocentric attitude of desperately searching to possess something for himself to a transpersonal attitude of seeking the Grail to serve a higher purpose. At that moment, the door to the Grail Castle opened and the Grail Cup appeared.

Parcival discovered, in this profound moment of insight, that the quest's purpose was not to serve *his own* desires, but rather to serve the king and the renewal of the land. The king is a symbol of our higher ruling Self. His land is healed when the king drinks from the cup of the Holy Spirit, and the connection between purpose and the self is made once again.

As did Parcival, many of us spend a lifetime in a dried-out kingdom of self-centered desires, searching for that sacred vessel that will satisfy our thirst for love. But do we know what we are really searching for? At moments when the land of our relationship seems empty or laid to waste, we, like Parcival, need to ask the question, "Who or what does this relationship serve?"

Finding the Name of Our Grail

Difficult moments in a relationship bring out our deep-seated beliefs, values, and desires about love and life. If we enter a romantic involvement with idealized fantasies of being constantly together, in time, we will feel lonely or angry when we are separated from our partner—when our partner takes vacations or goes out with friends. The inner voice that craves merging speaks out, "He goes out with other people too often; I want someone who is more *with me*." This person's Grail has become "Merger." Another person may, after courtship rituals are over, feel the desire to "drink from my own separate cup." On that Grail Castle gate is written "Separate Space," proclaiming a thirst for independence.

What is our Grail? The answers that our experiences with love reveal may be different from what we think or say is the object of our quest. If we are honest with ourselves, we may discover a deep-seated need for "Mirroring," "Security," or "Being Taken Care Of." We may say we are looking for love, but leave our partners because we're not feeling appreciated, secure, or taken care of.

Becoming conscious of what we are seeking—naming our Grail Cup and knowing its composition—is the beginning of forging ourselves into a suitable vessel. A vessel, according to the alchemical tradition, is a container where inner work can take place—where the stuff of life (the *prima materia*) can be mixed together, combined and transformed, and where lead can be transmuted into gold by secret processes.

For some, forging the Grail Cup involves letting go of unrealistic expectations of ourselves and our partners. If we are perfectionistic and afraid our partners will find our areas of vulnerability, we may feel mistakes are terrible and try to hide them. But if we believe that "the business of the universe is to make a fool of you so you'll know yourself for one and so become wise,"[1] then our mistakes become part of our quest. They become our teachers. To one tightly gripping the elegant Cup of Perfectionism with its limited supply of water, it's a liberating thought that mistakes are simply lessons in life's curriculum.

At difficult moments in relationships, when our partners' wishes oppose ours, the natural inclination may be to wish we could have avoided the issues. "Next time I'll be smarter and avoid this type of person," the embittered lover complains.

We may have forgotten to ask, "Who or what purpose does my relationship serve?" We may not have seen the fact that when our needs for mirroring, security, merging, or separation are unfulfilled, an opportunity exists to work on our wounded feelings. We may need reminding that our quest is to restore our barren or war-torn inner land.

It's this perspective that makes all the difference as to whether the door to the Grail Castle opens or stays closed. . . whether what appears is an empty cup or a sacred vessel.

Which Gods Rule Our Relationships?

The purpose of intimate relationship is our soul's growth. Symbolic language is a secret key to this golden door. As Mircea Eliade says,

> *The person who understands a symbol. . . succeeds in emerging from his personal situation and reaching a comprehension of the universal. Thanks to the symbol the individual experience is awoken and transmuted into a spiritual act.*[2]

There is a new movement in psychology[3] which is bringing back the pagan approach of personifying elements of the universe to resacrilize life. It is the premise of this movement that, by emphasizing one God (monocentric worship), our Western culture has lost sight that everything in life is an entryway into divinity (polycentric worship). "Resacrilize life by resacrilizing language" is written on this movement's banners. Capitalizing the initial letters of words is one aspect of the revolution. Though seemingly insignificant, there is a radical change that results from capitalizing a letter. By emphasizing the symbolic, ordinary words become deified and everyday aspects of our love lives are reconnected with a sacred universe of meaning.

At first it may be difficult to see our desires and beliefs about love as deities. Yet they do form such a central part of our lives that we may worship them like zealots who unquestionably hold onto our form of worship, not realizing that there are other temples in which we can worship.

Though at different times we have different ways of being in relationship (i.e. we worship many gods), many problems occur when we exist in a narrow area of ourselves and unconsciouly worship the god of one temple.

For example, one person in a couple may be an advocate of Happiness—"Let's do more fun things," while the other is a worshipper of Depth —"Let's share more about our life struggles. I feel like you don't share your deepest feelings with me enough." The first person here is worshipping at the Temple of Earthly Happiness, the second person is worshipping at the Temple of the Underworld.

By conceptualizing our relationship desires, beliefs, and resulting conflicts in terms of different temples at which we and our partner worship, we create a sacred language that respects each person's needs. We may then be able to say, "His desire for Earthly Happiness is a different need than my quest for Depth. Maybe we can grow and learn from our different 'temples' rather than arguing about who is 'right.'" Without this transpersonal attitude, our intimate relationships repeat the same mistake made by the missionaries and the United States government when they tried to convert the Native Americans to Christianity. They gained the land, but lost the opportunity to learn how to live in harmony with it.

A first step in developing an open mind is being conscious of what we name another's beliefs, attitudes, or ways of being. If we see another's way as "savage" it leads to self-righteousness; if we see their behavior as instinctual we are more likely to respect their values.

As we name our Grail Cup, so can we describe ourselves with the names of gods and goddesses, thereby making our ways of being sacred. We can create our own deities and temple names by personifying the nouns with capital letters and using classical mythological names.[4] For instance, if we point our finger at our partner, saying, "Why can't things just be easy around here?" we are praying at the altar of "Harmonia," the Greek goddess who was the daughter of Ares and Aphrodite. If we say, "I just wish the house was more comfortable when I come home from a long day," our wish for a warm, cozy home reveals our affiliation with Hestia, Goddess of the Hearth.

Some people worship at the Temple of the Mother Goddess,[5] believing that relationship is taking care of another's needs. Watch out though, for dark corridors in this temple have two-way swinging doors. Often we who open wide our doors to love will have an expectation that an equal amount will return. The door often swings back and hits us in the face.

Each temple has its own positive and negative qualities, and its own lessons to learn. Members of the Mother Goddess Temple benefit from the ecstasy of symbiosis and feelings of merging with another. Those who worship at this temple need to learn that giving too much to another at inappropriate times can stifle another's individuation; living up to an expectation to take care of another's needs can lead to drained or resentful feelings. Negotiating appropriate boundaries and making conscious the motivation for giving are part of the inner work of this temple.

At the Temple of Separate Space we must knock on doors to enter, and guards patrol the walls. The Gestalt therapy motto is written on the front gate: "I am not in this world to live up to your expectations, and you are not in this world to live up to mine. You are you and I am I, and if by chance we find each other, it's beautiful. If not, it can't be helped."[6] In this temple we have the blessing of room to individuate, yet we may miss the melting states of ecstasy found in merging with another.

The boundaries surrounding the Temple of Anti Co-dependency are clearly marked with no trespassing signs. Many of us were wounded by abuse or neglect in our early lives. We are very cautious about who enters our territory. Because we were caretakers of our families as children, we need to be conscious of the ways our old programming causes us to give from habit rather than love. The way we pounce on others' innocuous statements sometimes scares away people who would genuinely like to share intimacy with us.

In the inner sanctum of the Anti Co-dependency Temple is the Temple of Boundaries which contains a secret manuscript. In it is a zodiacal map which shows that Uranus and Neptune, the planets that symbolize higher connection between people, will be in the sign of Capricorn (ruled by Cronos—God of Boundaries, Time, Old Age, and Slow Movement) during much of the 1990s.[7] The members of this temple (many in our culture) practice Cronos' rituals of interpersonal relationship. Maintaining distance, they don't make eye contact with those they don't know; when approached with the possibility of relationship, they move very slowly. They have learned from their wounds, and exercise due caution; but they may not realize that they are imprisoned by the very God they worship.

For just as Cronos wanted to swallow up his children including Zeus, God of Light, Lightning, and Thunder, out of fear of being overthrown, so do modern worshippers of Cronos lose our opportunities to be with the light, lightning, and thunder of life due to their fear of being overthrown by the instability of passion.

Many men and women in our culture today live the myth of Cronos. As Rhea (Goddess of the Earth) hid the infant Zeus from Cronos in the Dictean cave until he was an adult, so is the light of love that many experienced in the 1960s and early 1970s[8] now hidden in the deep recesses of our own caves. From the perspective of psycho-mythology, Cronos (Boundaries) has led the light in many of us to hide out in the deeper recesses of our own caves. Here we are incubating the faculty of discrimination and learning to live in the isolated depths of our inner worlds. Perhaps it is only here that maturity in relationship can grow.

The temples at which we worship are usually not consciously chosen. Cultural beliefs, past traumas, and personal dynamics from our families of origin control our choices. For example, worshipers at the Temple of Victims may have suffered mental or physical or sexual abuse as children. Each visit to the temple takes us back to the inner geography where the wounding took place. We travel there to find healing.

In the Temple of Victims, our inner child finds a bewildering array of entitled rage, disappointed expectations, displaced aggression, projected emotions, all-or-none thinking, and the need for a selfless and, preferably, clairvoyant partner. If we were abused and then blamed for our abuse, we may reinforce our temple with chants of blame directed at our partners, and never realize that we are singing the same tune as our childhood abusers. A person who has been sexually abused during their childhood may demand that their partner transcend sexual intimacy for many months, "to show that they love me for who I am, not for my body." These are painful issues, and a partner needs to be sensitive during the time it takes to heal. Rather than blaming a partner, the survivor of child abuse must find the trapdoor in the temple floor. It is here in the healing realm of the underworld the journey begins.

Virgil said, "We make our destinies by our choice of gods," so it's important to be aware of which ones we worship. It is also crucial to know which gods or goddesses we deny or are biased against. In the story of Paris, Eris (Discord) was not invited to the wedding of the mortal Peleus and the goddess Thetis.[9] She attended anyway and threw an apple onto the table where the gods and goddesses were seated saying "for the Fairest." Paris was forced to choose between Hera, Aphrodite, and Artemis. He chose Aphrodite, Goddess of Beauty and Sensual Love. As a reward for choosing her, Aphrodite gave Paris the hand of Helen of Troy, the most beautiful woman in the land.

We are still digesting the lessons of this wedding feast three thousand years after the event. Paris's legacy is a culture that worships physical beauty and love above all other qualities. Like Paris, we are naive about our choices.[10] Paris learned the hard way that there were problems with Aphrodite's "gifts"; Helen was married to a Trojan prince and the most famous war in history was fought for her.

Hundreds of generations later, we are still trying to control the guest list of which deities we allow into our relationships. By attempting to eliminate Discord from our love lives, the universal law of opposites comes into play and she appears with all the more force, disrupting the sacred marriage between what is human and what is divine in each of us. Integrating Discord into our lives requires an awareness of our patterns when conflict arises. Do we retreat under pressure, like Dionysus, to an underwater hideaway? Do we confront and attack like a war god, or do we try to prove we are right and worship the Law?

We can see the clashing beliefs of two different temples in the example of one newly married couple. Mark said to Sylvia, "I did my share of the housework, why didn't you?" He was worshipping at the Temple of Justice which was almighty in the kingdom of his family. Mark discovered from his journey into his inner land that although Justice wore a Cloak of Fairness, it hid a Sword of Judgement. By contrast, in the kingdom where Sylvia was raised, domestic qualities were not valued. Her mother was a professional woman always on the hunt for a better job. Artemis, Goddess of the Hunt, was worshipped in her home.

Through speaking with our partners about the kingdom we came from, an opportunity is created to bring a new cup to our castles. We may find a cup running over with liquid compassion instead of judgments of our partner's foibles as we say, "No wonder, he speaks of Justice in such a jabbing way, that was the way it was worshipped in the kingdom of his youth." "No wonder she is so resistant in the kitchen; domestic chores were not respected as a valid part of the hunt in the kingdom of her youth."

By being aware of our origin myth, we can either transform it or play with it humorously. The man from the Land of Judgment may learn that more important than measuring equality, is to develop compassion. The woman resistant to domestic chores may learn to integrate them into her hunt, or at least learn to joke about her resistance to it: "I don't want to cook tonight, my life is about shooting pheasants out in the world, not being a peasant at home." Home can become a creative playground where archetypal deities reveal themselves and play the game of life with each other.

Think of those times when what we and our partners wanted were at odds. Remember when our partner pointed out one of our old patterns that we wished we could hide. If we put up defensive walls, in all likelihood, the difficulty grew. As the story of Paris teaches, if we try to eliminate Discord, she will most likely become an uninvited guest. War (not so civil) may result.

Inherent in relationship is a choice between temples. When unpleasant circumstances arise, will we leave the relationship in search of physical attraction (Aphrodite) and an easier time (Harmonia); or are we willing to invite Discord into our relationship and use the experience for our psyche's development?

If we look at the conflicts that arise in our relationship as an opportunity to work on our inner life and to transform old patterns, Parcival's question regarding the purpose of the Grail is answered by saying that relationship is a course in psychological and spiritual growth. Every area of conflict is a lesson—in communication, jealousy, possessiveness, commitment, assertiveness, or in balancing our own needs with those of another. Whether our relationship becomes a locked dungeon or a learning process in which the key to the Grail Castle is discovered, depends on the quality of our vision.

[1] Macdonald, G. *Lilith*.

[2] Arguellos. *Mandala*. Shambala Publications, 1972, p. 53.

[3] This movement is called Archetypal Psychology. See James Hillman's works beginning with *Revisioning Psychology*. Harper and Row, 1975.

[4] The tradition of Archetypal Psychology is rich in giving one an understanding of the ways of being of the various gods and goddesses. See Hillman Ibid., *The Myth of Analysis*, *Loose Ends*, *Facing the Gods*, etc.

[5] This is not to imply that the Mother Goddess Temple only involves taking care of others' needs. People of this temple also contribute positively to increasing *Gaia consciousness*—that we are all part of the earth and that each part of our web of interconnectedness affects every other part. Likewise, members of this temple are part of the movement to bring back the pagan rituals that bring participants into rituals of togetherness through music, dance, poetry readings, etc. A good beginning book on this movement is Star Hawks' *The Spiral Dance*.

[6] Perls, F. *Gestalt Therapy Verbatim*. Real People Press, 1969.

[7] Uranus entered Capricorn in 1988 and will enter Aquarius about 1995. Neptune entered Capricorn in 1985 and will leave shortly before the year 2000.

[8] It is interesting to note the synchronicity that in the late 1960s and early 1970s Uranus and Neptune were in the signs of relationship— Libra, Scorpio, and Sagittarius.

[9] Idemon, Richard. *The Hero's Journey*. Available from Pegasus Tapes, San Anselmo, CA.

[10] We shall discuss the archetype of "Aphrodite love" in the next chapter along with the Eros and Psyche myth.

CHAPTER 3
SHAFTED BY EROS'S ARROW:
PSYCHE'S INITIATION
INTO THE TRIALS OF LOVE

---

*From all other ills doth mine
differ. It pleaseth me;
I rejoice at it; my ill is what
I want and my suffering is
my health. So I do not see
what I am complaining about;
for my ill comes to me by my
will; it is my willing that
becomes my ill; but I am so
pleased to want thus that
I suffer agreeably, and have
so much joy in my pain that
I am sick with delight.*

CHRÉTIEN DE TROYES

The Psychological Purpose of Love

There is a force in nature imbued with purpose that draws all species into relationship. Like a bee drawn toward a flower, so are we drawn to our lovers. With human relationship there is a biological design behind the magnetic attraction we feel; there is also a psychological purpose, an inner pollination, i.e. creation of new inner life.

It's been said that "when all else fails, love may find the way." Love indeed is a transformative agent. I'm sure we can all remember a time when we were stuck in a long-standing life pattern, and a loved one confronted us with change as nothing ever had. Though it may have seemed that our lover's purpose was to sting us, like the bee pollinates the plant kingdom, we may have carried something away from the encounter that led to new flowering.

I remember Paul, a lawyer in his late forties who was confronted with his "need to always be right" and how it made his wife, Alice, continually feel belittled. She finally threatened to divorce him unless they sought therapy. Alice's pain initiated a process for Paul of finding something more important than being right—caring about another human being's feelings. Following his wife's confrontation, painful as it was, he began to work on his self-righteousness.[1]

Whenever we feel stung in a relationship, the pain and suffering that ensues initiates us on the path to the Temple of Psyche. It's becoming increasingly popular in our culture to proclaim that we honor the principal of psychological and spiritual development in intimate relationships. But, if a survey was taken asking people what purpose their relationship served, how would psychological and spiritual development compare to emotional stability, financial security, great sex, or fun? In no way should we denigrate the value of these other temples, but, as James Hillman puts it, "by relegating Psyche to the back seat, the wrong person is left driving the car."

Psyche should be given a prominent place in the territory of relationship because it is the relective soul in us who journeys through the trials of life, through times of emotional stability and instability, through ups and downs in our financial lives, through joy and suffering, pleasure and pain. At the end of our lives, it's not the gifts our lovers have given us, nor is it either pole of the emotional opposites that remains, but rather the psyche itself and whatever has been absorbed from these life experiences.

There was, at one time, a small, relatively unknown Temple of Psyche[2] where she was worshipped. More people worshipped at the Temple of the Earth Mother (Demeter) and the Sky God (Zeus) than at the Temple of Psyche. Even though today the Temple of Psychology is more well known, in the midst of hard times in a relationship, we do not pray there for guidance. As it has been through the centuries, more people pray to be taken care of in a relationship (by Mother Earth)[3] or want to transcend the problems of a relationship (by the sky gods) than want to enter into the temple of their own psyche and do inner work.

James Hillman defines Psyche[4] as analogous to "soul" and distinguished from "spirit." He defines the realm of spirit in relation to do with high places and transcendental religions, whereas the realm of psyche is a land of the wooded river valleys teeming with instinctual life. Whereas spirit is reasoned, soul is impassioned; whereas spirit is identified with logos, soul identifies with pathos; whereas spirit is identified with monocentrism, soul is polycentric; whereas spirit sits high above in moral judgment, soul lives in the dramas of everyday life; whereas spirit is eternal and unchanging in its perspective, soul enters into and is moved by the play of life.

Colloquial usages also tell us something about soul: We search our souls, play soul music, eat soul food, and our souls can be on trial. Some have thought that the soul was composed of a vaporous substance. Metaphysicians have proclaimed that each soul was composed of a unique combination of the raw elements of life: fire, earth, air, and water.

But, the further we go in seeking soul's nature, the more it recedes. Perhaps Heraclitus was right when he said, "You will not find the measure of the *psyche* by traveling in any direction, so deep is the *logos* of it."[5] Hearing this the seeker finds a clue and stops "traveling in any direction." In stillness we begin the journey of the soul.

If we allow ourselves to be stilled, and the imagination be active, we can explore what honoring this temple means to our relationships. For the mere words of what it means to "have soul," can only be a small part of the psyche's enormity .

Perhaps it takes an image to fathom her depths. In the Greek language, Psyche was pictured as a moth or butterfly. This is an apt description. For when we are in darkness struggling with a life issue, there is a psychological force that draws us upwards, like the moth drawn to the stars at night for illumination. If a lover has rejected us, hurtful though it may be, the psyche seeks understanding like the moth seeks the flame. Our psyches seek the light of knowledge, even if it scalds us to the core. We want to know, "Is it because I'm too pushy, or not assertive enough? Let me know. I'll change."

If someone we're dating has not returned our phone calls, we may call again and again though we risk further rejection. We ask them why? Our potential lover may say that he or she is overwhelmed by a busy life, or that a strong inner critic exists which makes him or her feel guilty, so guilty that they become frozen into inaction. We discover that their parents were so devaluing that now when they do something "bad," they feel overwhelmed with guilt and cannot face their "accusor". In hearing their story, maybe our psyche changes from burning anger to a compassionate glow.

But the path of Psyche does not mean having only nice, loving feelings. Sometimes going for the flame means being with the "fire in our bellies," getting angry at inconsiderateness, and setting firm limits about what we're willing to deal with.

The butterfly is the most common symbol of the psyche, for it represents the transformation possible in each human soul. At one moment, we crawl like a caterpillar, lost in the weeds of our pushiness or shyness. After a chrysalis period of inner work, something beautiful emerges in us, a potential waiting to be born out of the human condition. When an aggressive person leaves a therapy session with a newfound gentleness, or someone who is painfully shy finds playful self-expression, or a person disconnected from the power of their anger expresses it, that which emerges has wings of our own unique coloring. . . a coloring born from a long and arduous process of gestation, awesome in its vivid beauty. The color may be too rich for some or too muted for others, but love leads our psyches to create a beauty of our own design. The butterfly symbolism says, "Please handle the contents of our psyches with care, for they are delicate to the human touch, and are best approached with an open hand."

Perhaps the best way to explore the nature of Psyche (other than to reflect on our own) is to read her classic story. In ancient times she was thought of as a young maiden coupled with Eros. Our psyches and the God of Love do seem to be inextricably connected partners, dancing their dance together through the ages. Before relating this tale, let's delve into the cast of characters.

The True Name of Love?

In the Egyptian doctrines of the soul, the traveler in the un-
derworld must know the names of the gatekeepers in the nether
world, for only the knowledge of these names can unlock the
doors of Death's kingdom. He must call them by their right
names. For only by virtue of this appellation can he cause them
to take him to his destination.[6]

A first step in many initiatory traditions is to learn the secret names
of things. [7] For the name we call the force we are dealing with affects
the way we see it, and, in the case of love, it may determine whether
we can "unlock the doors of Death's kingdom and arrive at our
destination."

The FDA should require that "love" be properly labeled. "Meds"
is a euphemistic name for psychiatric drugs that hides their dire effects—so does the name "love." If we believe the outer label, we'll be
unprepared for the chemical reactions, volatility, implosions, and
explosions inherent to this drug; and we might take it without being
aware of its addictive potential.

We would be well served to take a course in relationships called
"The Psychomythology of Intimacy" early in our schooling, where we
learn the true names and stories of the phenomena we call love. There
we would learn about the "Whorfian Hypothesis"—how language
creates reality—and would hear how, for example, people in warm
climates are limited in their understanding of snow compared to the
Eskimos. The teacher would then further the analogy that we are likewise limited by our concept of "romantic love." We are waiting for soft
snowflakes, and are left unprepared for love's hailstorm.

In the course "Love 101," we would learn that there are many
different types of love. Love for a friend, love for a teacher, love for our
parents, love for country, love for a power greater than ourselves (God),
and finally, the type we are exploring here, romantic love.

When we say "romantic love," we may conjure up images of young
lovers gazing into each other's eyes before a sparkling fire, whispering
sweet words, caressing gently, ready to sacrifice anything to make their
companion happy. Using the word "love" to speak of romantic passion
is the problem. When stormy times come, we are disappointed by
our naive expectations. When we see a Valentine card with Cupid

portrayed as a chubby cherub, we are not prepared to deal with the force we are about to meet.

Apuleius was told in his initiation that the name of the force behind romantic love is *Eros*. Who is Eros? Webster's dictionary defines "erotic" love as sexual love, which vastly understates its power. Far from being Aphrodite's roguish little boy, as he appears in later writings such as Hesiod's *Theogony*, Eros greeted Aphrodite at *her* birth.

The creation myths tell how Eros is a primordial force in the universe. Eros existed almost from the beginning of time, and was born out of Chaos. We know this each time one of his arrows hits us and throws our well-ordered universe into Chaos. He forces us out of our narrow worlds, causes us to lose our bearings and knowledge of our own feelings, and makes the most conscientious of us neglect our daily responsibilities. When we "fall in love," we are repeating the creation myth of Eros; we are coerced into a *regressus ab origine*.[8] We regress to Eros's origins in Chaos.

> *In the Orphic creation myth black-winged Night united with the Wind and laid a silver egg in the womb of Darkness. Out of this egg came golden-winged Eros whom some call Phanes, the Revealer, who then set the universe in motion. Eros lived in a cave with the goddess Night, and outside the cave sat Rhea drumming, calling humanity to listen to the oracles of the Triple Goddess.*[9]

Through the image of Eros born out of Night, we can understand those times when love is not a smooth path filled with lightheartedness and golden smiles. At those times we feel like criminals sneaking around in the dark, hiding our attraction toward another out of fear of loss, or feeling intense, dark hatred. We are instructed how to proceed in this unfamiliar territory only if we can decipher the symbols.

The myth tells us that erotic love comes from the silver places of the moon, the places of emotional waves not of solar detachment, the places of dragons in caves, not the land of clear sunny days. Hearing where Eros originates gives us permission to visit our dark places when we enter his terrain.

Eros, born outside the cave of the Triple Goddess, was originally identified with the three phases of the moon: the Virgin of the waxing new moon, the Red Goddess of the full moon, and the Crone of the waning dark moon. So in the process of giving birth to Eros in our lives, we are secretly told, we shall meet a love of virginal innocence that is capable of sacrificing itself for something greater; we will meet our full-blooded, drum-beating wildness; and finally, we will meet the death of our old selves and a wise being will be born out of the darkness in ourselves.

Perhaps we will meet a dark repressed side of ourselves, with deep fears and amoral inclinations. We are told that if we can have the patience to witness this and incubate new life, golden-winged Eros will be revealed.

The nature of erotic love is defined by Eros' stories and images. He is often pictured as a winged being, which tells us that romantic love can transport us to a higher world. He's pictured as a hermaphrodite which can acquaint us with our contrasexual side. If we are identified solely with our careers, when love comes on the scene, domestic demands inevitably arise. If we have identified with being strong, a lover will no doubt challenge us to be more vulnerable; if we are vulnerable, a lover will express the need for us to be stronger. No wonder Eros is associated with the Creation. He calls us forth to create a new universe for ourselves.

Eros is the transformative force behind passionate love. He's pictured riding on a butterfly (Psyche) and burning it with a torch.[10] The butterfly, born as a caterpillar and changed into a flying creature by a miracle of nature, is a symbol for transforming our essential nature. The image of Eros burning a butterfly warns us that in Erotic love, forces arise that have the power to change us, but often leave us feeling burned in the process.

For those who fight to stay in control in the presence of love, the story of Eros, Apollo, and Daphne is a cautionary tale. Eros humbled the greatest of the gods, Apollo, by shooting him with a golden arrow and making him fall in love with the lowly nymph Daphne. And when Eros shot Daphne with a lead-tipped arrow, he made her resistant to Apollo's advances. The myth says that Eros knows no class prejudice; he makes the lowest and the most powerful fall in or out of love. Love makes us feel like gods one moment and humbles us the next.

The secret is beginning to unravel. Eros is a *daimon*. He is not quite of the human realm nor the divine realm; he's an intermediary between both realms not subject to the laws of either. Eros grabs us all when he wants and does with us as he will.

One image on an ancient gemstone shows Eros with Psyche tied to a column surmounted by a sphere.[11] In another image we see Psyche chained or bound to the chariot of love.[12] In Ovid's *Metamorphosis*, Eros had the transformative touch to make cold-hearted Hades love Persephone. So, Eros is a great torturer of the human soul and, at the same time, its great redeemer.

We can relate to the image of Eros tying Psyche to a pillar with a sphere on top, for Eros does indeed tie us to people we might not choose in order to introduce us to a larger sphere of being. And we can remember those times when we've felt cold-hearted, living in a hell when Eros touched our hearts and lifted us by our love for another. Eros has the capacity to transform the darkest aspects of our characters, as he did Hades. Daimon that he is, he has the potential to create many forms of love.

Jung knew of these powers of Eros when he said:

> *"Eros' range of activity extends from the endless spaces of the heavens to the dark abysses of hell. . . .We are, in the deepest sense, the victims and instruments of cosmogonic love. A man is at its mercy. He may assent to it, or rebel against it; but he is always caught up by it and enclosed within it."*[13]

The Tale of Eros and Psyche

This story is one of the last mystery plays of the ancient world, written in A. D. 125 by Apuleius but with roots in folk wisdom many centuries before that.[14] Just as the Rosetta Stone helped us decipher ancient Egyptian hieroglyphics, so interpreting this tale helps us dig into love's origins and mysteries.

This tale was told to Apuleius as he was on his way to initiation into the mysteries of Isis, the Egyptian priestess who said, "No mortal shall ever see beneath my veil." We can imagine that Apuleius, like us, was befuddled by love's mysteries, and welcomed the opportunity to peek under its veil.

> *Psyche was a maiden born from the sacred meeting of heaven and earth. "Heaven had rained fresh procreative dew, and earth, not sea, had brought forth as a flower a second Venus (Aphrodite)."* [15]

Symbolically, our psyches are born from something divine, and yet take root on earth with all of its limitations. As Psyche's birth was a challenge to combine the elements of heaven and earth, so is ours. When we are united with our beloved, it feels like a heavenly state indeed. But inevitably the time comes when we realize that we're married to a mortal, and then our beloved may seem like damaged goods.[16]

It's at these moments of earthly limitation that we are tested to see if we can keep our hearts open. Can we live with what we don't like? Can we keep in mind a larger perspective when our needs aren't met?

Different cultures have answers for why pain exists in "loving relationship" and why our failed heavenly ideals must come crashing down. The biological reason is given by Scott Peck who says the heavenly stage of love is "a trick that our genes pull on us to hoodwink us into marriage." In the East, the answer as to why we must experience the Great Fall is that it is meant to help us recognize that all of life is Maya or illusion, and the spiritual aspirant must learn to transcend the pain of earthly life. The Greeks give us another answer— the pain from failed ideals makes us do "soul work" and that soul work begins by meeting a dark figure from the land of the dead.

> *Psyche was so beautiful she rivalled Venus. Due to Venus's anger that divine honors were being transferred to Psyche and mortals no longer worshipped at her temple, Venus proclaimed that "this girl who has usurped my honors shall have no joy thereof." And so Psyche had no love. Men marvelled at her loveliness but did not ask her to marry, for they "looked at her as men marvel at a statue." Her distraught father went to the oracle of Apollo to ask for advice. But instead of being promised the eligible mortal for which he had hoped, the oracle said the father must put his daughter on a high crag dressed in funeral robes and wait for a being of the dragon breed from the darksome river of the dead.*

The oracle predicts that the psyche is destined to marry death when we choose intimate relationship. Our narcissistic attachment to our surface-self must be sacrificed or else we remain a statue, devoid of real life energy. On the path to intimacy we are destined to enter the realm of darkness, the realm where Pluto abducts the naive Persephone into the underworld. We are all left on the edge a cliff, wondering whether the dragon, our true selves will change as we merge with another, or whether we'll surrender the parts of ourselves that need to die. It's a rough edge.

For example, Harriet, a woman in her late forties, was married for over twenty years and yet never told her husband that she hated the colors he chose for their bedroom. Her self-expression and sexuality were repressed for many years until she could break the pattern of being a good little girl and finally speak the truth.

> Psyche was forbidden to look at her new husband Eros (God of Love) and see his face. She was warned not to yield to the impious promptings of curiosity, or she would exile herself forever from his embrace. For a while, she consented not to see her husband's face, and didn't know who he was or from whence he came.

This image captures well how we wish to see more of our partner's true self, and yet we want to keep the vulnerable aspects of ourselves hidden. It takes much trust to believe that someone could still love us if we revealed our true selves with all the tender spots, inadequacies, and dark secrets we may have. As did Eros, at the beginning of a relationship, we may hide our real self from our partner and show only our godlike self.

> Psyche held a lantern over Eros at night while he slept to get a glimpse of his face, and carelessly spilled a drop of oil on the great god, burning him. Eros awoke in anger with feelings of being betrayed. From the wounds he suffered, Eros retreated from the relationship, and as he flew through the clouds, Psyche held onto his leg until at last, overwearied, she fell to earth. Eros returned to his mother, Aphrodite, in heaven.

To experience the relevance of ancient myths, remember a time that a light was shed on a dark issue that we wished to hide. Our partner may have confronted a selfish, jealous, or emotionally detached aspect of our character. Just as the pupil of the eye initially closes up when a bright light shines, we may have also felt closed up from overexposure. If the confrontation was an attack, we may have felt burned by the lantern held up to our dark, vulnerable qualities, and by the affront to our divine image. At such times the wounded lover in each of us may dissociate and fly up to our mother complex which is the soothing, unconditionally loving representation of our heavenly desires. The young, inflated, godlike self in each of us feels threatened when our limitations are brought to light. As it did for Eros, this may lead us to create distance, psychologically or physically.

These times of separation in a relationship, whether it be for moments, hours, or longer, are times of self-reflection and growth for both partners—a time to find the light once again through the clouds of emotional dissociation. Eros and Psyche were both wounded by the separation. These wounds send both partners on a healing journey. What we uncover in ourselves, what we gain from others, and the suffering we go through, makes our psyches grow.

> *After Eros flew away, Psyche's soul was filled with lamentation and she flung herself headlong into a river. The kindly stream caught her in its current and laid her, unhurt, upon its banks. Luckily Pan, the God of Instinct came to her rescue and taught her to make sounds of every kind to express her pain. He told her that Eros could be won back through fervent prayer and tender submission because he was an amorous and soft-hearted youth.*

The tale tells us that the suffering of failed love leads us to the river of our pain. If we can let go of our emotional body, the inner currents will lead us to healing instincts. The catharsis that comes will help our "(pan)ic." By submitting to our pain, we'll find our way back to the softness of love.

As Psyche continued on her path, she went to Aphrodite (Goddess of Love and Eros's mother) to ask for help, just as we beseech the archetypal powers of love to help us when we are suffering from the wounds of one of Eros's arrows. Since Psyche had not yet been initiated into the secret stories behind Aphrodite's name, she naively assumed that Aphrodite was the Goddess of Kind Love and a member of her family, a mother-in-law that she could ask for help. She was unaware of Aphrodite's jealousy of her beautiful youth, and her hidden agenda for Psyche.

Who is the Aphrodite we call to when we want loving intimacy? Aphrodite's birth came from the foam of the sea that gathered around Uranus's severed genitals. The image tells us that love is inherently associated with the painful loss of male virility—with the loss of the part of us that wants to be in control of life. The image reveals a purpose in this wounding. When we lose our detached intellectual stance (symbolized by Uranus, the sky god) and suffer a wound to our virility, the vast array of feelings from the sea of the collective unconscious is born— humility, longing, betrayal, sadness, and the desire to share our lives with another. When our organ of potency is taken by the sea of life, there is a larger purpose than we are aware of. The emotional tidal waves and unpredictable patterns of this larger sea teach us to attune ourselves to its rhythms; to be aware of sharks in its depths, to be appreciative of powers more primordial and more powerful than our desires. We meet "love" when we let go to the waters of life.

Aphrodite's nature is inextricably connected with the wounds of love. When she sleeps with the mortal Anchises, he is lamed by a lightning stroke in one story, and in another version his eyes are stung by bees. For those who idealize love it may be disheartening to know that the Goddess of Love commits adultery, as is seen in her marriage to Hephaestus and subsequent affair with Ares followed by her capture in her husband's net. She is also associated with vengeance. Hippomenes was turned into a lion after he neglected to thank her for helping him win the race with Atalanta. Her love can be possessive and deadly, as in the story of Adonis.

From Aphrodite comes good and bad, pleasure and pain. When Aphrodite had children with Ares, they were Deimos (Fear), Phobos (Panic), and Harmonia (Harmony). She is caring, as is seen in the pity she felt when Ino jumped into the sea with her infant son, Melicertes, in her arms. Aphrodite benevolently adopted the orphaned daughters of Pandarus, and she helps mortals win their beloved as she helped Hippomenes win Atlanta. Aphrodite even helps the gods with love— she lent Hera her magic belt to win Zeus.

Aphrodite contains the dark and light sides of erotic love. She is called *Androphonos* "killer of men" and *Melainis* "the black one;" but also *Chruse* "the golden one" and "heavenly love." She infatuates, loves laughter, beguiles, and "steals the heart away even from the thoughtful."[17]

Out of the pain that Aphrodite brings comes growth—psychological and spiritual. Despite the fact that she seems to jealously oppose Psyche in the tale of *Amor and Psyche*, it is by accomplishing and by moving through Aphrodite's tasks that Psyche is initiated into womanhood.

> *After Hermes lead Psyche to Aphrodite, she was '"welcomed" by being introduced to Aphrodite's handmaidens, Trouble and Sorrow, who tortured her, scourging her with whips and racking her with other torments. In response to Psyche's request for aid, Aphrodite gave her four trials to perform to test her worth.*

Psyche's first task was to put into order a giant pile, full of many different seeds—before sunrise. Secondly, she was to find a way to contain the uncontainable waters of life from the river Styx. Thirdly, she was required to obtain a piece of hair from the unobtainable Golden

Fleece, and fourthly, she was sent on a journey to the underworld to bring back a beauty potion for Aphrodite.[18]

Psyche's First Task

After taking corn, barley, millet, chick peas, lentils, and beans, all jumbled into a heap, Aphrodite said to Psyche:

> "Sort that disordered heap of seeds, place each kind of grain in its own place, and see that you show me the completed work before evening." As Psyche sat in stupefaction, overwhelmed by the vastness of the task, the little ants that dwelt in the fields, understanding the difficulty of her huge task, pitied her, and abhorring the cruelty of her mother-in-law, helped her. They separated the whole heap grain by grain, each in its kind."

The metaphor of the seed and grain has many meanings. First, in order to work on the path of love, our Psyches need to put in order our priorities in order to decide what we want to sprout. Do I want someone from "my clan," someone who is well-endowed physically or financially, someone who shares my interests? Many people embark on the path with lists. Often the seeds of this list were planted in our youth. "I want someone who is intelligent"—but then dryness may come from the union. "I want someone who is emotionally expressive"—then the waves come that knock us over. Hermes, who teaches through opposites, often guides us to Aphrodite's door; in time we learn to tend the seeds we have "husbanded."

The seed motif tells us that intimate relationship continuously calls us to be aware of the small details. These little things, such as putting the top back on the toothpaste or putting the tea kettle on the stove before your lover comes home, take on symbolic importance. And aspects of ourselves that seemed inconsequential when we lived alone—leaving the socks on the floor or keeping the toilet seat raised—can become sources of contention. Our ability to be conscious of their impact shows that we care.

Love teaches us to be aware of the type of seeds we plant everyday with our partners. Each thing we say or do in a relationship plants a seed. If we are belligerent, one kind of seed is planted; by withdrawing, another kind is; and with clear communication, a flower blooms. As Virgil said, "We make our destinies by our choice of gods." Like Psyche, we must exercise our discrimination.

One aspect of the ant symbolism relates to their capacity to bear extraordinary weight for their size. Just as Psyche called upon the ants to aid her, when we have difficulties in our relationship, we may call upon friends to help us bear the emotional weight. Support from others is useful in an hour of need. The ants' symbolism also conveys that to have a healthy relationship requires finding the power in ourselves that can carry the responsibility of communicating with integrity, and thereby plant healthy seeds.

The symbolism of ants takes us to the heart of the ancient mystery traditions.[19] Unlike the concept notion that spirituality is about being "high," these esoteric traditions teach that spirituality is being "low." For instance, Taoists meditate on water and say, "The highest good is like water; it occupies the place which all men think bad (the lowest level). Oceans become kings of a hundred rivers because they are good at keeping low."[20]

In the story of Psyche and the ants, the message is clear. To make a relationship work we must be humble enough to realize that we don't have all the answers. Any couple who fights over household chores should watch the ants working together to lift a piece of food. Humbleness is one of love's great buried treasures.

Psyche's Second Task

And Aphrodite said to Psyche:

> "Do you see those sheep whose fleece shine with hue of gold?
> I bid you take a wisp from the wool of their precious fleece
> as best you can and bring it to me with speed."

Psyche's second task was to obtain a single hair of the Golden Fleece while it was guarded by fierce rams. In astrological symbolism, the ram is symbolized by Aries, the zodiacal sign of springtime, the time when new life awakens. The idea of zodiacal ages furthers the meaning of Aries and the birth of new life. Zodiacal ages are 2,160 years in length, and are measured by the place in the zodiac that is pointed to when the earth and sun are in alignment at the time of the spring equinox.[21] The Age of Aries followed the Age of Taurus (the sign of the bull), and symbolically began when Moses blew the shofar (the ram's horn). This signaled an end to the Hebraic peoples' worship of the idol of the Bull[22] and ushered in a new age.

The mythic tale of the Golden Fleece also adds to our understanding of Aries the Ram. The story begins when Phrixus's mother Ino convinced Athama to sacrifice his son. A miraculous ram appeared with a golden fleece and rescued him and his sister Helle just in time. According to one legend, the Golden Fleece was hung in a sacred grove; according to another story, the gods honored the ram's ability to give new life to Phrixus, and placed the ram in the sky as the constellation Aries.

So perhaps Psyche's task, like our own, is to free ourselves from what in our family dynamics could kill us and prevent us from individuating. By getting in touch with the ram power in us, we find the newborn light of springtime, blow our inner shofar, and a new age begins. We become who we are as individual persons.

In the tale of Jason and the Golden Fleece, Jason took the approach of stealing the fleece through fierce battle. In the tale of Eros and Psyche, Psyche is taught another way of obtaining the fleece—she is to take a reed from the water and play it like a flute, lulling the fierce rams to sleep. She is to wait for the sun to go down before taking the wool.

Psyche's second trial tells us that there are specific ways to obtain this golden softness that all lovers want . . .this presence that helps light the spark of our own individuality. Psyche's task to properly time her action is a good metaphor for the crucial role timing plays in our relationships. If we confront our partner too harshly when they are upset, we may butt heads as rams do. Instead of the *yang*, masculine powers of day, the more *yin*, feminine powers of nighttime are often needed.

To find this gentle way, Psyche must activate the powers of the water reed and the music that comes from it. Finding the right tune to play when we have difficulties with our partner is the key. If we assert ourselves forcefully like a headstrong ram, we may get our horns caught in the bushes, whereas if we keep in mind that relationship is a duet we have a much better chance of finding our way to the Golden Fleece.

For example, one of the common battlegrounds in partnership is cleanliness versus messiness regarding household tasks. Often this takes on the proportions of an archetypal battle or a crusade. One partner proclaims on her banner "cleanliness is next to godliness;" the other partner acts like he's fighting a crusade for "freedom from restraint." With such couples, the motifs in the above myth are helpful: First find time to reflect together on each person's family issues. Distance must be found and soft melodies played to find freedom from Aries-like rage. The first person may remember the rigid controls and value judgments of her parents regarding cleanliness; the "unbridled crusader" may remember rebelling against controls in his family. Sharing in a brother/

sister-like attitude is the key, the myth tells us. For like Phrixus and Helle, joined together in their quest to escape abusive parents and carried away by the Sacred Ram, so can modern couples find a brother or sister in their partner. This ally can help us leave the restrictive patterning of childhood. The Golden Ram from the heavens reminds us not to butt our heads against each other, and find a soft, golden presence to speak to of our differences. With much inner work we, too, may give birth to a new age that spins our different strands of life together into a golden fleece.

Psyche's Third Task

And Aphrodite said to Psyche:

> "Do you see the high mountain peak. . . where the swarthy waves of a black stream flow down till they flood the Stygian swamps and feed the horse streams of Cocytus? Go, draw me icy water. . .and bring it to me with all speed in this small urn." So saying, Aphrodite gave her a small jar carved out of crystal.

> As with all the other tasks, Psyche thought this one would be impossible to accomplish, for the mountains were of measureless height, rough, slippery and inaccessible, making the approach to the stream almost impossible. . .not to mention the forked-tongued dragons that stood on both sides of the stream. But Zeus sent an eagle who took Psyche's urn and flew to the mountains, and the fierce dragons let the eagle pass when he told them he was on a mission from Aphrodite, Goddess of Love. Thus the eagle gathered up the waters from the river Styx in Psyche's crystal urn and brought it to Aphrodite, fulfilling Psyche's mission.

Psyche's third task is about dealing with the black stream of underworld emotions—our own and our partner's—that emerges in intimate relationship. The symbolism of the eagle tells us what we need to activate in ourselves. The eagle is the highest flying of all birds and the most farsighted.

When our partner is breathing fire at us like the dragons at the river Styx for flirting with a member of the opposite sex, being far-sighted like an eagle means being able to see the vast terrain around a given problem from a larger perspective. We need distance from our own emotional reactivity, or we will burn in the fire of emotional hell. The eagle is king of the air. Taking a moment to breathe honors its power.

As Psyche felt her task was impossible, so do our psyches feel overwhelmed by the dragon's verbal attack that we are inconsiderate or disloyal for flirting. But the eagle's sight gives us a higher perspective—that our partner is in an inner child state, and fears abandonment. It takes this kind of sight to speak to our partner's inner dragons and tell them that we are on a mission from the Goddess of Love— that we did not intend to hurt them, that we love them, and that our speaking to another was a part of our inner eagle's free flying.

Adding to the story's richness is the insight that the crystal urn must be used to carry the black waters of the river Styx. Crystals are the symbol of clarity, a clarity born from the earth. When our partner is breathing fire, it does take grounded and clear vision to respond with love.

But natural crystals are not completely clear; they are clouded. Following "the crystal path" may mean admitting that we are not so clear about our motivation and intention. This is part of being "crystal-clear." We soul-search, we self-examine and finally we admit our flirtatiousness, narcissism, and possibly even our need to be worshipped by others. It takes this kind of honesty to deal with the black waters of jealousy—loving feelings alone will not suffice.

Then the deeper healing elements of crystal may appear. Crystals have been used for healing in diverse indigenous cultures. In our modern culture they are used to amplify energy and focus it into a narrow beam; and transform pressure into electrical signals in communication systems, computers, phonographs, and laser technologies. Even Western doctors are reporting success in using them for healing purposes, and some believe they can have an effect in balancing the human energy field.[23]

The crystal quality of the urn is a symbol of the capacity to direct healing energy to our loved one, and communicate in a clear manner. By doing so, balance can be brought to a couple's off-centered patterns, and, as in modern crystal technologies, transform a highly pressured situation through communication.

As the crystal cup was used to contain the uncontainable waters of the river Styx, so do we need to learn to properly contain the deep running emotions from our underworlds in a relationship. If we don't, we get overwhelmed, and our partner may feel poisoned. It is said that the waters of this river were so toxic, so penetrating that no normal vessel could hold them.

Psyche's Fourth Task

And Aphrodite said to Psyche:

> "Take this casket and descend to the world below and present the casket to Persephone and say, 'Aphrodite begs of thee to send her a small portion of thy beauty.'"Psyche was instructed not to open this box but to bring it back to Aphrodite. Psyche felt so overwhelmed at the prospect of such a trip that she was about to throw herself off a high tower to her death, but the tower spoke to her and told her how to survive the trip. She would be approached by a lame driver of a donkey who would ask her to hand him a few twigs that had fallen off. She was instructed not to help and not to say a word to him. Likewise when she crossed the river of the underworld, a dead man floating therein will ask her to take him into the boat. She was instructed not to be moved by pity for him and continue on her journey. She needed to carry cakes of pearl barley and mead to give to Cerebus, the three-headed dog that guards the entryway to the underworld. She was given two coins to hold in her mouth to give to Charon, the ferryman, for entry into and out of the underworld.

The tower's instruction to Psyche not to give the lame donkey driver aid and not to help the floating dead man mirors modern co-dependency literature. "Don't succumb to pity; for it will avert you from the focus on your path. And it isn't really helpful to others because it stops them from developing their own resources."

Certainly, there are times to stop and help those in need,[24] but now is a time stay focused, Psyche is told. So often we don't heed this advice and get distracted by the "lame asses" we meet on the path. So often we get dragged down by the emotionally dead, avoidant parts of our partners. Psyche heeds the advice from the tower recognizing that her soul is at stake.

The coins for the ferryman Charon stress the value of the thera-pist or guide that helps us traverse the waters of the dead; that helps us find the way to life. Psyche's instructions to hold the coins in her mouth, and have Charon take them, emphasizes oral expression. Speaking truth—whether it is with a therapist, a friend, or our partner— can be, literally, worth its weight in gold, and can help us cross the bridge to the beauty of our deepest feelings.

Feeding Cerebus with honeycakes of pearl barley is another rich metaphor. Normally, when one member of a couple barks, the other barks back. We don't realize that our partner, like Cerebus, is simply defending their territory. The initiate on the path of Psyche can hear these barks as defenses and has been advised to feed them, not bark back and escalate into a shouting match. Behind the bark is a great deal (three mouth's worth) of neediness. We need to deal sweetly with our partner's defenses, and approach them with pearls of wisdom that will nourish their underlying needs.

Psyche survived the journey to the underworld and took the black box of beauty potion from Persephone. Returning to the world of daylight, however, she succumbed to temptation and opened it saying,

> "Oh! what a fool am I, for I carry the gift of divine beauty and yet sip not even the least drop therefrom, even though by so doing I should win the grace of my fair lover." In going against the instructions of Aphrodite, Psyche fell into a spell of deep sleep. She laid motionless for a long time like a corpse. But the God Eros, who was recovering from his wounds, came back to her and wiped the sleep from her eyes. He woke her with a harmless prick from one of his arrows. When Psyche awoke, she brought the gift from Persephone to Aphrodite. Eros and Psyche then married and had a child called Pleasure.

Psyche's fourth and final task is a message that the heavenly love we seek in our idealized image of Aphrodite actually comes from Persephone, Goddess of the Underworld. To find the love we seek we must forge the path from heavenly bliss to emotional pain. Our psyches are being told that the final and most important death-defying task of relationship is to go into our underworld caverns and meet the dark forces within: our fear of abandonment, our attachment to the way we want things to be, and our heart-wrenching concerns about fidelity. "Soul" is found in grappling with these deep inner issues.

Beauty is found in this journey to the underworld, and its color is black, not the golden color we expected. Just as valuable gems are found in the bowels of the earth, so is our richness discovered in our descent to our depths. When a person finds their way on a difficult life issue, potent juices are found and deep beauty shines through. We can recognize the deep spark in the eyes of one who has taken that inner journey.

Like Psyche who used the beauty potion in daylight to win the affections of her love, most of us forget that there is beauty to be found in our underworld depths. Instead we become identified with a more earthly, superficial beauty; we put on makeup, or try to "look cool." We give up our quest for soul and become what the other wants us to be or tells us we should be. We become "nice," dissociating from our real experience like the woman mentioned earlier who, after twenty-five years of marriage, had never told her husband she hated the colors he chose for their bedroom set. By not being truthful, we lose the connection with the beauty of our own true selves. As Psyche did, we fall into an unconscious sleep. The sticky stuff of sleep seals our eyes shut and our psyche loses its way.

This sticky material is debris from our journey into the land of the unconscious, an apt metaphor for unconscious living. It is often unconscious beliefs that prevent us from seeing life as it really is: "He'll take care of me," says the naive maiden saddled with the myth of dependency. "I want someone to worship me," says the narcissistic young man who was overindulged in his childhood. "Marriage should be fifty-fifty," says the evenly-measured type before the journey of inequality in the Land of Unfairness. Bits of old matter that sealed our eyes shut are an inherent part of the eyes of love.

It's hard to let go of our own desires and love with divine purpose in mind. Psyche forsakes service to the Goddess of Love for her own self-aggrandizement when she steals the beauty potion. Like Psyche we often forget the importance of serving Love itself and suffer the consequences.

Don't worry. When we're feeling lost, the divine messenger of love (Eros) may come to our rescue. In a relationship that's committed to the path of the heart, our partner is there to remind us when we're off center. Our partner wipes the sleep from our eyes. Perhaps in the process, we'll feel pricked by the points made about our straying off-course, if our ego is attached to being right. Though there is some pain, the prick of Eros's arrow may help us awaken to something important to hear.

Inevitably, due to the limitations of our human nature, we fail on the path of the heart, but this is precisely what can bring our lovers closer to us. For when we can find compassion for our beloved's mistakes and our own, when two people can support each other's psychological growth by wiping the sleep from each other's eyes, pleasure is indeed born. This is the basis for *Hieros Gamos*, spiritual marriage.

What We Dislike Most About Our Partner is Our Greatest Teacher

As the myth of Psyche tells us, intimate relationship often feels like hot oil has been spilled on us. And though the myth tells us that we are awakened by the prick of Eros's arrow, it often feels like a deeper wound. In spite of the suffering that our psyche goes through, there's a higher purpose to the wounds we suffer. Wounds lead our psyches to evolve by subjecting us to trials of the heart.

Relationships are there to heal us, but not without maiming us first; for it takes this process of wounding to transform our deepest characterological patterns. It's amazing how we attract the person we need for our psyche's development; and though it is often difficult to see, our trials are precisely the ones we need to find our way back to Love. Two examples illustrate this vividly.

Case Study: Setting Boundaries on Abusive Behavior

Eli entered psychotherapy in order to deal with his drug addiction and his rage. He broke objects in his girlfriend's house and while under the influence of drugs, broke in through a window attempting to catch her with an imagined lover. He was angry and hurt that she would refuse to see him when he was high. "After all, I gave to her when she had hard times, why can't she be there for me when I need her?"

The pain Eli felt led him on a journey through to his emotional underworld. He remembered the psychological abuse in his family. On the day of his graduation from music school, his mother told him that he would never be a success unless he was a doctor or lawyer. His mother also took drugs while Eli was a child; no one had ever set limits on her behavior. Even when he was an adult, his mother reprimanded him before his own daughter and told him he was a failure. Still, he set no boundaries on her abuse.

In the course of therapy, Eli realized that he had been acting out the part of his intrusive, abusive mother and that his girlfriend, Karen, was doing what *he* needed to do in his own family—setting boundaries.[25] His psyche was working through buried feelings from his family. This realization gave Eli the strength to undergo an even deeper self-examination. He learned to put boundaries on his own abusiveness to others and to himself.

When Karen joined us for couple's therapy, it became clear that their life lessons were intertwined. Karen was "a pleaser," having learned from her family to agree with people to win their approval. It was difficult for her to say no to anyone, especially someone she cared for. With Eli, she was in a situation where her inability to say no meant danger to herself and her self-concept. Learning to set limits was a growth-filled experience for her.

Whatever in us was blocked in our family of origin is raised by our partners. Inevitably, people who developed intellectual defenses get involved with those who are emotionally reactive; people who learned to be overly neat pair up with those who are overly messy; and people who are starved for affection mate with those who are less expressive and warm. The list goes on.

It has been said that life is like a spiral.[26] Whatever was blocked earlier comes up again on succeeding turns of the spiral so that we can work through these emotional impasses. When we are younger we are unaware of the emotional resources available to cope with the people in our lives. Later, these same issues arise in our intimate relationships. As in fairy tales where the hero is visited three times before success arrives,[27] so we are visited again and again by the demons from our childhood wounding before we are successful. Our adult life is an opportunity to release the blocked energy and continue on the spiral journey on a healthier course.

There are partners whose demons monopolize conversation, or throw temper tantrums when their spouse doesn't return from work on time. Some appear downright "selfish." Our demons are, in turn, activated; we point to their lack of character and get caught in the net of accusation and counter-accusation. True intimacy calls us to carry a candle in the underground caverns of intimate relationship to illumine the ancient pictographs that tell us how to slay demons in a loving way.

Our caring for the soul of the other person demands that we explore what's beneath their behaviors. If we lose our candles and fall into darkness, we ourselves may be slain. We must discover the factors that created our partner's "demons."

The "selfish person" may have come from a very large family where he or she needed to grab things quickly for fear of losing them. The "monopolizing person" may be needing approval for his or her insights that were never properly mirrored in childhood. The "temper tantrum person" may be so frightened for fear of abandonment that he or she reverts to the patterns that were used in childhood when a trauma happened.

Case Study:
Resistance to Working on Negative Feelings

Harold, a very successful salesman in his late thirties, was a sociable fellow with an easygoing manner. He read books on positive thinking and desired happiness above all. He couldn't tolerate his wife's nega-tivity—her worries about their finances and her complaints. He became aware of underlying feelings of helplessness regarding his wife's com-plaining, and a desire to escape from "all this negativity." After deeper reflection, he realized that he felt the same way with his mother. When Harold was seven years old, his mother had a psychotic breakdown after his father was put in jail. Throughout his youth he tolerated her com-plaints, feeling helpless and unable to communicate with her. She responded to his indiscretions with irrational outbursts of anger, "You're no good; you're just like your dad!" Harold blocked his pain and learned to rise above negativity.

Harold's marriage opened these old wounds. Again he felt attacked. . .this time by his wife's complaints. But now as an adult, he saw that he had the power to descend into the underworld of his own deep feelings, and to hear his wife's complaints rather than react to by withdrawing. He realized that when his wife, Jane, was afraid of their economic situation, he heard his mother's voice criticizing, "You're no good, just like your father." Life with his partner gave Harold the opportunity to work through his reactions to abusive, critical messages.

He learned to empathize with Jane's vulnerabilities. Tired after a long day's work, she felt acknowledged when he listened. Instead of telling her, "Stop talking about negative things that we can't do any-thing about," he learned to ask her questions such as, "Let's look at your worst fantasy about our financial situation and see how we can deal with it" and, "What do you need from me in relation to your fear?" When Harold saw that Jane, unlike his mother, felt acknowledged when he listened, he began an exploratory way of relating that his childhood had not allowed.

---

[1] Later we will see how in the mythic journey process the power of myth helped Paul to work on changing his "critical sword of knowledge" that cut other people to shreds, to "a sword of compassion." See "Quest for Perfection" in the last Chapter.

[2] See Von Franz. *Apuleius' Golden Ass*. Spring Publications, 1976. Reitzenstein, R. *Das Marchen von Amor and Psyche*. Leipzig, 1912; and Collignon, M. *Essai sur les monuments grecs et romains relatifs au mythe de Psyche*. Thesis, Paris, 1877. Little is known about what actually happened at this temple.

[3] For an introduction into Mother Goddess literature see Neumann, E. *The Great Mother*. Princeton University Press, 1963; Stone, M. *When God was a Woman*. Harcourt Brace Jovanovich, 1976; Kerenyi, C. *Eleusis*. Shocken Books, 1977.

[4] See Hillman, J. *Revisioning Psychology, The Myth of Analysis*, and his article "Peaks and Vales" in *Puer Papers*. Spring Publications, 1979.

[5] Hillman, J. *The Myth of Analysis*. Northwestern University Press, 1972. quoting (Frag. 45 Diels).

[6] Cassirer, E. *Language and Myth*. Dover Publication, 1953, p. 49.

[7] See Mayer, M. *The Mystery of Personal Identity*. ACS Publications, 1985, where the author reviews the literature on the mystery and power of naming in ancient initiation traditions.

[8] See Eliade, M. *Myth and Reality*, Harper and Row, 1963, p. 13.

[9] Baring, Anne. *The Myth of the Goddess*, Viking Press, 1991, p. 307.

[10] See Hillman, J. *The Myth of Analysis*, Northwestern University Press, 1971, p. 93.

[11] Von Franz, M. L. *Apuleius' Golden Ass*, Spring Publications, 1970.

[12] See Hillman, J *The Myth of Analysis*, Northwestern University Press 1972, p. 93 quoting Reitzenstein *Das Marchen von Amor und Psyche bei Apuleius* Leipzig 1912.

[13] Jung, C. G. *Memories, Dreams Reflections*. Routledge & Kegan, 1963, p. 325.

[14] In the original text by Apuleius which mixed Roman and Greek elements, Psyche's husband was referred to as "Cupid." In H. E. Butler's translation of *The Metamorphoses or Golden Ass of Apuleius of Madaura*, 1910, Cupid is spoken of as Amor. In contemporary versions of interpretation by Erich Neumann and M. L. Von Franz, Amor is spoken of as Eros, the Greek name.

[15] The story here is paraphrased from Neumann, *Amor and Psyche*, Princeton University Press, 1956. We'll use Greek names throughout like Aphrodite, instead of the Roman Venus to keep with the deep archetypal realities that are connoted by the Greek mythic tradition.

[16] The idea of our partners as "damaged goods" I first heard from my Doctoral committee chairman Sam Keen.

[17] See Kerenyi, The Gods of the Greeks, Thames and Hudson, 1979.

[18] For a more complete version of the story see Neumann, E., Ibid.

[19] For more on the ancient mystery religions see Campbell, J., *The Mysteries*, Bollingen Press, 1955.

[20] Watts, A. *Tao the Watercourse Way*, Pantheon Books, 1975.

[21] The Zodiacal ages are determined by determining the amount of time it takes the pole of our earth to make a complete cycle through the heavens. This has been called a Processional Cycle or the Great Sidereal Year and lasts according to some 25,838 years. Dividing this by 12 signs, one Zodiacal age lasts approximately 2160 years. The time of Christ and "the fishermen," his disciples, was synchronistically the time of Pisces; also the time when sea powers ruled the world. Some believe that the age of Aquarius(an air sign) began when air power began to rule the world. For a more complete discussion see Rudhyar, D., *Astrological Timing*. Harper and Row, 1969.

[22] For a radical historical perspective on the overcoming of the Goddess worship of Astarte and the cult of the Bull see Merlin Stone's *When God was a Woman.*, Harcourt, Brace and Jovanovich, 1976.

[23] Crystals have been used for healing in diverse indigenous cultures. Oh-Shinnah Fast Wolf, a Mohawk-Apache Medicine woman I studied with for a time, uses them for healing and says she learned about them from

Mayans, Navajos, and from a Tibetan teacher. Dr. John Adams reports healing wounds with crystals, and being able to take stitches out in four days instead of the normal seven to ten days. Dr. Laskow, on the Faculty of the University of California Medical School, reports a decrease in the duration, frequency, and intensity of herpes lesions with their use. One hypothesis coming from these researchers is that the "weak energy fields" around the human body are affected and can be brought into balance by crystals.

Researchers who have experimented with the world famous Mitchell-Hedges crystal skull report hearing voices and music, and smelling fragrances while in its presence and believe the crystal has the capacity to store and transmit information. In our modern society they are used to amplify energy and focus it into a narrow beam, transform pressure into electrical signals in phonograph cartridges, and as frequency emitters in radio transmitters and in computer and laser technologies. Harley SwiftDeer says that in the body of the Earth Mother, "crystals are akin to brain cells, gemstones are the organs, rocks the muscles and trees the hair." And when Leonard Laskow M.D. wanted to corroborate this he looked at liquid crystals through a microscope and as he projected a certain thought into the crystal it shaped itself into a rough approximation of the object he had visualized. See *The Crystal Sourcebook*, Harford M. Mystic Crystal Publications, Santa Fe, 1987.

[24] See the story of Malik Dinar in the chapter on the Trial by Earth.

[25] In analytic literature this is called projective identification.

[26] For an excellent discussion of this subject see Purce, J., The *Mystic Spiral*, Thames and Hudson, 1974.

[27] For example in the Grimm's tale of Iron Hans the king's son's golden ball rolls into the cage of a wild man. He is given three opportunities to open the cage. The third time the boy does open the cage; and so begins his adventures with the wild man, Iron Hans.

CHAPTER 4
CROSS-CULTURAL METAPHORS OF THE HEART'S JOURNEY

How should we be able to forget those ancient myths that are at the beginning of all peoples, the myths about dragons that at the last moment, turn into princesses; perhaps all the dragons of our lives are princesses who are only waiting to see us once beautiful and brave. Perhaps everything terrible is, in its deepest being, something helpless that needs our love.

RAINER MARIA RILKE

The Medicine Wheel

The tapestry of stories of the heart's initiation into the Temple of Love is woven from a fabric that knows no limits of time and place. It has its dark and light threads. We can learn as much from negative examples as we can from positive ones. Each story we hear, each image from the past, adds another thread of meaning, and takes us another step on our grail quest to unravel the mysteries of love's nature.

In the last chapter we saw from Karen's issues regarding setting boundaries on abuse, and Harold's issues regarding working with negative feelings, that relationship provides us with a mirror to see a deeper part of ourselves. The richness of the American Plains Indians' tradition adds more depth to this idea.

Hyemeyohsts Storm in his book *Seven Arrows*,[1] discusses the oral teachings handed down by his Native American ancestors. These Plains Indians taught him that the universe was a Medicine Wheel—a mirror in which everything was reflected. "The Universe is the Mirror of the People, and each person is a Mirror to every other person." They believed that a fundamental purpose of life was to find one's place within the Medicine Wheel.

When they sat in a circle, they acknowledged each person's unique purpose on life's great wheel. This purpose was given a name based on an animal or an element of nature. It was emblazoned on their shield and expressed their part in the great spirit's creation. Names like Lame Deer: Seeker of Visions, Sun Bear, or Black Elk speak of the power of nature symbolism of nature, unlike modern names.

Another aspect of the Plains Indians' identity was the direction they represented. A tribe member's calm under pressure was like the cool wind of the North, another person's caring attitude reminded people of the warmth of the southern sun. The dynamism and courage of a young brave desiring to be first in battle was like the rising sun of the East, and the way a shaman sat alone looking within might be seen as the setting sun of the West.

Though each person had, according to tradition, a beginning place on the Wheel of Life; it was said that any one who perceived from only one of the Four Great Directions remained a partial person. The way a person became whole was through relating to someone who was from a different direction on the wheel of life. Meeting another person provided a sacred opportunity to turn one's own wheel. Thereby each person's "medicine" grows.

For example, an "eagle person" who resonates with the eastern direction of the rising sun will have the clear far-sighted vision of the eagle and the dynamism of the rising sun, but he might have difficulty maintaining close contact. On the other hand, a "mouse-like person" who resonates with the southern sun may have the warmth to be close to others, but may have trouble acquiring vision and distance.

We can imagine the issues that may arise in a relationship between the mouse person and the eagle person. "You're too friendly with others. Why can't you just keep an appropriate distance." "You're too reserved, why can't you be more open-hearted." With the vision of the Medicine Wheel, there are less judgments and criticisms, and a better chance that, even people today, could appreciate their differences as part of the wider natural order.

Metaphors from other cultures tap universal wellsprings of love and help us draw forth healing analogies, analogies that, like love itself, quench our thirst for anything that takes us out of our isolated lives and transcends time, place, and cultural boundaries.

Plato's Androgyne

In the classical Greek tradition, there is a potent metaphor for finding our wholeness. Plato's *Symposium* tells the story of the original Androgyne:

> *This primeval person had two faces looking in opposite directions, one male, the other female. The thoughts of their hearts were great and they dared to scale the heavens and attack the gods. For this, they were punished by Zeus to humble their pride and improve their manners. He cut them into two parts like an apple halved for picking. After the division, the two parts (the Androgyne), each desired the other half. They came together and threw their arms about one another, entwined in mutual embrace, longing to grow into one. They were at the point of dying from hunger and self-neglect because they did not like to do anything apart. They were about to be destroyed when Zeus, pitying them, invented a new plan; he turned the parts of generation around to the front, and after the transposition the male generated in the female so that man and woman might breed and the race might continue.[2]*

This image vividly portrays the primordial desire of people through-out time to reunite with our lost other half. There is something in us that senses a return to our original nature when we see someone who attracts us, when we become lost in an embrace, when we see the po-tential for a lasting union with another. Whereas the normal, "fallen state" of human beings is one of separation, in love we become uni-fied with another and feel whole again. Worlds away from each other, Plato's image of the Androgyne and the Native American image of the Medicine Wheel both lead to the insight that love can unite us with a wider dimension of ourselves.

Finding the Way Through Our Emotional Underworld: Ariadne's Thread

The classic story of Ariadne's thread represents the symbolic tools needed to deal with our demons.

> *There was a Minotaur, half man, half beast who lived at the bottom of an underground maze. Seven male and seven female children were fed to him as a sacrifice to appease his wrath. Many heroes tried to kill the monster, but none could succeed because they would get lost in the underground maze. Then one day, a hero named Theseus came along and one of the priestesses of the labyrinth, Ariadne, fell in love with him. She told him the secret way to survive the labyrinth.*

> *Ariadne gave Theseus a ball of thread and tied one end to a pillar at the opening passageway so that he could go down into the caves without being afraid of taking a wrong turn. If he got lost, he could always wind up the thread and find his way back to the world of light. So Theseus was able to descend into the labyrinth, defeat the Minotaur, and free the children of Athens.*

The story tells us that relationships exist to help us work through the bullheaded and monstrous parts of our personalities. We can liberate the fixated energies created by childhood wounds if we can evoke the love of the mistress of the labyrinth.

Ariadne represents the feminine principle that loves the hero with the courage to quest. She compassionately presents us with the thread that guides us into our deepest underground passageways. Here we meet those demons that hold our inner children captive. As the bullheaded Minotaur devoured the children of Athens, so does our stubbornness prevent us from doing the necessary work on our wounded inner child so our natural energy may be liberated and returned to the world of light.

According to Purce, in the *Mystic Spiral*:[3] "The symbolism of the original Cretan labyrinth was an initiatory hero's test of overcoming death at the centre and a subsequent return or rebirth into life." Remember Eli, whose inner child was wounded by his mother's abuse. His relationship helped him wrestle with this monster and find his own boundary-making function that had been lost in his childhood. His ability to put boundaries on his drug habit and his rage was indeed a rebirth into life. What is the demon that lurks in your underworld awaiting your Ariadne?

Time Traveling to Heal Our Childhood Wounds

As Theseus needed the magical tools to travel in the underworld, so do we. Three interwoven elements are helpful in underworld descent— a two-faced mirror, a golden thread, and the ability to time travel.

From the American Plains Indians we've seen that the ability to traverse the sacred land of relationship requires the ability to see how the issues of our partner mirror our own life lessons. A *two-faced mirror* can help this quest. Secondly, we need to find our own blocks as we meet an issue in our partner. To do this we need to be able to wind the golden thread back into the past to find what issue in our past parallels our parner's issue. Thirdly, through time traveling, we find the Minotaur from our past that is killing our ability to be fully present.

Time traveling is a useful method to the initiate of any age. In Steven Spielberg's movie *Back to the Future*, Marty McFly's father was a cowardly man, but when Marty revisited the past in his Delorean time machine, he was able to advise his father to confront the local bully. By defeating this bully in front of his wife-to-be, his father became more self-assured. As Marty McFly traveled into the past and helped to change his father, so do our relationships give us the opportunity to return to our roots and change those patterns.

It is interesting to note that in most science fiction movies, the hero is warned *not* to alter the past. Traditional wisdom says that could have dire consequences for the future. Spielberg broke the mold by having Marty influence his father's life with beneficial results. In psychotherapy, hypnotic regression, and in intimate relationship, the past is re-activated, which opens the possibility of altering the future.

For example, if we have pride in being independent and are in relationship with a person who is dependent, we might imagine the words "dependence/independence" placed on the search control panel of a time machine and travel back into our lives waiting for a light to go on.

"Where has dependence and independence been an issue in my early life?" we wonder. Regardless of what we call it—*parallel processing,*[4] weaving the thread of Ariadne, or time traveling—these gifts of the gods help us develop empathy for our partners and can keep the relationship together.

The Ancient Art of Scapegoating

Before weaving the thread of Ariadne back to the issues of blame and jealousy in a relationship, we need to add one more thread to our tapestry, an understanding of the ancient art of *scapegoating*.

An informal survey reveals that the most common source of conflict arising in couple's therapy is not sex or money as might be commonly assumed, but blaming. It can poison an atmosphere of intimacy, but if worked through, can make all the difference in changing the battlefield of love into a safer, more loving place.

It's no wonder that in our monocentric culture we see one right way and another way as wrong. The polycentric world view that imbued all life on earth with divine purpose was replaced by a monocentric culture that created a single God removed from earth in the heavens. In a relationship, a monocentric world view all too often manifests as self-righteousness—the assumption is that one is a God-like figure who can see the issues from an omniscient perspective.[5]

The problem with self-righteousness and blame is illustrated by the ancient art of *scapegoating*. The term comes from a ritual described in the Old Testament. Two goats are offered by the community as a purification sacrifice on Yom Kippur, the Day of Atonement. One goat is killed and the other is placed alive in front of the temple. A rabbi/high priest places both hands on the goat's head while confessing the sins of the community. The goat is then handed to a man who leads it away into the desert. In one tradition the goat was hurled down a ravine. Before returning to the community, the man must bathe himself and wash his clothes.

The ancient Greeks' equivalent of the scapegoat is called the *pharmakos*. A person with particularly grotesque physical deformities was chosen from the community. After a ritual meal he or she was whipped with fig branches and squills and was driven out of the town. During the festival of Apollo the Thargelia (the *pharmakos* complex) may have been associated with human sacrifice.[6] William Mannhardt has put forth the theory that the scapegoat was originally a vegetation spirit that must be whipped and chased and even killed in order for the earth to be regenerated.[7]

Modern psychologists see the scapegoating phenomena as a way to externalize blame and project psychological complexes onto another person in order to rid ourselves of anxiety, guilt, and the toxic effects of our own negative emotions. The Greeks called this procedure *kartharsis*, a purification to release "evil" from the mind, the body, and the community.

Couples Who Blame: The Two-Faced Mirror

To facilitate parallel processing in therapy with couples who blame or scapegoat each other, I ask both partners to imagine that there is a two-faced mirror between them, one face looking toward each person. When one partner points at the other's "problem with dependence" that person is asked to look into the imaginary mirror and journey within, examining what this issue means (or has meant) for them. This is particularly helpful with couples who blame because both want to prove the other person is wrong. We can imagine such a system energetically looking like this:

A > > > > > < < < < < B

Here both partners are pointing at the other, and each person's defenses keep the other person's statements at a distance. Energy is caught in the middle and no movement happens. Inner reflection is at a minimum.

On the other hand, with the two-faced mirror, both partners self-reflect. When one makes a statement, the other uses it as an opportunity to enter the underworld, explore, and share this exploration. The energy system looks like this:

In other words, when A says something to B, B reflects in his or her own inner mirror. This creates a dynamic for the other person receiving B, thereby creating a circular flow where A self-reflects, too. I call this process the "Circle of Communication."

Healing Jealousy

As an example, a woman with whom I worked named Nancy was threatened by her husband, Rob, looking at other women. Nancy had a history of raging temper tantrums and heated accusations of disloyalty. Rob usually became defensive, and when he tried to convince her that he wasn't disloyal, she wouldn't accept his reassurances. Like a hero of the past, Rob did everything he could to save the wounded maiden. He told her that she was beautiful and tried to rescue her from her painful feelings by giving her reasons why she shouldn't be jealous. He tried everything he knew. Finally, out of frustration, he angrily called her "a possessive bitch."

After two painful years, Rob and Nancy entered couple's therapy. In the course of their inner work, Rob and Nancy did the two-faced mirror exercise. The first thing Rob found inside was denial, "I don't have this issue in me. It's her insecurity about me connecting with others, and I don't care if she looks at another man." At the next level of descent, he realized that he wasn't insecure because she'd been so dependent upon him. Then he remembered the rocky times of his single life when he felt insecure, and the many relationships he lost. These memories felt like a "giant hole in his stomach." He remembered his own feelings of inadequacy.

There was a noticeable shift as Rob felt empathy toward his wife; for he had touched his own vulnerabilities. At that moment he realized that, while he had been co-dependently trying to rescue Nancy, he had an underlying frustration and resentment that she wouldn't transcend her feelings. Rob could now see that by denying his own feelings, he had contributed to Nancy feeling even worse about being jealous.

Next, Rob wound the thread back into his past and time travelled back to his family of origin. He reported an open-hearted feeling; but when I asked him about his upturned lip, he said that he felt exasperated and impatient. It said, "I am angry that you won't let me in." As Rob traveled back to his early life with this body sense, he remembered his disturbed sister who had been the object of the family's rescue attempts. His sister would never listen, and everyone felt exasperated.

Through a deep process of introspection Rob realized that none of his family members shared their vulnerabilities. "They were always on my sister, trying to help *her*." Rob's early life flashed before him. He recognized how his family had protected themselves from their feelings by making the younger sister into "the identified patient" of the family. They had all tried to help her, and when they were totally frustrated, they yelled at her.

Tears came to Rob's eyes when he realized how he had perpetuated this rescuing dynamic in his first marriage and now in his second one. He withheld his feelings and actually (though it was hard to admit) enjoyed being in this position. His sense of power in helping the vulnerable one enabled him to avoid facing his own vulnerable feelings.

Rob found his Minotaur, the bullish part of himself that refused to acknowledge his own vulnerabilities. He realized that this contributed to making Nancy's jealousy into a demon. Rob became an initiate of the timeless journey of the heart. Without knowing it by name, he looked into the mirror of the Medicine Wheel and found that his partner's quality of jealousy reflected something in himself. Without traveling to Greece, he traversed the difficult journey into the labyrinth and came up with a new sense of that wounded child that had been imprisoned all these years.

The rescue of the children of Athens from the Minotaur is an apt symbol for the process Rob experienced. We may have hidden parts of our real self in an underground labyrinth, because of the parent-child dynamics in our own family. We may have tried to please our parents by repressing our anger and hiding our weaknesses for fear of being abandoned by our primary caretakers. Or, conversely, we may have felt that the only way to be heard was to become overly reactive and indulge in wild tantrums. Later in life when we meet the person who is willing to play the role of Ariadne in our emotional quest (a therapist or a partner), we have an opportunity to find our way back through our emotional underworld. The compassion of our Ariadne leads us to the aspects of our inner child that were damaged, soothes the wounds, and opens up the dark chambers in the labyrinth, allowing the light to flood in.

Rob's deep sharing allowed Nancy to safely reflect in the two-faced mirror. She followed the thread into her past and explored the roots of her jealousy. Nancy relized that her parents always compared her to others. She thought she needed to be the best in order to be loved. Nancy's not meeting her parent's standards kept her in the place of being "not good enough" when compared to others. When Rob looked at other women, Nancy was afraid she wasn't good enough. This was the monster in Nancy's underworld.

By Nancy expressing her vulnerability, Rob could offer Nancy the tender compassion she needed and he, too, could receive attention for his vulnerabilities. For both of them, this was a long, arduous process, like mountain climbing with continued falls, but new awareness and new skills grew with every step.

Emotional Evolution

So often we go through the pains of relationship, unaware that our suffering is for a higher purpose—our own evolution in the divine play of life. Just as the evolution of the human species and our bodies' structure come from trials by the environment—changes in climate, geography, and consciousness—so do the trials of relationship affect our psychological evolution and structures. Psychological mutation takes place each time a lover's heart opens, and each time a critical partner finds compassion.

Like a giraffe whose neck elongates through evolutionary change, enabling his territory to be seen from a higher vantage point, for us, it is the soul that is stretched heavenward by the challenges of love, allowing life to be seen from a higher perspective.

The evolution of our very souls is the stake in the great game called love. This is Eros's purpose in shooting his arrows. From our heart wounds, from being stretched beyond our limits, emotional evolution occurs.

[1]   Storm, H., *Seven Arrows*, Harper and Row, 1972. Not all Native Americans had the same beliefs as the ones expressed here. As in our American culture, diversity existed.

[2]   Plato, *Symposium*, Benjamin Jowett trans., and reprinted in *Great Books of the Western World*, 7, Chicago: Encyclopedia Britannica 1952. Also see Singer J. *Androgyny*, Anchor Books 1977, p.109.

[3]   Purce, J. *The Mystic Spiral* ,p. 29.

[4]   "Parallel processing" is a term I use to speak of the process of reflecting on how our own blocked issues stand in the way of being present for an issue of another person. It can be used in a wide variety of contexts. I most often use it with my interns in clinical supervision training when their countertransference is evoked. Other therapists have used similar terms. For instance in Bugenthal's, *The Art of the Psychotherapist*, W.W. Norton, 1987 p. 95, he speaks of various ways "paralleling" can help the therapist deepen a session.

[5]   We shall have more to say about this throughout the book and particularly in the Trial by Air chapter under the heading of "either - or thinking" and the story of Nasrudin and the Donkey. Also see Baring A.and Cashford J. *The Myth of the Goddess*,Viking, 1991 for an excellent discussion of the mythic development of the patriarchal world view.

[6]   Burckert,W. *Structure and History*, op. cit.

[7]   Mannhardt,W. *Wald-und Feldulte*, Berlin, 1875, *Mythologische Forchungen* Strassburg, 1884. We shall have more to say about Frazer's research in the regard of the ritual killing of the King in the chapter Trial by Water.

SECTION 2:

TRIAL BY THE

ELEMENTS

Introduction to the
Trial by the Elements

---

*Oh, what a catastrophe for man when
he cut himself off from the rhythm of the
year, from his unison with the sun and the
earth. Oh, what a catastrophe, what a
maiming of love when it was made a
personal, merely personal feeling, taken
away from the rising and the setting of the
sun, and cut off from the magic connection
of the solstice and the equinox! This is
what is the matter with us. We are
bleeding at the roots, because we are
cut off from the earth and sun and stars,
and love is a grinning mockery because
poor blossom, we plucked it from its stem
on the tree of Life, and expected it to
keep on blooming in our civilized
vase on the table.*

D. H. LAWRENCE

Just as the psyche grows through its initiation into the temples of the various gods and goddesses, so does it awaken to its true nature through being "tried by the elements." "Elements" are the icons worshipped in different temples. Passion is worshipped in the Temple of Fire, Stability in the Temple of Earth; Merging in the Temple of the Water; and Space in the Temple of the Air.[1]

An understanding of the elements was central to healing practices in the ancient mystery traditions of the East and the West.[2] According to ancient Chinese medical philosophy, for example, the universe and the human body and mind were composed of five elements (fire, earth, metal, water, and wood). When a person was ill, an analysis was made regarding which element was in excess or deficiency. Then herbs were given, and points on the body were either needled with acupuncture or touched with acupressure to return the energies of mind, body, and spirit to harmony.

In Western esoteric traditions, the initiate was tried by the four elements: fire, earth, air, and water. The purpose of these trials was the evolution of one's personality—to become whole by coming into harmony with all the elements.

The ancient Greeks believed that the soul itself was composed of a vaporous substance formed out of the four elements. So, symbolically speaking, when we seek passion (fire), stability (earth), merging and deep feeling (water), and a higher perspective on life (air) in a relationship, we are on a quest for "soul." A "soul mate," by this definition, is one who unifies us with that element that we need for our wholeness: fire needs air to fuel it, air needs fire to move, water needs earth to contain and direct it, and earth needs water to moisten and nourish it. When Love initiates us through a trial by the elements, our souls are rounded and made whole. When we are with our lover, through *elemental osmosis* we become more of what our essential nature is, and what our potential fullness can be.

Osmosis happens when the initiate engages in a process that Jungian psychologists call a *symbolic attitude*. In this method of "outward introspection," [3] we see an object as a symbolic quality of the self. A tree becomes a symbol of groundedness, or a fluidly expressive dancer awakens our lacking water element. If we see our partner's qualities as an opportunity to develop them in ourselves, healing and wholeness can emerge.

Some of the ancient initiation rituals exposed a person to the raw elements of nature. And it was raw! Among the tribes of the Native

American Plains Indians, the young brave's stamina was tested by spending a long time alone in nature. And, as mentioned earlier, in the Sun Dance ritual, the initiate was hung on a pole with an eagle's claw tied to the breast muscle, exposed to the sun and the elements. In martial arts training, the acolyte would be tested for the ability to generate internal heat by being placed on ice without any clothes on; when a wet blanket was placed over him, the master would see if steam rose from the blanket.

Lovers may recognize metaphors for our trials and tribulations in these initiation rituals. If we stay tied to our lover long after the vital energy of the relationship has gone, we may feel the pain that the Sun Dance initiate did. Like the Indian brave, the modern initiate prays for divine aid for a task that seems beyond mortal limits. When our heart strings are pulled upon and torn, painful though it may be, we look to the light in the sky above to understand and withstand the pain. When our lovers throw wet blankets on our ideas, initiates into the trials of love are tested for their ability to sustain their life energy. Like the martial arts initiate, it's natural to steam a little under such circumstances.

One of my students went on a tour to the Temple of Komumbo in Egypt where, she was told, ancient initiates held their breath while passing through an underground tunnel filled with water. She didn't know if she could trust swimming through the tunnel and if she would come out alive. (Remind you of any relationships you've had?)

Though the following chapters have a particular order (fire, water, earth, and air) relationships do not present us with trials in such neat order. They come through a natural process of unfolding. What is seen along the way depends upon the path we choose and our openness. Likewise, in our intimate relationships, the trials by the elements present themselves in accordance with our chosen path and by noticing when the elements are there. We can appreciate the rain of love that appears after an emotional drought. And we watch in awe as lightning flares burn the forests below as it seems to do when human needs do not fulfill divine expectations.

---

[1] Chapters 3, 4, 5, and 6, respectively, go into more depth about the Trials of fire, earth, water, and air.

[2] See for example: Hall, M. *The Secret Teachings of All Ages*, The Philosophic Research Society, 1971; Campbell, J., *The Mysteries*, Bollingen

1971; Connelly, D. *Traditional Acupuncture: The Law of the Five Elements*, Center for Traditional Acupuncture, 1971.

[3] I heard this term on an album called *Planetary Peace* by Aurora, Beauty Records, 1981.

CHAPTER 5
TRIAL BY FIRE

People say that what we're all seeking is a meaning for life. I don't think that's what we're really seeking. I think that what we're seeking is an experience of being alive, so that our life experiences on the purely physical plane will have resonances within our own innermost being and reality, so that we actually feel the rapture of being alive.

JOSEPH CAMPBELL

Love and Passion

Love and fire are Siamese twins. It's hard to speak of love without using images of fire. Friends warn the starry-eyed lover that jumping into a relationship is "playing with fire." When we're impassioned, we say we are "on fire;" and when we care about someone deeply, "our heart is set aglow." Our attraction may be called "sparks" and our lover is our "flame." When we're angry at our partners, we "sizzle," and when we are humiliated, "our face turns red." When we're rejected, it's called "getting burnt." Romance is fostered by candlelight. In the embrace of a loved one, we are "turned on," "fired up," and glimpse "the eternal light."

Out of the darkness of our lonely nights, we are drawn, like moths, to the flame of love. The metaphor of the moth warns the traveler on the path of love to discriminate between love's many kinds of light and fire. When the moth goes towards moonlight, it spirals upward towards the heavens. Then the moth sees a beautiful fire, finds it difficult to resist on a cold night, and flies into the flame, burning alive.

There is deep meaning in the moth's and our own quest for light. The symbolism of the singeing moth teaches us that when we are drawn to love, we become aware of the nature of light that attracts us.

Unlike the moth which dies in the process, the initiate who impetuously moves too close to love's flame can learn something. At first we see a potential lover in a shimmering light. Perhaps a friend tells us complimentary stories about this person, or we glimpse him or her in a good light. But this is not love, it's infatuation.

In-"*fat*"-*tuation* isn't bad. It's nature's way of filling us to the brim with a loving experience. As fat is stored in the bear for the winter, nature gives us "fat" so that when our "winter" comes, we will have a stored memory of love to warm our hearts. As it does for the bear, these memories may sustain us through the rough winter ahead, when it seems that warmth will never return.

If we become blinded by the bright light of a courtship, chances are our evaluation of our lover will be less than objective. Like honey bees, we are attracted to a biological happening by bright colors. But if we want a relationship that lasts, we need to go beyond the dazzling light and vivid colors and see our potential partners under a normal spectrum.

Falling in Love with a God or Goddess :
The Story of Ixion

When relationships activate our inner fires, it's natural to feel longing and to project our unfulfilled needs onto the object of our desire. When we do, we get caught in illusion and become blinded to reality. In Greek mythology, Ixion is the story of one who fell in love with an image of a goddess, and learned a difficult lesson.

> *Zeus shaped a cloud in the image of his wife Hera, and Ixion tried to seduce this cloud-like image. Zeus punished him by chaining him to a a fiery wheel for eternity.*

This story speaks about idealization and love. As Ixion fell in love with a cloud that he thought was a goddess, so do we, at first, fall in love with a fantasy-filled cloud. Being chained to a fiery wheel is the price we pay when we fall in love with an idealized image. However, in mythology as in life, something positive is borne from suffering.

> *The cloud gave birth to the race of the Centaurs—half man and half horse—one of whom was Chiron, a great healer and the teacher of Aesculapius, the father of modern medicine.*

After falling in love with an idealized image, disappointment often follows. We mourn a lost ideal and let tears come, like a cloud dropping rain. Centaurs symbolize a time when people were more aware of their physical bodies. When the god or goddess we desire disappears, we become more aware of our physical bodies—we stomp and pace in frustration, we whinny in agony, and we become half man/half beast.

One of the most unacknowledged sources of illness in our culture may be the wounds of love—colds come when our immune systems are weakened, sore throats occur when we don't express ourselves, vertebrae are displaced when we are shaken at our core. If we're depressed, we may drink to numb our gloomy feelings; but this just leads to a fiery wheel that goes nowhere.

The myth tells us that, when we're lost in the clouds or wounded by love, we should go to Chiron. A great teacher, he was the founder of holistic healing. In Aesculapius' temple at Epidaurus, people would be healed by *nootherapeia* (therapy of the mind), theater productions (for catharsis and psychodrama), hot baths, herbs, gymnasium exercise, dream incubation, and hands-on healing. (Chiron's name bespeaks the origin of chiropractic medicine.)

When our bubble of idealization bursts, the myth tells us to seek that which will bring our lives and our spines back into proper alignment. We need to find our way to the temple where the spirit of Aesculapius lives holding his straight staff entwined with snakes.

For those who think mythology relates only to the past, here's the story of Arnold, an architect who fell in love with a fantasy of a goddess. Harriet was a beautiful actress who seemed to fulfill Arnold's dreams. Arnold was a creative man who needed to work independently, but felt guilty about it. In their courting days Harriet assured him that he would be free to do what he wanted. When they lived together, though, Harriet resented the late nights that Arnold spent working at his architectural studio.

Arnold felt the way he did as a child, held back from doing what he wanted. His father died when Arnold was an infant, and so he was raised by a family of women. When his mother went to the hospital for a nervous breakdown, he lived with his restrictive grandmother for most of his youth. Arnold angrily remembered how she wouldn't let him play outside, for fear that he would get dirty. Expressing feelings was out of the question. Often, when Arnold wanted something, his grandmother told him that he was fortunate she was taking care of him, and that he should be satisfied. Arnold felt guilty when he asked for anything.

With Harriet, Arnold became a modern-day Ixion, chained to his own guilt, tortured on the fiery wheel of resentment and festering rage. He drank alcohol excessively. Sometimes he was enraged and expressed his raw emotions, and other times he was submissive. When he used verbal assaults, Harriet would get upset; when he succumbed to her wishes and came home earlier than he wanted to, he felt tied down. His muscles tightened and the vertebrae in his lower back continually went out of kilter, a manifestation of his mis-aligned instinctual energy.

In time Arnold realized that he had not distinguished between Harriet and "the enemy" that he had perceived his grandmother to be. He learned to express in a deeper way how important his time alone was. He also learned to take Harriet's feelings into consideration and not sacrifice his freedom in the process. Her emotional aliveness gave him permission to open up to his own feelings. In time, his drinking lessened and his spine realigned. With his animal instincts set free, Centaur was born from the fiery wheel of pain.

Containing the Fire of Anger

Inner work is not always cathartic. Although in the Aries phase of psychological movements[1] (such as the men's and women's movements) we often see an emphasis on expressing anger, it is sometimes necessary to contain one's impulsive reactions.

The reactive fire of emotions can be like a forest fire. There are times when expressing anger is appropriate, but the adept needs to learn how to contain destructive, reactive emotions, like rocks surrounding a fire in the forest to prevent it from spreading. Placing appropriate boundaries around our reactive feelings contains an emotional fire.

In terms of Eugene Gendlin's focusing, it gives one a chance to have a "felt sense of what this anger is really about." When deep discoveries occur like Arnold's, we can feel a shift of energy. Gendlin calls this "a felt shift." The brain actually changes its EEG pattern when one finds the "felt meaning" of an energy blockage.

The Alchemy of Everydayness

When one's heart is open, energy flows; when it is not, energy is blocked. How do we find that life energy that is the nature of love?

Being in the moment is one of the key factors that makes energy flow. It's an intuitive sense of knowing what opens the door to passion at a given moment—telling a joke, reading together, giving or receiving a massage, being physical, going to a movie, doing a new activity, or even doing a regular activity and dramatizing how you're getting old together. But listing factors that make life energy flow is a futile exercise, for it is the quality of heart in the process of doing the activity, not the activity itself, that keeps love alive.

There is an alchemical concept that exemplifies how to flow with the life energy of another. Alchemists spoke about *the great round*, by which they meant knowing what operation was needed at a given time to turn lead into gold. Sometimes the material in the vessel needed more substance and the alchemist would add matter to solidify it (*coagulatio*); sometimes more fire was needed (*calcinatio*), water (*solutio*), or air (*sublimatio*).

The alchemist of relationship, likewise, needs to know how to turn the leaden burdens of daily life into the gold of intimacy. For example, if you have workaholic tendencies and spend long hours at the computer at home, "the great round" might consist of blending massage (earth, coagulatio), light-hearted humor (air, sublimatio), deep communication about the feelings regarding what's behind your compulsive working (water, solutio), and taking breaks for fun activities (fire, calcinatio).

Alchemists learn that when they apply "the great round," there must be sensitivity to the substance with which they're working, whether it be the prima materia[2] of the alchemical vessel, or the primal emotional material of your partner. If your lover is in a bad mood, being light-hearted (air) may produce an uplifting laugh. But, at other times, a joking response may make your partner feel misunderstood and the depth of their emotional need will not be met. There are no recipes; sensitivity is the only tool.

Creating Chi in Our Relationships

In the Taoist tradition, there is a training to flow with the energy of life. Cultivating *chi* is a first step and a life practice. Chi is the electro-magnetic energy that flows through the meridians of the body. After many years of skepticism in Western scientific circles, thanks to recent advances in our measuring tools, these channels are now scientifically measured.[3]

Without chi, the body becomes ill and love in our life withers away. When Lao Tzu, the great Taoist master and author of the *Tao Te Ching* was asked to describe "the way" to enlightenment, he said, "The way that can be spoken of is not the way." He then wrote a poetic treatise on it. Likewise, the chi of love is a mystery beyond words, and yet we can allude to its ways through poetry:

> *Trying to create chi in a relationship blocks it;*
> *letting go develops it.*
>
> *Rubbing together increases its fire;*
> *yet even in separation it exists.*
>
> *Chi lies at the center of yin and yang;*
> *it is experienced when we are not too soft with our lovers*
> *and yet not too hard.*
>
> *Chi moves in circles when two people listen to each other,*
> *and follow its meandering patterns to the center of things.*
>
> *At one's center is a vast reservoir to be tapped on;*
> *yet chi is everywhere waiting to be discovered.*

Some ancient traditions say that chi is centered in the chakras, and that the heart is the most important center. It flows freely through the body when there are no fears and emotional blockages.[4]

In ancient Taoist Temples, chi was cultivated in a practice still carried on today called Tai Chi Chu'an. "Push hands" is a practice for cultivating chi with a partner. Two partners stand facing each other, their hands joined in the shape of a Tai Chi symbol—one hand on the partner's forward wrist, the other on their rear elbow.

The touching is neither too hard nor too soft. The direction of the intention is to push towards the center of gravity of the other person, but not too far forward lest one leave their own center. For a moment, one person becomes yang (with a dot of yin, like the tai chi symbol) pressing toward the other, the other person becomes yin (with a dot of yang) and, without resisting yields to the pressure, neutralizing it by bringing the force back into their own center and then completing the circle back to the other.

The idea in this practice is to help your partner find fluidity in the midst of pressure, to find the center of his or her ball of energy in the midst of the application of force. Each follows the principles that create chi: not being too hard or too soft, finding the reservoir of chi that lies at our own center, and becoming sensitive to the center of our partner. Each person learns to be nondefensive to the other's force, and to follow the movement back to his or her own center of gravity. Force is played with as a child does with a ball—naturally.

Creating energy in the circle of togetherness is what love is all about. John Welwood says,

> "Passion arises at the boundary line where different worlds rub
> up against each other."[4]

Passion has its positive and negative manifestations. When the worlds of two different people meet, warmth is generated but friction occurs and sparks may fly.

Using Love's Fire

Throughout history, those that worked with fire knew that it was a metaphor for working on their personalities. According to Eliade,[5] the early alchemists, smiths, potters, and shamans all were on the path of becoming *masters of fire*. By working with fire, they learned to control the passage of matter from one state to another, and they changed themselves through the process.

The first potter must have felt awe when he discovered how live embers hardened the shapes which he had given to his clay; he had discovered a transmuting agent. Like the potter, love calls on us to transmute our psyches from one state to another, for the fire of our relationships can change the shape of our personalities into a beautiful vessel or distort them.

The damage of a distorted upbringing is illustrated by Marianne, a young woman in her thirties. After her mother died when Marianne was a teenager, she was continuously beaten by her alcoholic father to control her. He called her "a whore" when she wore "too revealing" clothes (skirts one inch above her knee). Marianne developed an extremely poor self-concept from her father's demeaning comments. Her path, like that of other battered survivors, led to a series of abusive relationships as an adult which reinforced her negative self-image.

When the sparks flew in Marianne's latest relationship, she came to therapy. Soon the fear and degradation she felt as a child resurfaced. Marianne was able to resurrect her buried anger as she was being physically battered by her husband. This began the process of building a positive self-image. She was ready to risk losing love by standing up for herself. She realized that the price that she had paid for "love" was too great. Her relationship gave her a chance to transmute her negative self-concept, and, like a potter, she began forging anew the vessel of her personality.

Currently, Marianne and her husband seem to have worked through the issue of violence in their relationship. They've been married for five years now, and report no more of the physical abuse that characterized the first years of their relationship.

Finding the Spark of Our Individuality

We explored how the myth of the Golden Fleece was a symbol of breaking abusive parental ties, finding our true feelings, and discovering ourselves. Phrixus escaped on a supernatural golden ram from the stepparent who wanted to kill him. This ram was sacrificed to the gods and became the constellation Aries, symbol of springtime.

When Marianne was allowed to express her feelings regarding being abused, something golden was indeed discovered. When we leave our parents' home and form relationships with others, we can begin a new life. With distance from parental programming, we can discover that unique spark within us. But the spark of individuality does not come easily, for our parents are still with us psychologically. We need to question and release old patterns. So begins the quest to discover the golden fire of the inner ram.

The ram is not afraid to butt heads with the world, and to climb for the peak experiences that life offers. The Golden Fleece represents the qualities obtained from the path of individuation—great softness, a golden glow, and the ability to carry ourselves and others to a magical world beyond ordinary life.

The qualities necessary to find the Golden Fleece were explored in the tale of Amor and Psyche. The path of Psyche was to approach the fleece when the sun was low, and to use the gentle, melodic sounds of the flute to tame this solar force. Her task was to bring back a small bit of wool, whereas Jason, in the tale that follows, takes the entire fleece. This tells us something about the difference between the archetypal masculine and the archetypal feminine, the yin and yang pathways to individuality.

Balancing Power and Love:
The Story of Jason and Medea

Finding the spark of individuality requires balancing love and power, for the desire to make a contribution to life is as fundamentally human as is the need to love. When power overshadows the love principle, the heart grows cold; when unconscious love overshadows power, our lives become mush. Worldly concerns and the desire for quiet intimacy may tug at us in different ways, forcing a choice.

Robert Bly has pointed out how modern industrial civilization affected the father-son relationship. It all but destroyed the mentoring that was possible when father and son worked closely together farming in the fields, or working in a craft. Economics have also affected our relationships, for today, the pressures to prosper in an economy that requires two-income households is often draining. The tale of Jason illustrates the problems that befall us when love and power are out of balance.

> With Medea's help, Jason grabbed the Golden Fleece and re-
> gained the throne that was usurped by his wicked uncle Pelias.
> He lived happily with Medea for ten years. But in time, Jason's

ambitions took over, and he wanted to marry Creusa, daughter
of King Creon. When he abandoned Medea, she killed their
children. Jason died when a beam of the rotting hulk of his ship,
the Argos, fell on him.

This tale serves as a warning about the overly masculine mode
of trying to grab everything around us. Modern civilization has made
us even more like Jason than Jason was. The corporate executive shifts
a piece of paper on his desk, and a thousand lives change. At home,
the news of the entire world is broadcast in half an hour, while lovers
tell their partners *shhh*. Images of the most beautiful women and men
parade across our TV screens, calling us more often (as fast as we can
hit our remote control devices) than Circe called to Odysseus to leave
his ship.

The trial of the Golden Fleece occurs in our relationships as it
did in Jason's. We are tested to keep Medea, or the feminine self, in
the center of our hearts or suffer the consequences. Medea was one of
the priestesses of the old Earth Goddess religion. Though we may not
realize it, our partners carry on the tradition of Medea when their touch
heals us at the end of a long day or when their cup of tea warms us
inside.

In daily life, we forget to honor this sacred gift. We ambitiously
try to grasp more and more—possessions or new lovers. Like wood
under a fire, love fuels us to go into the world and do our business. If
we forget to balance our love lives with our worldly desires, our partnership with love will be in danger. Only scorched earth will
be left.

Our lover may lash out, having felt deprived. Just as Medea killed
her own children, the relationship may be injured and its vital energy
destroyed. As the mast of the Argos fell on Jason's head, so do our
grandiose desires, when not in balance with love, come crashing down.

The adept of the Temple of Fire does not go overboard and
give up the fire of his or her outer life; for as easily as power
can stifle love, so can oversaturation by the waters of love lead
to a stifling of "the fire in the belly" we have for life. Over-
indulgence in love or work can turn our inner fire into a soggy
pile of embers.

When the Flame of Love Dies:
How to End Our Relationship

It's sometimes difficult to know to when to leave a relationship and when to stay. As in the story of Jason and Medea, if we do leave a kingdom, we should leave consciously rather than impulsively.

The Golden Fleece of relationship can give such a powerful spark to our life force that hubris can arise. This feeling of potency can lead us to grab at false ambition, or to pursue another challenge without respecting what is there in our relationship.

Of course there may be a time to leave a relationship. We must look into the embers of the relationship and see whether or not the fire can be reignited. Sometimes a relationship is so symbiotic that the fire is smothered, or so toxic that it destroys both partners' spiritual growth.[6] Then a period of separation can be helpful to get in touch with our own fire again. Breathing space (air) helps revive dying flames. Time alone or time with an objective observer (a therapist or couple's counselor) can be important to reflect on whether staying in the relationship is helpful to each person's growth. When we are considering leaving a relationship, we should ask ourselves:

- What does the relationship challenge me to work on in myself?

- What would I need to let go of within myself in order to make this relationship work?

- Does this relationship give me a sense of trust so that I can share, explore myself and my limitations, and grow?

- For long-term relationships, ask "Is this a person with whom I'd like to share the experience of dying?"

- If you are thinking of having an affair ask yourself, "What will be the consequences of my action? Are they worth the price I'll pay?"

In light of these questions we can determine whether the work to be done on the relationship or the sacrifice that would need to be made is in line with our spiritual path. Sometimes, however, even after facing these questions, we still may be unclear.

Dream incubation may provide an answer. It's helpful to keep a pen by your bed, and before going to sleep, feel the conflict and ask for a dream. Imagine your body being like a motion picture camera that is playing onto a blank screen.

I remember a loving yet dysfunctional relationship that I had a hard time leaving. After doing much inner work and therapy, a dream came that showed me the path that, reluctantly, I knew I had to take:

> *I'm trying to make a beautiful gold ring fit, but I've outgrown it. I go to the best metal smiths who tell me that this type of metal can only be fitted to my finger with much damage. One smith suggests that I give it away because someone else would find it lovely.*

Such is the power of the unconscious: it sometimes gives us the strength to do what our conscious minds cannot.

Developing a Tender Heart

In the course of loving, we move from the spark of individuality (Aries) to the fire of the heart opening to another (Leo the lion with a golden heart). The great Tibetan Buddhist teacher, Chogyam Trungpa, says that the path of the spiritual warrior is to develop "the awakened heart." One would think the warrior's path is to develop strength, forcefulness, and fearlessness. But Trungpa says that, the spiritual warrior's task is to develop a tender, sad heart:

> *If you search for an awakened heart, if you put your hand through your rib cage and feel for it, there is nothing there except tenderness. You feel sore and soft, and if you open your eyes to the rest of the world, you feel tremendous sadness. This kind of sadness doesn't come from being mistreated. . . .Rather this experience of sadness is unconditioned. It occurs because your heart is completely exposed. There is no skin or tissue covering it; it is pure raw meat. Even if a tiny mosquito lands on it, you feel so touched. Your experience is raw and tender and so personal.*
>
> *For the warrior, this experience of a sad and tender heart is what gives birth to fearlessness. Conventionally, being fearless means that you are not afraid or that if someone hits you, you*

*will hit him back. However, we are not talking about that
street-fighter level of fearlessness. It comes from letting the
world tickle your heart, your raw and beautiful heart. You
are willing to open up, without resistance or shyness, and face
the world. You are willing to share your heart with others.*[7]

Difficult issues in a relationship give us an opportunity to work
on opening our tender heart. For example, if a person has a child from
a previous marriage, a new partner may feel angry, sad, or jealous. It
takes the strength of a spiritual warrior to open the heart at these times
and feel our own and our partner's pain. Striking back in anger or
withdrawing in defensiveness damages our newly developing bond. The
real issue may be that both people need to give up the image of the
stable, less complicated one-family relationship we remember from our
early years. Searching for our "awakened heart" at such times is a quest
for the lion-hearted.

Trungpa offers the analogy that at sunrise, the sun provides beams
of light that provides a pathway. In the same way, when we follow
the tender heart, it provides a pathway of light. Opening the heart
burns away the reactive conflicts and can provide a means to what is
essential—tender caring for our deeper self and for another.

Burning Away Narcissism

At some time in every relationship, our self-centered desires must be
sacrificed and we adapt to our partner's desires.

New relationships trigger our deepest fantasies that our needs will
be met. Perhaps the first flames of love fan our primordial memory of
our idealized mother responding to our needs; yet, even in that relationship, a time came when we cried out and she was not there. A time
came when our feeling of omnipotence—standing on our own two feet
and ruling the world around us—changed. We learned to walk along
with another, sharing the world and adapting ourselves to another's
rhythm.

Our divine nature and our human limits are experienced to the
fullest in relationship. Surrendering to the spark of divinity in another
is depicted in the following story:

*A young student went to his yogi to ask how to find Truth.
"The truth is that you are one with Brahman," advised the*

*yogi. That gave him the feeling of great power. On his way
down the path he saw an elephant approaching. Now I shall
use my power and command the elephant to stop, he thought,
but the elephant came closer. "Stand aside," shouted the elephant driver to the student. But the student did not move,
whereupon the elephant lifted him from the path and set him
aside. The student was humiliated and complained to his yogi.
"The elephant is also Brahman," said the yogi. "Why did you
not stand aside?"*[8]

Relationships confront us with our narcissism. We feel our light
and power; but we need to let go if we are not to crush or drive away
the other. The life lesson of the astrological fire sign Leo, according
to Dane Rudhyar, is to realize that "the sun is also a star." This epitomizes the lesson of being narcissistically filled with our own sunlight.
We need to realize that our partner is an independent source of light.

This is the Copernican Revolution in the realm of intimacy!
Copernicus disagreed with the scientists of his age who thought the
earth was the center of the universe. He hypothesized that the earth
revolved around another center of energy, the sun. The adept of the
Trial by Fire makes the difficult shift from feeling we are the center of
earthly existence. We find a greater source of light as we open our
hearts to another.

Burning Away Old Patterns and Beliefs

One of the greatest fears that single people express entering into new
relationships is that it will end the way all others have—"in ashes."
They may be right, but not for the reason they think. In accordance
with the psychological law of opposites, where there is life there must
be death. What burns away is the unreal portion of our dreams.

Poet Robert Bly says, "Ashes do not belong to the sunlit crown
of the tree, nor to its strong roots. (They are) literally the death of the
trunk." When our most cherished dreams turn to ashes, the idealistic
youth is transformed into a mature lover. Ashes are a fundamental part
of the initiation into life and love.

Robert Bly describes the indigenous cultures of Australia, Africa,
and the near East, where a young boy between the age of eight and
twelve is taken from his mother and goes through "ashes time." The
elder male guides cover his face and body with ashes, the color of death,
to remind him of the inner death to come. He may crawl through a

tunnel (a vaginal symbol) made of brush and branches. The old men wait for him at the other end, and give him a new name. Similar to these initiation rituals, love takes us on a journey that can kill our infantile notions of being mothered the way we might like; we are born into a new maturity, forging a new identity from the pain and death of childlike ideals.

In alchemy, the end product that came from placing material in the fire of the alchemical vessel was white ash. It symbolized that which survived the ordeal. The history of symbolism contains many images of the ashes of love: the biblical image of the crown of glory which Isaiah gave the mourners of Zion was "a crown of ashes. . . praising the spirit of grief."[9] An alchemical text says, "Despise not the ashes, for they are the crown of thy heart and the ash of things that endure."[10] Both these images speak of the value of loss and mourning.

That value is best symbolized by the Phoenix. The Phoenix was a mythical bird of the Arabian desert, said to have a life span of five hundred years, after which it burnt itself to ashes on a funeral pyre of myrrh and frankincense. These twigs were ignited by the sun and fanned by the bird's wings. Ancient fables say that the Phoenix would then emerge from the ashes of the fire, and be reborn to live another five hundred years.[11] In the Bible it says, ". . . I shall die in my nest, and I shall multiply my days as the Phoenix."[12]

In the nest of relationship, a process of death and rebirth does indeed take place; our old patterns can be alchemically transformed. We saw how Marianne developed a pattern of taking abuse, believing this was what she deserved. Continual scolding by her violent, alcoholic father molded the vessel of her personality with introjected feelings of shame and compliance. When Marianne's partner was angry, her old feelings and reaction patterns returned, but recognizing this helped Marianne alter her self-sacrificing ways. A sense of her own value was reborn out of the pyre of inner work.

Arnold, the architect tied to Ixion's wheel, underwent the process of changing the way he shackled himself by his own guilt. After mourning a time when he couldn't express feelings, he began the rebirth process of finding a centered way to express them.

What first attracted us to our partners undergoes a Trial by Fire, burning away our early expectations. If a person's body excited us, eventually we tire of it or it changes with aging. If we were attracted by a warm smile, inevitably a cold scowl takes it place. Intimacy burns away our desires and turns them to ash.

As a forest fire burns away the outer layer of old, decayed wood and opens up a process of new seeding, so does the superficial level of initial attraction burn away. Our devastated feelings of loss burn away our attachments to old beliefs, desires, and expectations. New seedlings emerge from the ravaged forests; from the rich soil grows a deeper capacity to love.

For example, a woman may believe that a man should take care of her. She may marry a handsome wealthy, man. Then he loses his money in a bad business venture, and she is faced with the death of an ideal she cherished since childhood.

The emotions that are expressed by feelings of entitlement, "I deserve to have someone who will take care of me financially," are subconscious messages of our materialistic culture, and are rooted in our universal fears, insecurities, and childlike desires to be mothered. These examples, and our own, show that out of suffering, new wisdom can arise.

One of the lessons of the *calcinato* process is called *extractio*. In alchemy, the white ash symbolizes the wisdom which remains after surface values are burned away. After a Taoist master is cremated, legends say that a pearl is often found in the remains— a powerful symbol for the beauty we hope will emerge from our suffering.

Guarding Against Inflation: Riding Phaethon's Chariot

As the nature of fire's heat is to rise, so there is a natural inflation under the influence of love's fire. The young lover feels that there will be bliss forever. Some people forget their old friends and neglect all earthly concerns. Like Phaethon, who boldly asked his father, Zeus, to drive the sun chariot for one day, the inflated lover rides a fiery chariot in the sky defying all limits.

> *The four horses sensed an unsure hand on the reins, shot upward, and scorched a great scar (creating the Milky Way) across the sky; then they plunged downward until the earth was ablaze from the sun's heat. In order to save the world from destruction, Zeus had to kill Phaethon with a thunderbolt. Phaethon's flaming body fell into the Eridanus River.*

Love impels us to go beyond our limits. We may perform physical feats to impress our lover and stretch ourselves in many psychological ways, too. Inherent to heat is its expansive nature; inherent to love is an expansion of our capacity to care about others. This expansion is healthy and widens our narrow limits. We give more than we thought we could.

The negative consequence is that love can take us too far too soon. Impulsive movements in inflated moments can create injuries. Vertebrae can become unhinged and internal organs taxed due to love's excesses. We may give in ways that are not in anyone's best interest. Feeling the power of love can fill us with a sense of specialness that can lead to arrogance. We may forget our human limitations and ride the chariot too high into the sky.

When love's rising fire inflates us, we must learn to master Zeus's chariot. To ride in the abode of the sky gods requires humility. We must keep our hands surely on the reins enjoying the ride, but being aware of the earth below. Most importantly, we must remember to respect the divine force that lent us the chariot, for at any moment, some divine hand may take us or our lover away.

Finding Compassion:
The Story of Heracles and Iolaus

The high moments of intimacy are balanced by the demons that jump out at us from the underworld. From these caverns emerges the many-headed monster—jealousy, household struggles, waning passions, and differences between our desires and our partner's.

At such times, we feel an affinity with Heracles, who dealt with the many-headed monster.

> *Heracles tried to sever the Hydra's many heads, but found that another one always grew back. Finally his friend and charioteer, Iolaus, held a torch to the severed head and cauterized the wounds.*

When we meet the many-headed monster that emerges in relationship, we respond as Heracles did. We try to slash the dragons that we perceive in others and in ourselves. After the slashing doesn't work, eventually we find, as Heracles did, that changing our reaction pattern was the purpose of this trial. The tale tells us that we need to find a torch, not a sword, to cauterize the dragon's heads.

The torch is a symbol for the light of consciousness and compassion. Unlike a match, it can light our way into the underworld without blowing out and it can cleanse and cauterize our partner's wounds.

The ancient gods bequeathed to humanity potent mythological images to deal with our difficulties. Perhaps in the story of Heracles and Iolaus we're being told that we need a torch to help us battle with biting emotions, to find the way through love's emotional underworld, or to touch our lover's wound to cauterize it. Only then will a sword sever the old reaction pattern.

Communicating with torch in hand to a jealous partner might sound like this: "I know you're jealous, but the way you're attacking me makes me want to withdraw. Sure, there was a momentary attraction to the person that walked by. But, please accept my reassurance; it's you that I love."

If we can find compassion for our partner's limitations instead of slashing them, we will have a friendly rather than contentious basis for relationship. Heracles' friend Iolaus is a symbol of the inner charioteer who has the power to put reins upon our instinctual pattern of blaming others. His torch helps to cleanse and seal the wounds of love and sheds light on the pain behind the dragon's roar.

Slashing is not only directed outwardly towards our partners. When something goes wrong in a relationship, our instinctive response is often to slash away at ourselves: "How stupid I was to get involved!" "I never make the right choices." "I'm no good." "This time I'll be smarter than in my last relationship; I won't be fooled again, I'll just cut the whole thing off."

The initiate must face other people's dragons as well as our own. For many of us it is easier to forgive others than ourselves. We need to find Iolaus's torch to bring light to our self-criticism and our family's patterns that grow like stalagmites in the caverns of our underworld. These stalagmites give our old fire-breathing dragons a place to curl around and feel comfortable. "If you were a real man (woman), you'd be married by now." or "If you were psychologically together, you'd be satisfied in your marriage," or "If you were smarter, you wouldn't have chosen a relationship like this."

It takes a strong torch to cauterize the wounds of self-blame and shame. It takes courage to put the fire of awareness directly on the sore spot. It takes the light of compassion, not a judging mind, to work through the woundedness.

Mythology has a soothing function by showing us that love and pain go hand in hand. And the images explain the purpose of love's wounds—to introduce us to the path of healing.

Becoming a Healer to Our Partners and Ourselves: The Story of Prometheus and Chiron

The myth of Prometheus further develops the theme of love, fire, and healing. The story is like a four-act play. Act One covers some of the problems involved in attracting love and how we fall into co-dependent patterns. After empathizing and identifying with Prometheus's failures, in Act Two, Epimetheus gives us hope. In Act Three, Chiron gives us a mythic solution to the age-old archetypal battle between of giving and receiving in relationship. Act Four discusses sexuality from the viewpoint of Prometheus and Chiron.

Act I: Attracting the Fire of Love (Prometheus)

The Titan Prometheus was a great lover of humankind. Out of his love, he wanted humanity to have the pleasures of the gods. He stole the fire of the gods and gave it to humankind. In a further affront to the gods, he attempted to deceive Zeus by hiding the best part of the sacrificial meat in a bad-looking animal stomach, and wrapping the bones in rich-looking fat. He gave Zeus his choice of parts, tricking him into choosing the inferior part. Prometheus was punished by being chained to the Caucasus Mountains, while an eagle pecked at his liver for eternity.

The message of this story may be that the fire that Prometheus wants to give to humankind is love itself. Each time we fall in love we partake in a *regressus ab origine* (regression back to the original). We re-enact Prometheus's deed of giving the fire of love to our human selves, and in the process, we betray our deepest values and connection to higher truths (symbolized by deceiving Zeus).

Like Prometheus many of us deceive to acquire love. When we tell "a little white lie," exaggerating our accomplishments to win a prospective mate, we may try to rationalize our behavior by saying it's all part of "the game of love," but when we do so, we're "playing with fire." Like Prometheus, we, too, get fixated on getting the "meat of life" solely for our own nourishment. At such times we commit the Promethean sin of hiding the best portion of the meat, and show only the bare bones of who we really are.

Violating our connection to the sky gods seems to be part of the fire of love. We "lose our cool" and get "hot under the collar" when our partners foil our expectations—when they weren't as excited as they should have been after we arranged that special outing, or when they didn't show us the public attention we wanted. The fire of love makes us lose our connection to our observing self, and we, like Prometheus, get tied to the rocks of our human concerns.

What is the myth saying by using the image of Prometheus's liver? The liver symbolizes the cleansing of excesses from the body that abound in the pursuit of bringing love into our lives. When we go to extremes, we violate the divine truth written on Zeus's son's (Apollo's) Temple at Delphi—"Nothing in excess." Our livers can be damaged when we consume too much alcohol, drugs and junk food, or get involved in the emotional excesses of festering anger or out-of-control rage. We suffer like Prometheus did, chained to the mountains of our off-centered patterns, pecked at by the high-flying eagle, a symbol for a higher perspective on life. It may seem as though the gods are against us; yet the pain we feel is a result of being out of alignment with our higher source.

Another lesson of the myth is about giving and co-dependency in a relationship. The very definition of co-dependency seems to have originated from this myth, for it is the betrayal of our own truth in order to take care of another's needs.

It is awe-inspiring to dig into this ancient Greek myth and find the modern principle of co-dependency. It is a rich treasure to discover that centuries before Western psychology created a label for overly giving to others at the expense of ourselves, our ancestors encapsulated the image.

A common pattern of co-dependents is that they learned to give up their needs for another's and in the process, their own self-development was thwarted by avoiding their own painful, vulnerable feelings. Many develop an inflated sense of being able to heal others. We all have this co-dependent self in us when we think we can "fix others." We think we are Promethean Titans, bigger than the rest of humanity. "She's so messy. I'll try to help her be more conscious so her life gets organized." "He's so cerebral. I'll try to get him in touch with his emotions, so he'll be healed." "I can heal my partner's wounds; I have the fire that will heal my partner."

From Prometheus's attempt to give fire to humanity, we are reminded that when we want to give to another, we must not forget to acknowledge the higher source of our healing energies. As Martin Buber would say, "It is not I who heal, but Thou." Or, as the Taoists believe, when healing happens it is borrowed from the chi of the universe.

Act II: Reflecting on Suffering (Epimetheus)

To avoid Prometheus's mistake we must ask what it means to consult with Zeus, God of Light, Lightning, and Thunder before giving to others? First, the gods represent a higher view of the human condition, a knowing that on earth, growth takes time and suffering. But the gods' compassion doesn't necessarily extend to making us comfortable. Prometheus wanted humans to have the comforts of gods; Zeus did not. As a matter of fact, so that humans wouldn't profit from the more comfortable conditions of their lives after Prometheus gave humans fire,

> Zeus sent Pandora (whose name means "all gifts") to Prometheus's brother Epimetheus (afterthought). Out of her box was released all the evils of human existence— only hope was left in the box.

Zeus might advise us that before trying to ease another's uncomfortable feelings, we should consider the "gift of suffering." Instead of being impulsive (Prometheus is a symbol for forethought and the quick mind) in our judgments of our partner, we need to realize that their suffering is a "Pandoran gift from the gods." Like Epimetheus (who symbolizes the reflective mind) we must reflect on this "gift." The wise King of the gods might warn us not to interfere in God-given suffering and not to abuse the power of light and thunder, the tools of the gods.

On the other hand, the God of Lightning would probably not let our partner find their way slowly. Perhaps Zeus would know that humans inevitably will try to get the tools of the gods for themselves. If we go to his temple with the proper attitude, then Zeus may allow us to borrow lightning and thunder—if we agree to use them for our partner's healing rather than our egotistic desires.

We make our destinies by our choices, so we must choose the path that will further our higher destiny. Perhaps we decide never to use the lightning of the gods because it's too hot to handle, and thus, we let our partners be. Or perhaps we choose the mystical path of saying that the gods are within us, and hope to be true to Zeus's spirit as we hurl our thunderbolts. In the latter case, we must exercise the highest degree of consciousness or else we will become like Semele, Zeus's lover who asked him to show himself to her and was consumed by lightning and burnt to death.

Framing feelings in terms of poetic images is a way to bring a bolt of lightning into an interaction with another; it illuminates the mythic background of a life impasse. "When I see your stuff all over the place, it's like Pandora's box has opened and spilled onto the floor. I find not only dirty socks but Judgment, Chaos, Anger, and I hate to admit it, but also a desire for Vengeance. How can we find Hope again? I wonder if we can break the way we're chained to our rigid viewpoints." Using this mythic imagery, our suffering turns into a mythic quest, and our hearts can unite in our shared anguish and pain. The uncomfortable feelings that we have are "gifts of the gods" to help us develop self-reflection. It is here that hope is found.

Act III: Healing Our Partners (Chiron)

The imagery in this act involves issues in healing—the balance between being co-dependent versus rigid in not giving to others. We left Prometheus chained on a rock for betraying of the gods in helping humankind.

> Chiron the Centaur came to Prometheus's rescue. Chiron was an immortal, half man, half horse, and a great healer who taught Aesculapius the healing arts, yet he could not heal himself of a wound he suffered when one of Heracles' arrows accidentally struck his foot. This arrow had been dipped in the poisonous blood of the Hydra (a many-headed water monster). One side of the Hydra contained blood that could heal disease, and the other side caused death to mortals and mortality to immortals. Since Chiron was immortal he had to bear this pain forever. To be relieved of this pain, he agreed to change places with Prometheus, giving Prometheus a chance to live again.

The wound to Chiron's foot by Heracles's arrow is a symbol of thwarting the hero's grandiose fantasies of healing, the part of us that feels able to leap over obstacles and rise above the human tragedies. Heracles causing the wound tells us that if we have heroic expectations of being able to heal others, we will wound the immortal healer in us.

Our inner healer is lamed, and brought to earth, and thus, becomes humbler and aware of human limitations.

As Chiron becomes mortal due to the Hydra's blood, so does the modern healer, due to the blood of emotional encounter. Our pain makes us recognize our own need for healing. Our compulsive giving changes. We realize that our lovers' lives are their own; they need to work on changing and healing themselves and we need to work on ourselves. Chiron was made mortal by the wound to his foot, which suggests that if we want to be Chiron for another, we must pay attention not to overstep our boundaries. If we don't ask first if our partner wants to look at their issue with us, the door may be slammed on our intrusive foot.

On the other hand, there are those that take the modern-day lessons of co-dependency to an extreme (members of the Temple of Anti Co-dependency) and become overly careful of giving to others. These people boomerang back into a withholding stance, having been overly giving in childhood. "It's your problem; deal with it yourself." As a result, they become like Prometheus, hiding the nourishment they have to give others. This robs the gods of the gift of openheartedness, and chains the Prometheus in us to a cold, isolated mountain. Many people who are "working on their co-dependency" fall into this trap.

Chiron represents conscious sacrifice on the path of love. To understand this we need to distinguish between *neurotic sacrifice* and *loving sacrifice*. Neurotic sacrifice takes many forms. There is co-dependent giving that is not truly in the other's best interest. This is exemplified by a parent who stifles a child's development by doing it for them; or the partner of a substance abuser who "gives" to another, not expressing how the abuse impacts them. This enables their partner's pattern to continue.

But, the myth tells us, there is a path of loving sacrifice. It originates from heartfelt compassion, represented by Chiron taking Prometheus's place in the underworld. As did Chiron, the healer in us often makes sacrifices out of compassion for another's suffering. When our partner is in pain and we arrive home after a long workday, we may feel that we don't have energy to deal with problems, yet we may choose to do so anyway. We become Chiron, the healer who changes places with our lover.

We know we are neurotically giving if we can't be firm when we feel tired and say, "Listen honey, I just don't have the energy now."

Setting limits is particularly important if we always felt responsible for everyone else's comfort in our family of origin. We may become conscious of our rescuing pattern when our partner finally pushes us beyond our limits—asking for our attention after a difficult day at work. By being aware of our patterns healing takes place.

The Chiron/Prometheus myth leads to mutual exchange. Chiron's wound from the Hydra's blood was taken on by Prometheus, and Prometheus's wound was taken on by Chiron. A balanced relationship gives the opportunities to exchange healing roles as Chiron and Prometheus did, from being a giver one moment and a receiver the next. By relating our feelings and listening to each other, exchange happens. "I'll do it your way today. How about doing it my way tomorrow?"

Every time we see our partner suffering, whether it's chaos, depression, or limitations and we help them deal with it, our own wounds get activated and we come down to earth. We are neurotically giving if, in supporting another, we are out of touch with our own wound. The hero in us shoots our higher self in the foot unless we are working on our own value judgments about messiness, our uncomfortableness with tears, and our inflation and self-criticism regarding our own limitations. Chiron's path of mutual exchange unfolds when we realize that in helping others, we gain something. We come down to earth, healing the wound of isolation that comes from a pretense to be immortal, above suffering. We find the very heart of love and solve the Promethean riddle. Each time we see our partner's limitations, we have the opportunity to transform our suffering into the flame of our divine compassion. We are not merely giving for our own nourishment, but we are giving something back to the heavenly forces. Then we consciously, and conscientiously, borrow rather than steal the fire of love from the gods.

Act IV: Orgasm: The Lightning of Love

The physical culmination of the fire principle in relationship is orgasm, the lightning of love. In a culture like ours that is so goal-oriented, it is no wonder that we become obsessed with passion's highest point of ecstasy. The roots of the orgasm's importance in lovemaking go beyond culture. Orgasm feels like a divine gift, a bolt of lightning that electrifies the atmosphere, and raises us to a higher plane of life.

When it doesn't happen, it feels like a reverse Prometheus myth, like the God's have stolen fire from us. If we don't blame the gods, we may blame our partner. These are projections, the way the psyche protects itself from having to admit painful truths. It's natural to be defensive when the most vulnerable organs in the body, and the most tender areas of our selves are involved.

When fireworks do not go off in our love lives, despair enters. Instead, it may feel like a flare in a battle zone, magnifying our most vulnerable defenses. The initiate's path is to use the flare to help the relationship find its way over difficult terrain. The flare must be gently held over what *is* in our relationship; flaring up with accusations makes it painful, and our eyes shut instinctively to protect ourselves. When physical intercourse is blocked, verbal love-making is the antidote.

Orgasm is a living paradox. There is nothing that we as individuals try to make happen more than this, and yet here we tap a force beyond our control. It happens in a moment of complete fullness when we hold onto our partner with the utmost desire, and yet it happens only if we completely let go.

If there is a block in physically letting go, maybe we're trying too hard. Western sex therapists tell us that "trying" is the root of many orgasmic problems. And Taoists tell us that if we try too hard to possess something it eludes us. Just as surrender is needed for sexual orgasm to happen, so is psychological surrender to allow love-making to happen. Sometimes we need to surrender the desire to have our own personal needs met.

On the other hand, many orgasmic problems are caused by not allowing ourselves to be honest about what we desire. Whether we like to be held firmly or caressed gently, where we like to be touched, the fantasies that arouse us are all expressions of our unique energy. If we block our inner desires, we hide the truth of ourselves and hide the best portion of the meat that feeds the God of Lightning and Thunder. It is no wonder at such times orgasm is stifled and the fire of the gods disappears.

The *Tao Te Ching* expresses the paradox of the need to acknowledge and to transcend desire like this:

Rid yourself of desires in order to observe its secrets,

But always allow yourself to have desires in order to observe its manifestations.

Another paradoxical element of orgasm is that sex is the most personal of life's treasures, and yet the most transpersonal. Orgasm is a part of the primordial fire that Prometheus stole from the gods. To ignite it requires an honest appraisal of what kindles our own passion, as well as what brings lightning to our partner. The focus in our lovemaking cannot be only our own needs and desires, but must be our partner's as well. Some lovers enjoy playing on the edge of sado-masochistic sex, in part, trying to gain control over the pleasure, pain, and power issues that have been a part of their lives. Others who have felt deprived of demonstrative affection in the past may want gentler, prolonged physical contact. If we look at the peak moments of lovemaking as a Promethean theft of divine fire, the myth reminds us not to forget that such a blessing often requires a sacrifice of our personal needs.

Paying proper homage to the gods does not mean prudishness or sacrificing our needs. Quite the opposite—it means that we need to honor our temple: the tenderness and sensuality of Aphrodite, the joy and abandon of Dionysus, the communication of Hermes—and be in alignment with a power greater than ourselves. Rituals that honor the sacred nature of sexuality are one such alignment. We can create a sacred atmosphere with candles, music, massage, looking into each other's eyes and speaking from the heart, or whatever activates the lightning and thunder between two people.[13] When sex is divine, it is all the more personal; when it is personal, it is all the more divine.

Despite our best attempts to serve others, the myth tells us, inevitably the desire to possess love's fire leads us astray. We get swept away by the passion, as Prometheus did and lose contact with our higher selves. The myth says that the Chiron in us needs to come to the rescue bringing the sacred healing ways that fit the problem. Sometimes we need to let go of a particular goal and feel our love expressed through touch or massage, expressing our instinctual feelings, or being straightforward and truthful.

Finally, Chiron points the way to mutual exchange, for sometimes, our partner, like Prometheus, strays off the path, falling into egocentricities and we come to the rescue. The next moment the roles reverse. In exchange, healing takes place.

Sexual difficulties can quickly become negative explosions of charges and counter-charges, or with a shift in inner awareness, a light illuminating the dark sky. If one can find a torch of compassion to shine on sexual difficulty, what seemed like a flare in a war zone can become a guiding light to a pathway of even greater unity.

The culmination of the psychological/spiritual initiation into the Temple of the Fire is to become like the sun, using our light to help another grow. When we enter into a relationship, a light gets activated in ourselves. At our best moments, we reflect that light to another human being and help them grow, as the sun gives light and life to the earth.

When we give to another, our own personality, as well as our partner's, is transformed through the warmth we exude.

Remember the Divine Principles Our Relationships Serve

It is easy to become addicted to the warm glow we feel at healing moments in a relationship; and it is difficult to deal with those times when the relationship turns on its axis and nighttime appears. The beauty of the Greek mythic tradition is that not only lofty deities are worshipped; the Greek worldview is a polycentric one (worshipping many gods). This means that when we choose not to give in a "loving way," we may find that a deity is being served.

Choosing not to give to our partner after a hard day and respecting our limits breaks an old rescuing pattern and serves Saturn/Cronos, God of Limits. If we have difficulty in expressing anger, allowing ourselves to be constructively angry honors the Fire God, Mars.[14] By being conscious of the gods behind our actions, and paying the proper respect, we fulfill a higher purpose and destiny. We then solve Prometheus's dilemma, to give in to our earthly passions as well as to the realm of divine principles.

Through Eros's wounds, we have the opportunity to transform our desires, develop wisdom from the ashes of our disappointments, develop compassion towards the other, develop the ability to befriend ourselves, become connected to our higher selves, and transmute old patterns. Like the sacred fires of alchemy, the fires of our love contain the potential to "burn away our base metal;"[15] and the smoke may carry us to a higher perspective on the human condition.

In one ancient alchemical text, the trial of fire is poetically described this way:

> *The fire that is within us, imitating the energy of divine fire, destroys everything that is material. . .purifies the things which are offered, liberates them from the bonds of matter, and renders them through purity of nature, to the communion of*

95

*the gods. It likewise liberates us. . . assimilates us to the gods,
causes us to be adapted to their friendship, and conducts our
material nature to an immaterial essence.*[16]

---

[1] For example early in the 1960s, though many practitioners benefited
from Primal Scream therapy, many others alienated close significant
others, and at the extreme, some had psychotic breaks because their ego
structures could not handle the shock. Likewise, in early phases of the
women's and men's movements, though Aries-like release happened
that was healing to practitioners, many got their horns caught in butting heads with others and got their horns caught in the bramble. In the
butting, hurt feelings are experienced by members of the other sex, but
consciousness evolves in the process.

[2] The alchemical idea of *prima materia* posits that before any alchemical
operation can take place, a given substance must first be reduced to its
original undifferentiated state. This can be seen to be the seed idea that
rules western psychoanalytic psychotherapy, where the patient regresses
back to their childhood wounding—and then the work begins.

[3] Becker, R.O. *Electromagnetism and The Foundation of Life*, William
Morrow, 1985. We shall have much more to say about the glowing ball
of energy in The Trial by Earth chapter.

[4] Welwood, J. *Journey of the Heart*, Harper and Row, 1990, p. 58.

[5] Eliade, M. *The Forge and the Crucible*, The University of Chicago Press,
1956, p. 79.

[6] For more on the question of when to stay in a relationship see Halpern,
H. Ph.D., *How to Break your Addiction to a Person*, Bantam Books, 1982.
He discusses how "attachment hunger"—the same kind of infantile
hunger that one had when one was an infant—often keeps one in a
relationship beyond when it is spiritually useful to both partners. Then
we become like an infant and feel like we did when we were an infant
—that we can not live without our partner (mother), that we will die
without our partner, that we will never find another. Halpern discusses
how to analyze your relationship to see whether attachment hunger or
genuine need is keeping you in your relationship.

[7] Trungpa, Chogyam, *Shambhala: The Sacred Path of the Warrior*, Shambhala Publications, 1984. p. 45.

[8] This story was told by the late Dr. Chaudhuri of the California Institute of Integral Studies. CIIS Newsletter, Vol 3, #4, 1985.

[9] Deuteronomy 61:3

[10] Jung, C.G. *Mysterium Coniunctionis*, par. 247.

[11] See *The Complete Oxford English Dictionary*, Vol II, p.787.

[12] Ibid, *Oxford English Dictionary*, quoted from 1885 Bible, Job xxix.

[13] See Anand, Margo. *The Art of Sexual Ecstasy*, Tarcher, 1989 for some beautiful ideas on sacred sexuality.

[14] For more on constructive expression and communication of anger see the chapter "Trial by Air."

[15] Isaiah 1:24.

[16] Iamlichus on the Mysteries of the Egyptians, Thomas Taylor, London, Stuart & Watkins, 1968, p. 247.

CHAPTER 6
TRIAL BY EARTH

---

*"Stirring the oatmeal" love represents
a willingness to share ordinary human
life, to find meaning in the simple,
unromantic tasks: earning a living,
living within a budget, putting out the
garbage, feeding the baby in the middle
of the night. To "stir the oatmeal"
means to find the relatedness, the
value, even the beauty, in simple
and ordinary things, not to eternally
demand a cosmic drama, an entertain-
ment, or an extraordinary intensity in
everything. Like the rice-hulling of the
Zen monks, the spinning wheel of
Ghandi . . . it represents the discovery
of the sacred in the midst of the
humble and ordinary.*

ROBERT JOHNSON

Withdrawing Our Projections: Being with What Is

An important step in the earth initiation is to withdraw our projections about love, and be with what is. In Martin Buber's terms, we need to distinguish between an *I-Thou* and an *I-It* relationship.[1]

> With an I-it attitude the world and our relationships are seen as objects for our own needs, desires, fantasies, and fears. With an I-thou relationship, we experience the otherness of our partners as they are, as a whole subject.[2]

All relationships have some measure of I-thou and I-it. Some people try to fit their partners into their images, while others have learned to be an object for another's needs. In both cases, I-thou is sacrificed. For example, if we were not allowed to be children and instead, had to take care of our parents, we may become caretakers in later relationships. We may replay the role of being an "it"—seeking worth from supporting others at the expense of our own needs. We become an object for our partner's needs. On the other hand, we may respond the opposite way to a childhood of taking care of our parents, desperately searching for someone who will finally take care of us. Our partners then become objects to fulfill our needs. In either case the whole person is lost.

The aim of the earth initiation is to find a place solid enough to express our needs and fertile enough to nurture another's growth. From this ground true intimacy can grow.

In order to be present for another or for our deepest selves, we must first find the ground beneath our many fantasies about relationship. First our parents, then television and the media send us these images, hypnotizing us into buying their views. The beliefs that permeate the airwaves are not often recognized as dogma. We accept them as truths. "Happiness is the goal of partnership." "If a relationship takes work it isn't meant to be." "Find the right man or woman, your dreams will be fulfilled, and you'll live happily ever after." "No one wants to hear your problems." "You should be completely honest with your spouse. This is what relationship is all about." "Extramarital affairs will destroy a marriage." "Extramarital affairs are good for a marriage."

We must train our eyes to be aware of beliefs and myths about relationship.[3] By doing so, the quicksand of popular opinion is circumnavigated, and a more difficult solitary path is taken—to question and find where our own ground.

Robert Johnson, in the book *We,* states that the foundation of our Western romantic ideals emerged from courtly love in the twelfth century, and that the archetypal myth, *Tristan and Iseult,* captures the world view of this period. The problems of romantic love he speaks of are insightful and relevant to the Trial by Earth.

> *Tristan falls in love with Iseult the Fair who is to be the king's bride. He loves her even though it's forbidden to consummate this love. Another woman, Iseult of the White Hands, loves him very much, yet Tristan will not be with Iseult of the White Hands; he suffers tragedy because he will not accept love where it is.*

Johnson believes that tragedy enters Western culture because we try to bring to earth that which is of heaven. We try to make our husbands and wives into gods and goddesses. Our culture is ruled by idealized images that make it difficult for us to settle for less than the ideal.

Discovering Sacredness in the Ordinary

There is a biochemistry of love that correlates with the movement of the Trial by Fire phase to the Trial by Earth. Michael Liebowitz discusses in his book *The Chemistry of Love* how the euphoria and energy of attraction correlate with natural amphetamines in the brain's emotional centers. He posits that this is why infatuated lovers can stay awake all night talking, why they become so optimistic, so gregarious and so full of life. With time, the brain can no longer tolerate this continually revved-up state, the nerve endings become exhausted, and exhilaration wanes.

As the excitement subsides, the brain exudes a new chemical, endorphins—natural, morphine-like substances that calm the mind. Liebowitz maintains they usher in the second stage of love—attachment, with the accompanying sensations of security and peace. Helen Fisher, in *The Anatomy of Love,* says that these emotions occur in people around the world. Nisa, a Kung woman of the Kalahari, says, "When two people are first together, their hearts are on fire and their passion is very great. After awhile, the fire cools and that's how it stays. They continue to love each other but it's in a different way—warm and dependable."

Leibowitz proposes that these two distinctly different chemical systems in the brain evolved for survival purposes.[4]

"The first was to have males and females become attracted to each other long enough to have sex and reproduce. The second was for the males to become strongly attached to the females so that they stayed around while the females were raising their young and helped to gather food, find shelter, fight off marauders, and teach the kids certain skills. . . . When humanity went into the grasslands, a woman needed a male because if a woman was carrying the equivalent of a twenty-pound bowling ball in one arm and a pile of sticks in the other, it was ecologically critical to pair up with a mate to rear the young."

Living in the present is not easy in our culture. Our entire early conditioning is oriented toward the future. In our early school years, we sacrifice current pleasure for a future goal. Our materialistic paradigm teaches us that a better product is always possible; all we need is more money or patience to wait for a newer model to come along. In the supermarket, we get overwhelmed by the many choices.

Marshall McLuhan's insight that "the medium is the message" is relevant to the problems that couples have in grounding their relationships. Since we are a reflection of our throw-away materialistic culture, it's no wonder that people today have difficulty staying with their partners "through thick and thin."

This is not to imply that this difficulty is unique to Western culture today. In most psychological literature, the eternal youth (*puer aeternus*) who wants to explore all possibilities is discouraged. It has become synonymous with dilettantism and instability.[5] This may be based on a pervasive cultural self-hatred—that we are ungrounded with an addiction to new and stimulating possessions and products, always on the move for something "better."

Greek mythology presents both positive and negative aspects of the puer aeternus.[6] When Icarus impetuously defied his father's instructions and moved too closely to the sun, his wax wings melted and he fell to his death. On the other hand, Hermes, a positive puer figure depicted with wings on his feet, forever chased the nymphs. He never settled down with one partner; instead he chose to travel and experience the many intricate pathways of life. He became one of the major gods of the Greek Pantheon and used his mercurial talents to guide and awaken others.

It is natural to resist limitation and want to roll like the ball of energy we are into all areas of life's terrain. This is the hunter archetype who enjoys expanding the knowledge of a wider territory of life and honing his or her skills in the pursuit of "a fresh meet(sic)." And it is just as human to want to stay in one place and feel the security beneath our feet. This is the farmer archetype who enjoys watching the fruits of his or her hard labor grow and bloom into a beautiful flower or a sustaining meal.

Even further back in the roots of Homo sapiens, we find various models for pairing between the sexes. Ninety percent of all birds form pair bonds; but only three percent of mammals form a long-term relationship with a single mate.[7] Among these are some muskrats, some bats, Asiatic clawless otters, beavers, deer mice, dwarf mongooses, a few antelopes, some seals, a few South American monkeys, and all of the wild dogs. Foxes, wolves, coyotes, jackals, and the raccoon dog of Japan all form pair bonds and raise their young as "husband and wife." Gorillas usually pair for life but they also try to accumulate a harem. And among our early human ancestors, *Australopithecus afarensis*, who lived on the plains of East Africa some four million years ago, we have a model for serial monogamy.

> *They traveled in bands of twelve to twenty-five. Friends and relatives formed pair bonds shortly after puberty, shared food with a mate, remained paired for the infancy of a single child (about four years), and often parted when the child became old enough to join community activities. Then, typically, each formed a new pair bond with a partner in a neighboring group and bore more young.*[8]

After surveying a number of different cultures, Helen Fisher found evidence of a divorce peak among couples married for four years, and hypothesized that there may be a planned obsolescence of the pair bond in the human species. Like foxes, robins, and many other species, we generally stay with a partner for as long as it takes to raise a child through infancy. Her research also shows that divorce is not just a phenomena of the industrialized world. For instance, among the Ngoni of South Africa, divorce peaks between the fourth and fifth year of marriage. The rainforest-dwelling Yanomamo tribe of Venezuela shows a similar pattern. Fisher supports her hypothesis with data from a wide variety of sources including a United Nations study that surveys cultures ranging from the Truk Islands of Micronesia, to the Kung Bushman of the Kalahari, as well as a number of Muslim countries.[9]

Should We Settle Down?

As we have evolved, our inner voices and our choices, though rooted in biology, have been colored with psychomythological themes. The theme of "moving on" occurs in the motif of the puer aeternus. Peter Pan, one of our culture's archetypal puer figures says, "I never want to grow up" because he didn't want to face the limitations of adulthood. To stay in one place for a long time feels suffocating. The puer feels that the voice of the *senex* (the father principle) stands in the way of his sense of adventure.

The senex represents limitation and claims that without focus and groundedness we never accomplish anything in life. "You'll have nothing to show for your lighthearted ways in the end. Maturity requires limitation, sacrifice, and denial of one thing to get another." Regardless of the period of human history, biological or moral compulsions, we all face the puer-senex debate within ourselves and must take a stance.[10] Moving from one pole to another throughout life is a choice, as is choosing to be "free of any one partner." Each choice has its own limitations. Again, we make our destinies by our choice of myths.

What the puer misses on his or her quest for the ideal is expressed beautifully in "The Story of Malik Dinar":[11]

> *After many years of philosophical study, Malik Dinar wanted to travel in search of knowledge. So he searched for the hidden Teacher that he had read so much about. Leaving home with only a few dates for provision, he came upon a dervish plodding along the dusty road. He asked the dervish if he could walk with him, and if the dervish could help him find his hidden Teacher.*
>
> *"Can I help you, can you help me?" said the dervish in a joking manner. "The hidden Teacher is in the self. How he finds him depends upon what use he makes of experience." They came to a tree which was creaking and swaying and the dervish stopped, proclaiming that the tree was saying, "Something is hurting me, please stop awhile and take it out of my side so that I may find peace."*

"I am in too much of a hurry to meet the Teacher I'm to find down the road" said Dinar, "and besides, how can a tree talk anyway?" They went on their way. After a few miles, the dervish said, "I thought that I smelt honey. Perhaps it was a wild bee's hive which had been built in the tree that was hurting it." Dinar then wanted to go back so that they could collect the honey, eat some, and sell the rest for the journey.

When they arrived back at the tree, they saw other travelers collecting an enormous amount of honey. "What luck we have had" these men said, "This is enough honey to feed a city." A depressed Dinar and the dervish went on their way again. Soon they came to a mountain where they heard humming. The dervish put his ear to the ground. Then he said, "Below us are millions of ants who are crying out for help. They say they are excavating, but have come across strange rocks which bar their progress, and they are pleading for us to help dig their way."

"Ants and rocks are not our business, brother," said Dinar, "I have more important things to do because I am seeking my Teacher." When they stopped for the night, Dinar noticed that he had lost his knife and thought that he must have lost it near the ant hill. The next morning they retraced their steps, and when they arrived at the ant hill, they couldn't find Dinar's knife. Instead they found a group of people covered in mud, resting beside a pile of gold coins. "These," said the people, "are a hidden hoard which we have just dug up. We were on the road when a frail old dervish called to us, 'Dig at this spot and you will find that which is rock to some but gold to others.'"

One of the men remarked, "The dervish with you looks strangely like the one we saw yesterday." "All dervishes look very much alike," said Fatih. Dinar and Fatih continued their travels and came to a beautiful river bank. As they sat waiting for the ferry, a fish rose to the surface and mouthed to them. "This fish," said the dervish, is saying, "Catch me and give me the herb on the bank there next to you. Then I will find relief and give it back. Travelers have mercy!"

*At that moment the ferry boat appeared and Dinar, impatient
to get ahead, pushed the dervish into it. On the other side of
the bank, the next morning, the ferryman appeared while they
were drinking tea. He kissed the dervish's hand in deep
appreciation. The ferryman explained that last night when he
saw them on the opposite bank, he resolved to make one more
trip, even though they looked poor, for the 'baraka'—the
blessing of helping the travelers. As he was about to put away
his boat after dropping them off, he saw the fish which had
thrown itself on the bank. It was trying to swallow a piece of
plant. The ferryman put the plant into its mouth and the fish
threw up a stone and flopped back into the water. The stone
was a huge and flawless diamond of incalculable value and
brilliance.*

*"You are a devil!" shouted the infuriated Dinar to the dervish
Fatih. "You knew about all three treasures by means of some
hidden perception, yet you did not tell me at the time. Is that
true companionship? Formerly, my ill luck was strong enough:
but without you I wouldn't even have known of the possibilities
hidden in trees, anthills, and fish—of all things!"*

*No sooner had he said these words when he felt a mighty wind
sweep through his very soul. And then he knew that the reverse
of what he said was true. The dervish touched Dinar lightly
on the shoulder and smiled." Now, brother, you will find that
you can learn by experience. I am he who is at the command
of the hidden Teacher."*

*When Dinar dared to look up, he saw his Teacher walking
down the road with a small band of travelers who were arguing
about the perils of the journey ahead of them. Malik Dinar
became one of the early classical masters, a companion and
exemplar of the "Man who Arrived."*

The tale of Malik Dinar captures clearly the essential earth initiation task that is so often forgotten in our intimate relationships.
Though we may have a biochemical pull to "move on" in life after our
phenylethyamines have worn off or after our infants have matured to
childhood, if we do we may miss the psychospiritual depth that comes
from remaining in one place. Like Dinar, when we feel that what we

are looking for is always down the road, we miss the hidden treasure in the present moment with our partners. We miss the sweetness, the gold, and the brilliant gems hidden in our everyday lives.

Finding Our Stance

A young man of thirty five, whom we'll call Peter, engaged in much self-reflection about his relationships over the years while studying for his Master's degree in psychology. But Peter still couldn't decide what to do about his relationship—stay or leave? His dilemma was familiar; this same sense of emptiness led him to leave many past relationships. As usual, he wondered whether his current lover was "good enough" to finally allow him to settle down.

In Peter's therapy, he grew to understand that his quest for "an ideal goddess" had roots in his family mythology. He was raised as "a prince," continuously pushed to be better than he felt he was deep within. It was no wonder that in his relationships now this same "striving for something better" arose over and over again.

The way we were "loved" as children and the myths we were told set the stage for the way we love as adults. I remember the perfectionistic, yet lonely, middle-aged beauty queen who never married and whose father told her, "No one is good enough for you," and the self-effacing young man told by his parents "you're no good," so critical of himself that his last two partners couldn't cope with his constant self-flagellation.

Becoming conscious of our ruling myths is the beginning of a process of reclaiming the power to sculpt our own destinies. Becoming conscious of our ruling myths is the beginning of a process of reclaiming the power to sculpt our own destinies. For Peter, the power of old myths was so great that he could not bring himself to let go and be with his current lover. It was as if no human effort, no insight, no emotional outpouring was strong enough to clear the way through the dam built by many generations of his family mythology. In ancient times, at this point, a person may have prayed for divine intervention. If he or she was in Ancient Greece, a trip may have commenced to The Temple of Aesculapius to incubate a dream.

Peter's dream went like this:

I'm playing poker for high stakes. In this poker game there are more cards than usual and as I pick each one up I'm happy

*because there are many wild cards that I know I can make
into anything I want to. The only solid cards are a Queen of
Hearts and a seven. So I can put together a Royal Flush down
to a seven. But still I'm not sure that this will be good enough
to win the game.*

After awakening Peter immediately felt the connection between
the dream and his love life. "Wow, I'm sitting with a Royal Flush with
a queen (my girlfriend) and I'm still insecure that this isn't good
enough!" The emotional impact of this message from his inner world
was a new perspective on how rich his relationship was. He realized
that it was a relationship with a "queen of hearts," and that his wild
nature (symbolized by the wild cards) could be integrated with his
queen to give him a winning hand. A path of commitment to live in
everyday life with his partner grew from this dream.

The basic postures of life provide a way for the initiate into the
Trials of the Earth to discover the sacred in the ordinary. The Buddha
said that there were four noble postures through which we could discover enlightenment: lying, sitting, standing, and walking. Many know
about sitting meditation and lying meditation (yoga); but the practice
of standing meditation is less known as a way to cultivate the human
spirit. It is a beautiful way to find the treasures that exist beneath our
own feet.

How beautifully John Welwood captures the significance of the
standing posture,

*Standing on the earth and raising our head upward exposes
our heart to the world. Four-legged animals carefully protect
the vulnerable, soft front of the body. But as human beings,
we walk around with our heart exposed, allowing the world
and other people to enter, touch, and move us. Only in this
tenderness and openness to the whole of reality do we start
to become fully human. Only in exposing the heart do we find
a path.*[12]

Developing the Golden Ball of Energy

Throughout time, initiates have practiced circulating golden light
through the body and forming it into a circle or a ball. This knowledge
was hidden in fairy tales and folklore. The Iron Hans tale, popularized
by Robert Bly, tells of a king's son who loses his golden ball, and in the

fairy tale of the Frog King, a beautiful, bored princess loses hers. During May Day celebrations in Ireland, villagers carry hoops from which are suspended a gold and a silver ball that represent the sun and moon.[13]

Developing a golden energy has been a quest of esoteric training traditions.[14] Carl Jung spoke about how fifteenth century alchemists meditated on the spherical light to develop "the shining or illuminating body that dwells in the heart of man."[15] By doing so, the adept strove to be like the sun in the macrocosm and like God in the supracelestial world. One of these alchemists was Michael Maier who, in his 1616 treatise *De circulo physico quadrato*, spoke of weaving gold into a circular form like a snake biting its own tail.[16]

The practice of standing meditation and Tai Chi develops the sense of the body as a golden ball of energy, "under our own feet."

This book will not explore these meditation practices as it is extremely important to have the guidance of a teacher while doing them.

Finding the Primordial Self: The Story of Iron Hans

The loss of the Golden Ball is a major theme in the Grimm's fairy tale called *Iron Hans*. Since Robert Bly's bestseller[17] many are now familiar with the symbol of the loss of the golden ball as it relates to a man's lack of connection with his primordial self. A closer examination of the *Iron Hans* tale will expand upon Bly's interpretation and focus on how the story can reveal deeper insight not only about men, but about our collective history. Here is a synopsis of the first half of the story.

> *Once there was a king who lived by a great forest, and his huntsmen did not return on three successive occasions that they were sent out for food. An unknown huntsman agreed to go alone into the feared forest with his dog. While the dog was chasing some game it came upon a deep pool. A naked arm stretched itself out of the water, seized the dog, and drew it under. The huntsman went back to the castle, got three other men, and returned to the forest with buckets. They began to bail out the water.*

> *At the bottom there lay a wild man whose body was brown like rusty iron, and whose hair hung over his face down to his knees. They bound him with cords and led him back to the*

castle. They put the wild man in an iron cage in the court-
yard and forbade the door to be opened on pain of death. The
Queen herself took the key into her keeping.

The king had an eight-year-old son who played in the court-
yard. Once, while he was playing, his golden ball fell into the
cage. The boy asked the wild man for the golden ball and the
wild man replied, "Not until you have opened the door for
me." The boy refused because the king had forbidden it. The
boy came back the next day and still the wild man refused.
On the third day while the king was out hunting, his son went
to the cage and the wild man asked him to open it. The boy
replied, "I cannot open the door even if I wished, for I have
not the key." The wild man replied, "It lies under your
mother's pillow, you can get it there." The boy wanted his
golden ball back. Casting all thought to the winds, he brought
the key, unlocked the door, and set the wild man free.

The story of Iron Hans symbolizes the many dimensions of the Trial by Earth. While exploring its meaning, we will see how it speaks to cultural issues still relevant in our world and relationships today. Each symbol contains meaning and is a living lesson that tells us not only about our collective history, but how that history lives in us.

The story begins as the king is out hunting, when one of the hunting dogs is pulled down into a pool by the iron-colored wild man. For Bly, the wild man in the pool represents a moment in history when Western males of the Industrial Age became separated from male initiation traditions, when our instincts became rusty, when we lost touch with our fathers working in the fields. Bly has been a catalyst for getting men back in touch with this wild man that lives deep down within us.

In the 1960s and in the 1970s men were told that the golden ball (symbolizing the unity of our personalities) was hidden in the watery feminine side of the male, the *anima*. Using the images of the fairy tale, Bly says that now it is time for civilized man to remove this water bucketful by bucketful, contact the more primitive side of the male psyche, and find the inner wild man. "This does not mean to go back to an old shallow macho image of man, but rather to find that deep instinctual energy that has been underwater for ages." Bly sees the solution to this loss in the symbol of the wild man and the lost male initiations by male mentors.

To be sure Iron Hans is a tale of the loss and finding of instinct and male initiation. But how does one find the key to his instinctual energy? The king's son is told that the key to the wild man's courage is hidden under his mother's pillow. Bly points out that a man's empowerment is taking back the power that he gave his mother to win her approval (likewise with a woman, the power that she gave her father). In the process of doing so, we are led into the woods, into a new reality of our making.

The psychological symbolism of the ball is described by Bly as "the unity of personality we had as children —a kind of radiance, or wholeness, before we split into male and female, rich and poor, bad and good." (Whether we literally experienced this as children, is not the point. The ball is a symbol of the transcendent function of the human personality capable of uniting all opposites.)

From our viewpoint, the golden ball that the boy has lost is bigger than psychological reality. The golden ball is also a symbol for the secret knowledge of ancient traditions, masculine and feminine.

In Western alchemical and Taoist traditions cultivating chi and the golden ball of light is a part of secret initiations. This fairy tale may well be telling us about these and other ancient traditions that the king's son and we, in our modern culture, have lost. The fact that the golden ball is lost in a cage with an iron man may be referring to the loss of the Goddess religions by invaders like the Kurgans, Aryans, Acheans, and Dorians during the beginning of the Iron Age in Europe.[18]

The historical representations in the story are varied; three different time periods are represented. First, we have post-Iron Age industrial Europe out of touch with instinct. Through the king (symbol of the ruling personality of the era) we see a time when humanity became overly civilized and lost its sense of instinctual energy in a pool of civilized comforts. Then, there is Iron Hans who represents the brute force of the early Iron Age conquerors "getting rusty" using the non-instinctual ways of modern life. Finally, we have pre-Iron Age technologies—the ways of the golden ball.

The people of the post-Iron-Age industrial culture saw the Iron Man, symbolized by Iron Hans, as a negative image—"The iron man pulls huntsmen and dogs under the water." The old instinctual ways that were hidden in the pool of the collective unconscious of these modern men were seen as a threat to their modern lifestyle.

The golden ball, held in the cage of the wild man, may symbolize how the members of the Goddess-worshipping tribes felt when they
were forced into submission and separated from their religious practices of worshipping the cyclic forces of nature by patriarchally-oriented
tribes with weapons of iron, and by the industrial age of "the king's cage
of linear bars." There has been much debate surrounding the conclusions of Marija Gimbutas,[19] one of the great scholars of this period of
history. In her view Europe was changed by a series of invasions from
4300 BC to 2800 BC which imposed a culture that was "patriarchal,
stratified, pastoral, mobile and war-oriented" upon a culture that was
"matrifocal, agricultural, sedentary, egalitarian and peaceful."[20]

The story of Iron Hans brings together the concepts of the lost
golden ball of the earlier era, and the instinctual ways of the men of
iron (Iron Hans) through the symbolism of the king's son. It is a lesson in how to regain the golden ball of pre-technological eras. The boy's
possession of the ball at the beginning of the story is the ball we all
possess unconsciously as children. We are alive with our own energy
and unaware of our own mortality. When we lose this ball, as the king's
son did (all myths pivot upon a fall from grace), the pain of loss leads
us on a quest where we will discover an even greater golden ball that
has rolled through history and gathered a greater collective wisdom.

It contains a rapprochement; the king's son learns something from
this iron man —and is initiated by him into an important awareness
of being a man. The story integrates themes of raw male instincts
and holism (the golden ball) that our culture is still in the process of
integrating.

Through the king's son the fairy tale takes us on a journey of
developing consciousness, its symbolism showing us how to heal the
imbalances of civilized life, how to reverse the polarization between
masculine and feminine, and how to find our way to personal love. The
story tells us the king's son (and each of us) must reconnect with the
wild man. In the Industrial Age, the wild man, who is still in touch
with instinct, is one connection back to our primordial reality. It can
be both instructive and healing for our culture, and for men in particular, to read this story. In an effort to reverse the imbalances of the patriarchal era, there is a major movement that tells men the answers lie
in the feminine sphere. In the story of Iron Hans we find a solution
in the image of an instinctual man.

The fairy tale also takes us into the area of the feminine. To find
the golden ball, we must retrieve the key from under our mother's

pillow. Bly interprets this as a need to individuate by looking at the psychological issues where men symbiotically merge with their personal mothers. He feels, as do psychodynamically-oriented therapists, that a man in the world must take back the power that he once gave to his mother in order to please her and win her approval. (Similarly, a woman may need to recover the power that she gave her father). Though this psychological interpretation is fundamental to personal healing of men in our culture, I believe that when the story tells us that the key that we children (the king's son) of the ages of metal have lost is under our mothers' pillow — this key is bigger than the one of our personal mothers. The story says that we all (men and women) need to find a key that's beneath our personal mothers, under her pillow where her dreams come from — in the feminine collective unconscious. This is the place where Goddess mythology and pre-technological (male and female), rounded ways of worship live.

The story may have been created at a time in history when our European-based culture drowned the old ways in a pool of prejudice and locked away the ball of life into a cage of iron. The evolution in consciousness that led away from unity and *participation mystique* with the world turned an important part of our history to rust. We become caged by a linear world view. The key to unlocking this cage is in the collective unconscious of the pre-technological era.

We can not look at the personal healing of men and women in our culture without examining the world we now inhabit and how the loss of the golden ball impacts our love lives. A ball is a symbol for the unity of opposites, and for men and women an image of being equidistant from a central point can be an important step in healing the polarization that currently exists between the sexes. The metaphor of the golden ball avoids relying solely upon the Goddess traditions for the answers for which our out-of-balance culture is looking.

Many authors have searched for a term to represent an egalitarian relationship between the sexes. Gimbutas suggests the term *matristic* to avoid the term *matriarchal* (denoting female power or rule), and Eisler offers *gylany* (*gylne* referring to women, and *andros*, man), to denote that during the goddess-oriented age one sex did overpower the other. Others have described those times as *matrilineal* (that descent took place through the mother). But all of these terms are gender-specific with emphasis on the feminine.

By employing the image of the golden ball we find a nongender-biased term to describe traditions where men and women can find a golden unity of spirit. Some of these traditions may historically have been more male or female oriented. But by speaking of the golden ball we implicitly represent the spiritual crux of the matter—that sacred traditions belong to and are originated from a point in the center of us all. This does not mean to advocate a premature synthesis of the sexes; for there is a purpose in the differentiation of the sexes and their separate initiation traditions.

Perhaps the Oriental yin/yang symbol most closely represents the balanced juxtaposition and interrelationship of the sexes. Here we see the yang, (light, masculine) and the yin (dark, feminine) equally contained within a circle divided by an S-shaped curve rather than a straight line. This tells us that the relationship between the sexes is one of complementary energetic interplay, not straight division. Each half contains a point of the other's light and nature; the female is in the male and the male in the female. Rather than one dominating the other or revolving in opposition to one another, they dance around each other—a dance that keeps revolving and evolving around a center point deep in their midst.

Working with the life force or energy is a concept prevalent in many ancient cultures such as the Kung of the Kalahari. Members of the tribe activate *num* (analogous to the Chinese concept of chi), an energy force that was given to the Kung by their gods. To be a healer is part of normal socialization, not the function of a special class. A frequent event in this regard is the all-night healing dance that happens approximately once a week and activates num. Rock paintings depict the dance, its origins stretching far back into their culture's past.[21]

Ecstatic rites were performed throughout the ancient world as men and women came together and experienced a sacred joining. Sexual union and revitalization of the earth were often intertwined, and symbolically acted out in a serpent dance—human and animal vitalizing each other. The serpent still survives as a symbol of healing entwined around the staff of Aesculapius, the symbol of Western medicine.[22]

Until recently, our culture did not acknowledge the existence of an energy force in the human body. [23] This denial has affected many areas of our health, including the way we touch or don't touch each other. People of early cultures felt the body's energy and used touch to heal. Systems of healing like acupuncture and acupressure came from such experimentation. When a point on the body's blocked river of chi was touched, energy circulated once again where stagnation existed before and the golden ball of health was restored.[24]

Today, few health insurance companies recognize these ancient methods of healing. We are like the king's son, separated from the golden ball by the cage of our own linear thinking. Although we must be careful not to idealize pre-modern cultures, and though participation mystique created a beautiful experience of oneness with life, it also contributed to blood sacrifices to "the Great Mother."[25] Also there are many so called "holistic methods" that are quackery. There are benefits to consciousness evolving into a scientific attitude in the area of human relationship and in medicine.

We know much was lost when the pagan mysteries went underground due to the suppression by the church to promote the idea of Christianity.[26] The holistic healing temples of Aesculapius were destroyed all over the Mediterranean area; the Wickas, who held much ancient healing knowledge, were burned at the stake, and, until recently, energy systems such as acupuncture were scoffed at by Western scientists. But sociopolitical analysis goes beyond our purpose. We are using the image of these pre-modern cultures to symbolize a connection with our primordial self and natural energies that people of all ages have desired.

By ignoring these systems, we have suffered the consequences. We are reminded of the legacy of the doctrine of *manifest destiny* imposed by white men upon the Indians: We occupied the land, but we lost the knowledge of how to live with its sacred treasures. This loss affects our ability to love in tune with each other and with the great circle of creation.

In our love lives we lost the knowledge of how to be a circle flowing with our partners that the ancient Taoist temples taught so well. Now we take classes in Tai chi; but Tai chi is not a class to take or a thing to do, it is a way to be, a way to flow with the yin and yang of life. It is a way to find our center in the midst of adversity, a way to maintain a rounded attitude in a linear world.

Today, we sit at video display terminals, forced to adhere to linear time schedules, removed from our body's natural rhythms—carpal tunnel syndrome is our reward. Trapped in huge, hermetically sealed high-rises, workers suffer from sick-building syndrome. We come home from work exhausted, with only enough energy for a microwaved meal and an hour or two of television.

The loss of the golden ball is evident in the way we see our lovers. Ancient cultures looked at the human personality itself as an expression of the great cosmic Wheel of Life. When we look at the personality of the one we love, we may see a fun person or a deep person. We

115

have lost sight of these gifts from the cosmos itself—our fun-loving partner is a gift from the fire element of the universe, our deeply emotional partner is a gift from the Temple of Water. The human personality itself was, in these ancient traditions, seen as part of the great circle of creation.

Is there a larger intelligence that directs our lives from the heavens? The fact that Saturn (symbolic of walls and boundaries) and Neptune (symbolic of dissolving) came into conjunction on November 9, 1989, the same day that the Berlin Wall came down, makes us wonder what mysteries may lie beyond our minds and how we can use the timing of events such as this to dissolve the walls between ourselves and our loved ones. The adept of the Temple of the Earth uses the metaphors of the heavens to live the symbolic life.

The loss of the golden ball may be even more significant than our culture realizes. Though Robert Bly makes an excellent case that the golden ball symbolizes the loss of our connection to instinct and to male initiation ceremonies, it is crucial that our culture becomes aware of this metaphor as a symbol of both the male and female ancient wisdom traditions. These traditions have so much to say about how to cultivate that energy which enables us to love life and others and how to live in an ensouled world.

The Golden Apple of Intimacy

This fairy tale brings together the key of the feminine relationship to the collective unconscious (the mother), the instinctual ways of the men of iron (Iron Hans), and the concept of holism (the golden ball). As we continue the story of Iron Hans, we will see what the king's son learns from his initiation by this man of iron and from his own journey.

> The boy was afraid that he would be beaten by his parents for letting the wild man out so he followed him into the woods. The man made a bed of moss for the boy and the next morning took him to a well and ordered him to be careful that nothing should fall into it. The boy disobeyed after the wild man left, and put his finger into the water. It turned gold. No matter how hard he tried to get rid of the gold on his finger it remained, and the wild man saw it when he came back.

> The same thing happened the next day with a piece of his hair; and the wild man said to him that if anything fell into the well

the next day, that the boy would have to leave. As the boy reflected upon himself in the water, his long hair fell in and turned gold. When the wild man returned that day, he said the boy must go. "But since you have not a bad heart, and as I mean well by you, if you ever fall into any difficulty, come to the forest and cry 'Iron Hans,' and I will come and help you."

The boy went on to another kingdom where he worked as a cook's apprentice for another king. He always hid his golden hair under a cap, for he did not like to let it be seen. He got in considerable trouble for not taking off his cap before the king and was demoted to a gardener. One day the king's daughter, in jest, pulled his cap off, and his golden hair was splendid for her to behold.

Not long afterwards, the country was overrun by war and the king's defeat by a superior army seemed imminent. The boy went back to the forest and called "Iron Hans," asking for help. Iron Hans gave him a horse and a great troop of warriors entirely equipped in iron. The youth rode to the king in battle and saved the day. Then he rode off so the king couldn't identify him.

When the king returned to the castle, his daughter complimented him on the victory and the king explained how a strange knight saved the day. They wanted to find this knight and so they proclaimed a great feast where the king's daughter would throw three golden apples on three successive days. They hoped the elusive knight would show up.

The boy returned to the forest and again called to Iron Hans and asked his help in catching the golden apple. Iron Hans gave him a suit of red armor and a chestnut-colored horse. When the apple was thrown to all the knights, the boy disguised in red armor caught the apple and quickly rode away. On the next day, Iron Hans gave the boy a white horse and white armor and again the boy caught the apple and quickly rode away. The king became angry and said, "This is not allowed, he must appear before me and tell his name." He gave the order if the knight rode away they were to pursue him and even cut him down.

On the third day, he was given a black suit of armor and a black horse by Iron Hans. The boy again caught the apple and when pursued by the king's men, one of them wounded him in the leg, and as his horse leapt up, his helmet fell off so they saw his golden hair.

When the king's daughter heard this, she went back to the gardener's boy and identified him by the three golden apples he had, the wound he received, and his golden hair. He then disclosed his identity as the son of another king, and was given the hand of the king's daughter in appreciation for how he had helped her father maintain his kingdom. At the wedding ceremony, a stately king entered and approached the groom and said, "I am Iron Hans, and was, by enchantment, a wild man, but you have set me free; all the treasures which I possess shall be yours."

Through the second part of this fairy tale we can appreciate how important the earth initiation is to a child's (the child in each of us) pathway to himself and to relationships with others. The theme of gold repeats three times. First, the golden ball, symbol of the old ways; secondly, the goldenness of the boy's hair (male virility); and finally, the golden apples (female virility—the juicy virility of relationship with another). Each reflects the other. For when we are in love with another (and find the golden apple), we find our own virility and encounter the old ways with our loved one. When this *coniunctio*[27] takes place, and the gold is experienced on all three levels, the wild man in us is freed and the golden ball is found, allowing us to be intimate with another and play the game of life.

By repeating the theme of gold, the story is telling us that when we dip our hair into the golden pool of our own instincts, we find the goldenness of the old ways. We may learn to touch the acupressure points that bring healing to our mates, or we may discover our natural instincts by walking in the woods at night with our partners, listening to the mystery around us. We may explore the healing arts of touch and play, and become wild with our instincts, or find a sacred relationship to the earth by experiencing the gold in the simplicity of everyday life. We need to find the ways that work for us, the ways of rounded perception, of the ancient sacred tradition that we need to heal our lives. We need to bite into that juicy apple to be whole.

Many people have idealized the Iron Man from Robert Bly's story. And certainly he did much for the boy. But let's not overlook the fact that the Iron Man forbade the boy to go into the pool as many men in the Iron Age of technology do. Though well-meaning, they are often anti-experiential. Even though the Iron Age of technology often forbids us to go into the golden pool of our collective unconscious, our curiosity draws us there, sometimes at the risk of losing our relationships.

For example, I've heard many children of parents with a mechanistic world view express pain due to their parents attacking in the old ways. Whether it's about environmental protection, meditation, or interest in spiritual practices that differ from their upbringing, many relationships break up over it. At a certain stage in such children's (sometimes adults') individuation process, their parents' value judgments are perceived as lead weights. Such children need to go through their alchemical process to find their gold. They need to dip their hair into the pool and individuate, finding what feels right to them, and thereby find their virility. Some are able to communicate with their parents; others must return after they have made their own life.

A supportive parent gives the child just enough help and guidance so he can make it in the world himself, and says, like Iron Hans, "go out into the world and fight your battles, but if you get into serious trouble, all you need to do is cry out for help and I'll be there for you." Like Iron Hans , a supportive parent can equip us with a spirited chestnut horse by giving us room to recognize and live with our instincts. The gift of a white horse supports our spiritual nature. The black horse allows room for our dark side. With these gifts we learn to ride through the trials of life, gaining the self-assurance we need to reach for and catch the erotic fruits that a prospective mate may throw our way.

Our parents can help us solidify our defenses (the armor). In unhealthy relationship, a parent may expect a child to always comply with their wishes. A wise parent (like Iron Hans) allows room for differentiation. The gift of red armor gives us a safe space to express our anger. Discovering our inner vision within our own boundaries is the gift of white armor. Black armor allows us to explore the dark feelings within our real selves.

Creating appropriate boundaries with our parents equips us with the ability to shield us from our partner's father complex. In our battles we often meet the forces that threatened our princesses' fathers. These forces are the enemies of the king that the boy must fight. If the princess's father suffered from lack of money, issues about money will be projected upon her partner. If her father was physically abusive or used anger destructively, our assertiveness or anger may be seen as a threat. The psychological and spiritual strength symbolized by the red, white, and black armor is needed to catch the red vital juicy stuff that's thrown at us by our lovers.

The story has much to say about male psychology and tells us that in a patriarchal culture, it is often through contact with a man (father, father substitute, or male mentor), that a boy gets in touch with the goldenness of his own virility (the golden hair). This gold is found through self-reflection in the deep well of our own being. We let our hair down and dip it into the waters of our own natural expression, and find our way out of the forest and into the world of our making. From the deep self-reflection we've done in our inner forest with its furry and ferocious creatures, we are able to take the powers of our primordial energies into the world.

Also, the story gives us potent symbols of what a boy needs to succeed in the realm of relationship: A boy becomes a man through his spiritual virility (dipping our golden hair into the pool), the fruitfulness of his sexuality, his ability to seed a relationship with another (the golden apples), and the boy's wounded leg. As with Chiron's wound from Heracles, injuries to the leg symbolize the way the wounds of relationship bring us down to reality and feel our humanity. All these things help him to find a loving relationship with the king's daughter and win a kingdom in the adult world.

Unfortunately, there is an absence of meaningful initiation rites for boys[28] in our modern world. When men in our culture today search their heart centers they often find only an empty cage. As the story of Iron Hans illustrates, the golden ball has been lost, and the ability to flow with life has become constricted. Robert Bly and others in the men's movement are crystalizing Western culture's lack of initiation into manhood by other men. Bar mitzvah gifts heaped upon the adolescent, the license to drive a mechanized vehicle, and getting drunk don't quench the thirst of the primordial adolescent soul who longs to be initiated into life's mysteries.

Robert Bly has given men in our culture the gift of reminding us that other men can help to find and liberate the golden ball in us even when they seemingly oppose us and say, don't dip your hair into what you know is gold. In ancient Greek culture, a young man would often leave his family to study the ancient traditions with an older man. Among the Hopis a boy is taken away at the age twelve and down into the kiva; many months may pass before he sees his mother again. He learns the dances of the animals, how to move in ways that heal his soul and attract members of the opposite sex by his connection to his animal nature. Other Native American cultures send their young braves into the woods alone to seek a vision, and to align themselves with their purpose in life. A person's name was often based upon this vision and they could call on it in times of crisis.[29] Primordially-based cultures used rituals like these to help initiate boys into the male world.

I have heard Robert Bly criticized for calling for a return to pre-modernism. Stressing the value of pre-modern cultures, however, is simply paying respect to our ancestors, as we want to be respected after we pass away. The knowledge of the plants we eat and the medicines we use today comes from the knowledge and sacrifices of our ancestors who ate these substances so we could learn from them. Likewise, the mistakes that our fellow sufferers made in the trials of life and love can benefit us if we take time to listen to the ways and rituals they developed.

Many battles in our relationships today center around the ways of the ball versus the ways of iron. How much touching should there be? Is eating a meal or making love with our partner going to be a rushed or a savored, romantic experience? Many relationships have parallels with the Iron Hans story. Keeping up with the house payments or not having the energy to make love after a long day at the office doesn't make it easy to liberate the ball from the cage of our responsibilities and obligations. Hundreds of years after this story was first told, the boy in us is still seeking the way to freedom from the iron cage imprisoning our love lives.

Today the ancient ways are making a comeback and reversing the cruelty of monocentric attitude. To be healthy in a relationship requires connecting with our whole instinctual selves. And the knowledge of our ancestors is one important way to do this.

In our culture today, body therapies proliferate, joggers run over concrete streets, backpacking and other outdoor activities abound. Martial arts training is spreading as Westerners get in closer touch with their own bodies. A wide variety of other practices are coming to the West and all parts of the world. A recent poll in the *New England Journal of Medicine* said that one third of Americans have experience with alternative medical treatment. Exercise and health centers are appearing in corporate offices. Americans "fire walk," Native American sweat-lodges are constructed at psychological conferences, and in the movie *Karate Kid*, a young boy receives instruction from a Japanese mentor and introduces a generation of young people to the values and practices of the martial arts.

We still have a long path to follow to heal the wounds of centuries of cultural repression against the spiritual practices of our ancestors. Our civilized culture is like the kingdom of the Iron Hans story, something is hidden deep in an ancient pool. We initiates, men and women, travel to explore the old ways found in the pool of collective memory. We take out its waters bucketful by bucketful and renew ourselves and our culture. Like the boy in Iron Hans, we must begin by looking into the well of our own being.

It's not so esoteric. At key moments in a relationship we must tap into this natural sense of aliveness, to be true to who we are. Finding our primordial self is an everyday event—essential to the most basic of aspects of relationship. Being in touch with our primordial ground and goldenness means to accept ourselves, our human limitations, and our place in the universe.

[1]   Buber, M. *I and Thou*. Trans. Walter Kaufman. Scribner, New York, 1970.

[2]   Jacoby, M. *The Analytic Encounter*. Inner City Books, 1984, p. 64 quoting Gordon, R. "Transference as a Fulcrum of Analysis, p. 116.

[3]   For a discussion of common marital myths see Lazarus, A. Ph.D. *Marital Myths*. Impact Publishers, San Luis Obispo, 1985.

[4]   Liebowitz, M. *The Chemistry of Love*. Little, 1983. Fisher H. *The Anatomy of Love*. W.W. Norton, 1992.

[5]   The puer (masculine) or puella (feminine) aeternus is a term meaning the eternal youth. See for example, Von Franz, M.L. *Puer Aeternus*. Spring Publications, Dallas, 1970.

[6]   For a more extensive discussion of this issue see Hillman, J. *Puer Papers*. Spring Publications, Dallas, 1979, and Von Franz, M.L. *Puer Aeternus*. Spring Publications, Dallas, 1970.

[7]   Fisher H. *The Anatomy of Love*. W. W. Noton, 1992, p. 150.

[8] Fisher, H. op. cit. p. 141.

[9] Fisher, H. op. cit. p. 114–116.

[10] Hillman, J. *Puer Papers.* "Senex and Puer."

[11] This classic Sufi teaching tale is paraphrased and retold from Shah, Idries, *Tales of the Dervishes*, E.P. Dutton & Co. 1970, p. 148. This version is that of Emir el Arifin.

[12] Welwood, J. *Journey of the Heart.* Harper and Row, 1990, p. 38.

[13] Frazer, G. *The Golden Bough.* Collier Books, 1922, p. 140.

[14] The golden ball, to my knowledge, has never been specifically spoken of in the Tai Chi tradition but *the golden pill, the golden elixir,* and *the golden bath* are common designations for the experience that comes from Taoist meditation. In the book, *The Way of Energy* by Master Lam Chuen, Gaia Books, London England 1991, are many exercises to develop the ball of energy, though he does not specifically mention the golden ball. These exercises are from the *Zhan Zhuang* (standing like a tree, or the root of the tree) style of Chi Gung which is part of the *I Chuan* (the intentionality behind the various systems of Chuan) system that I have had the good fortune to have been trained in for many years by Fong Ha and Han Sing Yuen. The I (pronounced Yi) Chuan system was originated by Wang Xiang Zhai who lived in Beijing in the early 1900s. He was a weak sickly man in his youth and travelled throughout China studying with various masters until he synthesized their knowledge into the I Chuan system. He used this method as a way of healing as well as a martial art, ultimately becoming one of the greatest martial artists in China. My experience of doing the exercises is a feeling that's like a golden ball of energy, and I started to wonder whether this might be the lost golden ball that is spoken of in the fairy tales of Iron Hans and the Frog Princess.

[15] Jung, C.G. *Mysterium Coniunctionis.* Princeton University Press, 1977, paperback ed., p. 47.

[16] Jung, C.G. Ibid.

[17] For a more extensive discussion of the Iron Hans tale see the interview by Keith Thompson of Robert Bly, *What Men Really Want.* Revision Magazine, May 1982, and Robert Bly's book, *Iron John: A Book for Men.* Addison-Wesley, 1990.

[18] The Kurgans, whose homelands were the steppelands between the Dneiper and Volga rivers, invaded Old Europe in three waves: 4300-4200 B.C., 3400-3200 B.C. and 3000-2800 B.C. They imposed a culture that was stratified, pastoral, mobile, and war oriented on a culture that was agricultural, sedentary, egalitarian, and peaceful. See Gimbutas, Marija's many works on this including *The Goddesses and Gods of Old Europe*, University of California Press, 1989; and Baring, A. *The Myth of the Goddess*, Viking Books, 1991, p. 81–2. The peoples of the matrilineal cultures had little defense against the taller, stronger, well-armed and mounted invaders and gradually succumbed to them. The Bronze Age matrilineal cultures were almost totally extinguished by the Iron Age warriors. (Baring, op. cit. p. 82 and 144).

[19] We will discuss one of the critiques of Gimbutas's conclusions further in the Trial by Water chapter. In the section on "dismemberment" we wonder how a culture that sacrificed some of its male members could be considered to be egalitarian toward the sexes.

[20] Gimbutas, Marija. *The Goddesses and Gods of Old Europe*. 1989, see preface. Also see Eisler, R. *The Chalice and the Blade*. Harper and Row, 1988.

[21] Parabola Magazine. Spring, 1993. The *Kung Approach to Healing*, by Richard Katz.

[22] In the Asclepeion temples throughout the ancient world, and particularly in Epidaurus there was an integration of healing modalities; nootherapeia (mind-healing), hands-on healing, dream incubation, musical therapy, psychodrama, physical exercise, and herbal remedies. See *Epidauros* by Papadakis, T. Verlag Schnell, Zurich, 1988.

[23] For a discussion of the recent discoveries of scientific measurement of the acupuncture meridians see: Robert Becker M.D.'s *The Body Electric*, William Morrow, 1985; and Ted Kaptchuk O.M.D., *The Web That Has No Weaver*. Congdon & Weed, 1983.

[24] Teeguardan, I. *Acupressure Way of Health, Jin Shin D*. Japan Publications, 1978.

[25] See Graves *The Greek Myths I and II* op. cit.; Frazer *The Golden Bough* op. cit.; Gimbutas, M. *The Goddesses and Gods of Old Europe*, University of California Press, 1982, p. 74 and 199; Campbell, J. *Primitive Mythology*, Penguin Books, 1978, p. 151–169; Baring, A. *The Myth of the*

Goddess op. cit.; and Walker, B. *The Women's Encyclopedia of Myths and Secrets* Harper San Francisco, 1983, p. 10, where there are numerous examples
of male castration, sacrifice, annual regicide of the king, etc. that happened during the epoch of matrilineal civilizations. We will discuss this further in The Trial by Water Chapter on Dismemberment.

[26] Achterberg, J. *Imagery in Healing.* New Science Library, 1985.

[27] The *coniunctio* is the alchemical designation for the final stage of union of opposites. See Edinger, *Anatomy of the Psyche Open Court.* 1985, Chapter 8.

[28] The same could be said about the effect on women of being separated from their ancient mystery rites. Being a man, this is not something I can speak of; but what I do know is that we're all in the cage of modern life together.

[29] See Storm, H. *Seven Arrows.* op. cit.

CHAPTER 7
TRIAL BY WATER

---

*Our falling apart is an
imaginal process, like the
collapse of cities and the fall
of heroes in mythical tales—
like the dismemberment
of Dionysian loosening
which releases from
overtight constraint,
like the dissolution and
decay of alchemy...*

JAMES HILLMAN

Letting Go to Something Larger than Ourselves

It is perhaps one of the most basic needs of being human to let go of our boundaries and to embrace a larger life. The ecstasy and dissolving that we feel in meeting a beloved are biological, cultural, psychological, archetypal, and spiritual in nature. All areas have deep implications for the evolution of humankind and for our personal development.

One of the effects of being hit by Eros's arrows is that distinctions between levels dissolve. We can't be sure upon which level our attraction is happening or why. But when struck, we set sail on an odyssey in a multidimensional sea of meaning where we are responsible for determining the purpose of our mythic journey.

The biochemical force that makes us loosen our boundaries and ourselves for another is not unique to the human kingdom. A moose trailed a cow in Vermont for seventy-six days before he gave up his "amorous come hither gesturing."[1] The male praying mantis endures decapitation by the female during mating. Mary Batten, in her book *Sexual Strategies*, says that,

> *"The male praying mantis becomes a better lover when he loses his head because the center of copulatory control in male insects is located in the ganglia of the abdomen, and the brain's role is primarily inhibitory. . . . Thus freed from inhibition, his headless body bends in intense copulatory movements."*

In the biology of our species is a force that expands our very nature, sometimes in ways that our rational minds resist, to help assure our survival. This biological force seems to have a mind of its own. It draws us together not only to procreate, but also to assure our survival and evolution on other levels. According to current anthropological thought, when the primeval forests were receding and the human left its safety and went into the savannah to survive, the female became more dependent on the male for protection. At this time, the female's biology shifted from estrus to being available for sex throughout the month. The expansion of her biological parameters had a purpose: to secure a pair-bond with a mate and to allow additional lovers to be interested throughout the month. Her continued sexual availability ensured her survival and helped her get the necessary protection. (When male chimps kill an animal and all the other chimps beg for pieces, estrus females receive extra portions.)[2]

In humans, one way the biochemical level of infatuation manifests is phenylethylamine (PEA), a chemical which causes feelings of elation and euphoria.[3] This results in an addiction to our lovers for the biological purpose of procreation. When psychiatrists gave lovesick people monoamine oxidase inhibitors which break down PEA, one perpetually lovesick man began to choose his partners more selectively and to live more comfortably without a mate.[4] In a study of thirty-three people who were happily paired, all were found to have high levels of PEA. When going through a divorce, PEA levels are low.[5] Rhesus monkeys who are injected with a PEA-like substance make courting gestures. But PEA levels soar in parachute jumpers, also. Infatuation cannot be reduced to biochemical exhilaration alone.

Love involves a spiritual dimension that is more than an urge to copulate. Robert Johnson expressed in his book, *We*, that Western culture's notion of romantic love can be traced to the "courtly love" of the twelfth century. "Courtly love was based upon a completely new view of love. . . which idealized a spiritual relationship between men and women."[6] Johnson says that this love was an antidote to the rough patriarchal attitudes of that era.

Though I do not agree with Johnson that romantic love began at the time of the troubadours, the notion that love acts out qualities of the collective unconscious of a given period of history is key to our understanding of the Trial by Water. First, it seems that romantic love has existed throughout the ages. In *The Song of Songs*, Jews of biblical times likened the adoration between husband and wife to the love between the peoples of Israel and the Lord. A wife's hair, teeth, lips, and breasts were all celebrated before God. In the Talmudic period, the first few centuries A.D., sex within marriage was seen as holy. It was said that God decreed husband and wife to engage in the marital act on the eve of the Sabbath.[7] In the *Kama Sutra*, between the first and sixth centuries A.D., there is much instruction on making sexuality a spiritual experience, "The abode should ideally be situated near water . . . it should be surrounded by a garden. . . at the head of the couch should be placed fragrant ointments, perfume, and flowers."[8] In Hindu teaching, the purpose of love-making is to awaken the great Goddess Kundalini, the pure energy of the self that resides within. In ancient Taoist and Tantric practices the initiate withholds ejaculation so that energy can be circulated and heightened between lovers in an ecstatic spiritual union.[9]

Indigenous cultures are replete with examples of romantic passion and the self-sacrifice that often accompanies it. In Japan, lovers sometimes chose double suicide, *shin ju*, when they were betrothed to other partners. Occasionally, among the Mangaians of Polynesia, young men

129

killed themselves when they were not permitted to marry their girl-friends. In Bali, men believed a woman would fall in love if her suitor fed her a certain leaf incised with the image of a god who had a very large penis.[10] William Jankowiak was able to find direct evidence for the existence of romantic love in eighty-seven percent of vastly different cultures.[11] Romantic love is a universal and transtemporal trait; possibly, as the Orphic myth of Eros says, "it existed from the beginning of time."

The idea that love is a manifestation of the collective unconscious is central to understanding love in the Trial by Water. We are a drop in the water, part of a larger sea. Romantic love expands this drop to an ocean. A culture is a sea of beliefs and values, and when it is missing an essential ingredient of life, personal love expands boundaries to heal the imbalance. Courtly love, where the knight, theoretically, had no involvment sexually with a lady, was a metaphor for the patriarchal attitude that separates us from the world. The knight was insulated by his invincible armor that no arrow could pierce. When struck with Eros's arrow, however, he felt an overwhelming desire to merge with another. The knight who had finely-honed skills for conquering land and possessing what he wished, was not allowed to fulfull his longing or consummate his passion. He was thus initiated into the path of transcending possession.

The Tristans among the troubadours saw something divine in the Iseults of the time. Their worship of the feminine helped them worship the gentleness and beauty absent on the battlefield. Transported out of the gross conquering realm, they cultivated refined feelings of poetry lacking in their warring culture. Identity was expanded by love.

Our patriarchal culture was founded on the suppression of paganism and the ancient mystery religions where ecstasy was a greater part of everyday life. Primordial peoples of the world lived in participation mystique with the world and felt deep reverence for all life.[12] Initiates in the Eleusian mysteries felt their ego boundaries expand through the use of psychedelic drugs. These rites sometimes involved as many as ten thousand people.[13]

Today in our alienated culture where more people live alone than at any other time in history, we seek this euphoric state of unity with our lovers. In the moment of release after an orgasm (and hopefully, at other times), we transform into a state of pure energy; the distinction between self and other dissolves into a sea of ecstasy. By merging with another in love-making and in love, our life recovers the feeling of interconnectedness, intensity, ecstasy, and transcendence we miss in our culture. Romance becomes our religion.

Though sexuality and romance have always expanded ego boundaries, so did the rest of life. By our world shifting from *anima mundi* (the world ensouled) to a world of *anima personalis* (love of an individual person)—our lovers must now bear the weight of our love for the world. Johnson believes that we suffer today because we seek in love what earlier generations experienced in their religions. When we seek a vision of perfection, a sense of inner wholeness and unity, when we strive to rise above the smallness of personal life to something extraordinary and limitless, we become spiritual aspirants looking for God in our beloved's eyes.

Johnson emphasizes the need to separate our soul's desire for union with the divine from union with our lover, or great problems will arise. When we put too much weight on our lover, we become intoxicated with love.

In the Trial by Earth we discussed the problems that arise when we do not separate the divine and the human. From the perspective of the water initiation, love enables our ego boundaries to dissolve so that we can incorporate a larger part of the wheel of life. On the biological level, we expand our boundaries to bring in a suitable mate for propagation. On the cultural level, we correct the imbalances of our materialistic world when we experience the divine in our partners and are willing to give up anything for love. On the spiritual level, love expands our boundaries to bring to earth the love and compassion in our divine hearts.

Our relationships may act out transpersonal archetypal forces symbolized by the Processions of the Equinoxes as Eros dances through the zodiacal signs.[14] It is interesting to note that during the third and fourth millenia B.C., the spring equinox was in Taurus (a female sign symbolized by the bull). This was the time of vitalistic religions when natural fertility was deified, human sacrifice to the earth took place, and the Goddess religions were prevalent.[15] Likewise, in the Age of Aries (a male sign symbolized by the ram), when Moses sounded the shofar (the ram's horn), biological paternity rights dominated and the child was named after the father rather than matrilineal civilization where children were in the line of the mother.[16] It may make the scientist in us wonder whether our lives are influenced by larger forces

131

than we are aware. Consider that the Age of Pisces (an idealistic water sign symbolized by fish) was ushered in by Jesus and his fisherman disciples and our current era has been ruled by idealized love.

How far does this sea of love extend? By looking into the archetypal symbols of our age, we wonder if the ocean we are swimming in is related to a larger cosmic sea of possibilities. The beauty of exploring this sea is that we can't be sure how much the system is composed of our projections, or we of its. By diving in, we are caught in the currents of the *mysterium tremendum*, the great mystery that through the ages has addressed the enigma of human existence and calls forth meaning.

Did the Age of Pisces (generally thought to be the most spiritual sign because of its association with the sea, merging, and compassion) cathect the energy of love into the spiritual dimension where the beloved was worshipped as a divinity? And now that we've moved into the Age of Aquarius (an air sign ruled by Uranus, God of Sky and electricity), is the area of communication and personal psychological qualities cathected in order to move the circle of life still one more evolutionary step?

On the psychological level, one purpose of love is to expand the boundaries of our personalities and round ourselves out. When we meet another human being we open to a larger vision of life. Jung was working in therapy with a man who dreamed that he fell into Lake Zurich. And, as as John Gray says in his book *Men are from Mars, Women are from Venus*, "meeting a member of the opposite sex sometimes feels like being abducted to another planet."

Fear of falling into something larger than ourselves is a common experience in relationship, and a cause of resistance. On the other hand, our partners are often able to handle the problems that are our greatest difficulties. If we are reserved, our partner may be extroverted. If we have difficulties handling financial matters, our spouse may do this with ease. Whatever our philosophy of life has not included, this is inevitably the part to which our partner introduces us.

This was certainly true for Paul, a minister of a local church, who felt threatened by his wife's desire to express her sensuality. This was repressed in his religious upbringing and in his family of origin where there was virtually no touching. When his wife had an affair with another man, he finally had to examine his marriage. He saw that the lack of his physical expression of love and affection contributed to her affair. After much soul-searching, he and his wife began to integrate physical contact into their relationship and even took a massage class together. The pain he experienced introduced him to a more inclusive philosophy of life.

Love takes a journey through the territories of life where we each need to find our own mythic solutions. We travel through the realms of earth (biochemical and procreative), heaven (the spiritual/archetypal), and the underworld (psychological/emotional).

Interestingly enough, the symbol of Aquarius has two different meanings that philosophers debate. It's portrayed as a human water bearer, symbolizing the emotional dimension of being human; and it is an air sign which emphasizes meaning and communication. In the Age of Aquarius, both definitions are needed in our relationships.

The biological level was the focus for our ancestors to meet many security needs. We are now moving into a psychological age where interpersonal difficulties and emotional issues have become the focus of our romantic evolution.

Loosening Fixed Ways of Being

In alchemical symbolism, the water element is called solutio, turning a solid into a liquid. One of the ways our psyches experience this is as dissolution. The alchemists believed that a substance could not be transformed unless it was first dissolved or reduced to prima materia, its original undifferentiated state. One alchemical recipe for solutio said,

> Because sol and luna have their origin from this water, their mother, it is necessary, therefore, that they enter into it again, to fit into their mother's womb, that they may regenerate or be born again, and made more healthy, more noble, and more strong.[17]

The dissolution of our adult personality structure has, throughout the ages, been spoken of as part of the spiritual quest. For instance, Jesus said, "Truly, I say unto you, unless you turn and become like children, you will never enter the kingdom of heaven." (Matthew 18:3) In intimate relationships, this dissolution takes place one way or another; but we often are unconscious of the purpose of this "turning back" the clock, or worse, we resist or are repulsed by it.

For instance, many couples notice themselves talking baby talk to each other or making up childlike nicknames. Sometimes a partner

133

becomes uncomfortable with this, especially if it leaks out into the world of other relationships. "I can't believe you called me 'sweet cakes' in public."

Regression to an earlier state of development is a part of initiatory traditions around the world. The acolyte is put through this process as a rite of renewal. Among the Hopis, a young boy is taken to a kiva, an underground hut like the womb of mother earth. He is taught that although he was born through his parents, his true parents are universal entities, Mother Earth below and Father Sky above. As he completes his stay in this earth womb, he returns to a more primordial layer of himself.[18] He unites with the plants, the four-legged animals, the insects, and all the elements of the surrounding universe. Through the initiation the brave merges with Wakantanka, the Great Mystery that is woven into everything where nothing can be separated from another.

In the Taoist initiation tradition of Tai Chi Chuan the student practices a series of exercises to reach the primordial self. One exercise is called *Tai Chi Chih* (Tai Chi Ruler) which involves rocking motions while holding onto an imaginary fluid ball. An hypnotic state is induced like a baby rocking in a cradle. In another Taoist exercise, the initiate practices "embryonic breathing" (t'ai-si) while imitating the circulation of blood and breath between mother and child. The preface to the *T'ai-si Keou Kiue* (oral formulas for embryonic breathing) states, "By going back to the base, by returning to the origin, one drives away old age, one returns to the state of a fetus."[19]

In relationships we "return to the origin of things" and wind back to our childhood, with early wounds resurfacing. Many people are repulsed by the regression that takes place in ourselves or in our partner. If we were abandoned by our parents, the issue of abandonment arises again. Our partner may have a hard time dealing with our childlike needs and feels, "I don't want to be with someone who has such abandonment issues!" We forget at such times that we are undergoing an initiation like the Hopi boy in the kiva who is learning to become one with all elements of the universe, or like the Taoist who is regressing to meet childhood ways of being once again. We are dissolving our present self in order to be renewed.

Couple's counseling helps people suffering from the wounds of Eros's arrows to reflect upon what's bothering them, and they may be regressed back to the source of that wound. In the example of Rob and Nancy, we saw how, at first, Rob was angered by Nancy's feelings of abandonment whenever he would talk to another attractive woman.

He was trapped in a pattern of trying to rescue her from her feelings, and resented it more and more. Rob gradually realized that this was the same way he had tried to rescue his disturbed sister throughout his childhood. By continually playing the part of helper, he had maintained a position of power in his family and had paid the price of not having anyone support his vulnerable feelings. By regressing to the early memory of his family, Rob became more conscious of the pattern that ruined his first marriage and threatened to ruin his second. With much hard inner work, Rob found a new way of relating to Nancy's vulnerability without rescuing and opened a channel into his own insecurities.

If we imagine personal development as a spiral, a block on a given issue will cause the energy to skip a space and continue its journey. Later in life, when we meet this issue again, the energy regresses back to the earlier place on the spiral. One analogy is, in weaving a spiral design on a fabric, we may miss a stitch; later when we notice it we unwind the tapestry and pick up the missed stitch.

In intimate relationships, it is inevitable that our fixed ways of being are given the opportunity to loosen. If they don't, the relationship develops hardening of the arteries—and we fail the Trial by Water. Single people learn that they must change their ways in order to live with another. This refers not only to the mundane aspects such as the way we wash the dishes, but also to the very deep and basic ways of appreciating the world. Love challenges us to let go of old patterns.

The Fear of Merging

The Trial by Water tests our willingness to merge. The story of "The Frog Princess"[20] expresses the fear that we have of merging and the solution.

> *A king is dying and says that whichever of his three sons brings back the most beautiful woman will inherit his kingdom. He helps them find their direction by performing a ritual where he blows three feathers into different directions. The oldest son follows the feather to the east, the second follows the feather to the west, and for the youngest simpleton son who never succeeds at anything, his feather doesn't go anywhere. It falls to the ground. Sitting there depressed, he notices a ring and when he pulls on it, an underground passageway opens up. He meets a frog half way down and explains his quest for a*

beautiful woman. The frog apologizes that he can't help the boy, all he can offer is his daughter, a frog.

Because the boy is open-hearted, he accepts the elder frog's offer and meets his daughter. She is very slimy, a frog one might be afraid of catching warts from. But since he is a trusting fellow he agrees to stay with her. She says that if he wants her to return with him to the upper world, he needs to embrace her, hold her close to his heart, and jump in the water with her. He does and she is transformed into a beautiful woman.

She tells him that a curse was put on her long ago where she was turned into a frog until someone loved her for who she was. The spell was now broken and when they returned to the boy's father, he won the kingdom with his new wife.

This story captures well a common experience in relationship. Our critical mind often gets in the way and judges our partner. He or she isn't affectionate enough, intelligent enough, and so on. "The Frog Princess" tale presents us with a path to approach our dissatisfaction. Jumping into the water with another while opening our hearts unlocks a magical door which transforms the ugliness into beauty. Intellectually-oriented people who marry feelings-oriented people sometimes change their focus on the intellect. What was once repulsive in our partners looks more and more beautiful.

The Purpose of Merging

A story that further develops the theme of merging is "The Stream and the Sands," loosely paraphrased from Shah's *Tales of the Dervishes:*

Once upon a time a stream passed through varied terrain. It fell over great cliffs, and twisted and turned, but it enjoyed the adventure of traveling alone. It had acquired considerable skills in overcoming barriers, but one day it reached the sands of the desert and found that as soon as it ran into the sand, its waters disappeared.

The stream was convinced that its destiny was to cross the desert, and yet there didn't seem to be a way. Then a hidden voice from the sands whispered, "The Wind crosses the desert and so can the stream. By hurtling in your accustomed way you cannot get across. You will either disappear or become a marsh. You must allow the wind to carry you to your destination by allowing yourself to be absorbed in the wind."

This idea was not acceptable to the stream. After all, it had never been absorbed before. It didn't want to lose its individuality. How could it be regained? The sands replied, "The wind performs this function. It takes up water, carries it over the desert sands, and then lets it fall again. Falling as rain, the water again becomes a river."

"How can I know that this is true?" "It is so, and if you do not believe it, you cannot become more than a quagmire, and even that could take many, many years; and it is certainly not the same as a stream." "But can I not remain the same stream that I am today?" "You cannot in either case remain so," the whisper said. "You are called what you are even today because you do not know which part of you is the essential one."

When he heard this, certain echoes began to arise in his thoughts. Dimly, he remembered a state in which he—or some part of him—had been held in the arms of wind. With this thought, he let go for a moment and lo and behold, he started to rise. It was scary. . . as if who he had identified with for a long time was evaporating away. But this awe-filled evaporation process did indeed bring an experience of a deep, long forgotten part of his identity.

As he continued to rise with elation, the memories of his long journey alone began to return. He remembered how he shut down after early hurts and how he had bound himself between river banks. With this realization, he noticed his form again change into a dark cloud, and he felt very sad about the time he had spent alone, not being open and loving.

Tears started to roll down his face, and he noticed that they fell as rain to the sands below, beginning the process of watering new seeds which would eventually grow into flowers.

He realized that the cycle of his journey had not been meaningless. He appreciated the cycle of creation and learned something from every part of it. At this moment he felt electricified with appreciation for the cycle of aloneness and togetherness, merging and separating. Lightning and thunder filled the heavens as he felt the wholeness of his essential nature.

The stream's journey is familiar to any person who walks the path of love and meets the issues of merging with another. We go through a process of solutio, dissolving our previous identity and discovering an even deeper part of our identity.

This process is often painful because we do not let go easily of a lifetime of patterns. At first we may resist. As Heraclitus says, "To souls, it is death to become water."[21] After our initial defensiveness, when our partners challenge a part of ourselves with which we're identified, the sadness that we feel from not living up to a loved one's desire may melt something inside. A seemingly innocuous statement by a partner who says "you're too intellectual," or "you're too emotional" can precipitate a process that alchemical metaphors vividly describe as *mortificatio* (an annihilation of oneself, or a dismemberment). As the process continues, eventually the intellectual person discovers emotions that were hidden. The overly emotional person finds their forgotten detachment.

Though the purpose of the Trial by Water for the initiate is to learn merging, it is equally important to know when to merge and when not to merge with another. Sometimes our quest requires that we resist the call. Remember how Odysseus, in Homer's *The Odyssey*, had the crew plug their ears with wax so as not to hear the Sirens? Odysseus survived this by lashing himself to the mast of his ship and turning a deaf ear to their seductive song.

Each time we lose our bearings—whether it's as simple as asking our partner what we should wear or, more significantly, relying on our partners' perception of our own feelings, we run the risk of drowning and losing our own uniqueness. We must learn to recognize when to tie ourselves to the mast in order to maintain our own individual selves, and when leaving the ship will bring us to a closer understanding of another's world.

In finding our way through the Trial by Water and discovering the balance between merging and separation, individuated growth can be an overwhelming task. The experience of coming together with another may feel, ironically, more like a painful death than an ecstatic conjoining. Jung captures such an experience in the following horrifying image:

> *The man is chained fast to the woman; and the more he winds and coils himself around her, the more will he be cut to pieces by the female weapons which are fashioned in the body of the*

*woman. And when he sees that he is mingled with the limbs
of the woman, he will be certain of death, and will be changed
wholly into blood.*[22]

Dismemberment

The theme of being torn apart by relationship has its roots in pre-
history. With the rising tide of popular interest in goddess-oriented
traditions, current research has focused on the Upper Paleolithic Era
(beginning approximately 40,000 years ago), into the Neolithic Era
(from 11,000 years ago), and into the Bronze Age (beginning approximately 3000 B.C., ending 1200 B.C.). Theories have been put forward
that there were peaceful, agricultural, egalitarian, and matrilineal cultures in Europe and elsewhere. This research points to the destruction
of these cultures by nomadic, patriarchally-oriented tribes between
4500 and 2500 B.C. This interpretation of historical events has been
used to fuel the ongoing battle of the sexes. Some historians claim that
acts of dismemberment are always attributed to male gods who replace
the Goddess in each culture.[23] In India, Indra killed the goddess and
scattered her body parts all over the countryside. In Babylon Marduk
tore Tiamut in two. In Mexico, the Aztec war God Huitzilipotli killed
his sister, the Goddess Coyolxauhqui, and threw her body from the top
of a mountain. And there is a myth about Zeus that tells of his devour-
ing Metis (the ancient goddess of insight) and giving birth to Athena
through his forehead. This story is often used to symbolize the co-
optation of the teachings of the Great Goddess. But to argue that barbaric acts have been unidirectional tells only half the story.

Many scholars think that during the Neolithic Era, blood of a
sacrificial victim that saturated the earth was believed to fertilize it,
making crops flourish.[24] We might begin to understand how such a
thing could have happened if we realize that events were based upon
the lunar worship of the Great Goddess and the cultural belief was that
there was no such thing as death. The death-rebirth cycle was seen to
be the basic fact of life. It was witnessed each month in the gradual
disappearance and death of the moon and its subsequent reappearance.

Anne Barring and Jules Cashford reconstruct the ritual in *The
Myth of the Goddess:*

*The gradual swallowing or dismemberment of the moon during
its dark phase may have offered an image of the idea that death*

139

was necessary to renew the principle of life. So by imitating the moon's apparent death, people would themselves assist in restoring fertility to the earth. Enacting the dark phase literally, the tribal practice would be to kill and dismember a 'sacred' victim who personified the dying moon as an image of dying life, burying the parts of the body in the earth, the Mother, to ensure that the life principle would persist and the crops would reappear. [25]

In his seminal work, *The Golden Bough*, James Frazer described the ritual sacrifice of these kings and princes in a wide variety of ways, one of which was dismemberment. [26] The period of grace granted to them varied greatly, from every eighth year to one year or even less.[27] Death was perceived as a necessary step to his renewal or resurrection in another form.[28] It was believed that if the man/god was allowed to die of sickness or old age, his divine spirit might share the weakness of his body, thereby bringing weaknesses (poor harvests, illness, or other calamities) to befall the whole community. The king was put to death while he was yet in the full vigor of body and mind, his sacred spirit uncorrupted by decay and his potency transferred to his successor.[29]

These practices were wide-spread. Froebenius reports that in the rituals of sacral regicide in Africa the king bore the name "moon," and, following his death, all the fires in his domain were extinguished. Later, the fire was rekindled by a pubescent boy and girl who, after copulating for the first and only time, were then tossed into a prepared trench and buried alive.[30] Joseph Campbell says that "The most vivid example on record of an immolation of the sacred king is in the south Indian province of Quilacare in Malabar, an area having a strongly matriarchal tradition to this day. . . The king had to sacrifice himself. . . . He took some very sharp knives and began to cut off parts of his body— nose, ears, lips and all his members and when he was about to faint he slit his throat."[31]

These types of acts may have been passed down in the form of myths throughout the European and Mediterranean areas. As with the era of the Great Goddess hypothesis, that we discussed in the Trial by Earth chapter,we may never know how historically accurate the stories are, how much the anthropological evidence is influenced by conjecture, or how the biases of researchers have skewed conclusions. We may never determine how many of these sacrifices took place during Goddess-centered or patriarchally-centered times. Some have

140

hypothesized that they are just psychological allegories for the spiritual process of death and rebirth, or that they are rituals for the changes of seasons, transposed into historical images. But many scholars believe that there is a measure of objective truth in the actuality of ritual sacrifices that are spoken of these myths.[32] Even Marija Gimbutas speaks of human sacrifice in Cucuteni culture of the Western Ukraine whose classical period was 4500-4000 B.C.

A wide variety of authors believe that the Sumerian version of the myth of Dumuzi, the son-lover of Innana, is a coded story of ritual sacrifice. This theme reoccurs in the Babylonian story of Ishtar's descent into the underworld and the death of her consort, Tammuz. It appears again in the tale of the Goddess Cybele and her lover, Attis, whose genitals were dismembered in sacrifice to fertilize the earth.[33]

The great scholar Walter Burkert adds weight to the reality of these rites when he says that "castration and throwing into the sea are presumably connected with sacrificial rituals." He also cites physical evidence of human sacrifice in the Knossos region, where children's bones were found with clear knife marks which he says may be related to a cannibalistic feast of the Minotaur.[34] Burkert says that the barbaric origins of Taurian Artemis presided over human sacrifices. In later times, this custom was symbolically reenacted by "a man having his throat scratched with a knife."[35]

Lest we think that ritual sacrifice was reserved only for men, let's not forget about the story of Iphigeneia when Agamemnon killed a stag in Artemis' sacred grove and the goddess demanded the sacrifice of his daughter. And there were seven male and seven female children sacrificed in Crete to the Minotaur.[36]

All over the ancient world the bull was depicted as the son/lover of the reigning Goddess, in part, because its horns looked like the crescent moon, a symbol of the goddess. In one of the earliest surviving written myths comes to us from Babylon (around 2900 B.C.), King Gilgamesh refuses to mate with Ishtar because he wanted to escape his death, a fate ordained for Dumuzi and her other lovers. In revenge, Ishtar sent "The Bull of Heaven" against Gilgamesh. The last Goddess-worshipping civilization of the ancient world was at Knossos in Crete. The Minotaur, with the body of a man and the head of a bull, was the son of the Goddess. The sacred marriage ceremony between the priestess/queen and the priest/king of Knossos was probably enacted in the costumes and masks of a bull and cow. This ritual evolved from the myth of Pasiphae, the Cretan moon goddess, who coupled with the sacred Bull of Poseiden and gave birth to the Minotaur. Though we cannot be sure of exactly what took place, one can imagine the ritual slaying of a bull, athletes testing their skill by leaping through the bull's horns (as the famous fresco in the Akrotiri museum depicts), the sun setting through the great carved stone horns in the western promenade of the temple (where they remain to this day) along with a sacred marriage ceremony of the bull/man and temple priestess. If accurate, this would have been a powerful evocation of the renewal of the earth through the union of opposites—male and female, death and life, sun and moon.

Regardless of their historical accuracy, these images give us insight into one dimension of the unconscious fear that men have of the female sex, shed some light on the subjugation of women in the patriarchal era,[37] and balance the idealized perception some have of the era of the Great Mother Goddess. It is certainly of psychological interest to note how many authors describe the era of Goddess worship as "egalitarian," [38] while ignoring or mentioning as an aside that men were ritually sacrificed, or rationalize it as an act done in the context of "sacred ceremony."

These sacrifices may have been performed as part of a world view that didn't experience death as an act of finality as we do today. The ritual sacrifice of a human being may have been seen as part of the cycle of death and rebirth of the moon each month and the dying and rebirth of the seasons. Still, imagine how a patriarchal culture would be perceived if it practiced (and it could be argued that this is, in fact, being done[39]) the killing and dismembering of women.

But our purpose in bringing up the historical and political dimensions is not to focus on the abuses by one sex of the other. There has been enough blaming going on between the sexes, with dire consequences for Love and the polarization between men and women.

The important psychomythological issue is how we, as a culture, are to deal with the fact that women have living in their unconscious an image of barbaric persecution. These images may date from the times of the destruction of the Goddess-oriented cultures during the rise of the Iron Age, and the torture and murder of millions of women during the Inquisition.[40] Similarly, how are men to deal with the images of male sacrifice to the goddess in our collective psyche?

Though the major thrust of our interest is psychomythological, anthropological history does have relevance to the understanding of the modern male and female psyche. Just as our culture is becoming conscious of the results of early sexual abuse on current relationships between the sexes, and just as women are becoming conscious of the results of patriarchy on suppression of women, so does the myth of male sacrifice by the Goddess-oriented cultures have import for understanding the collective psyche of men. Looked at from this viewpoint, our patriarchal culture may be caught in an unconscious "acting out" behavior against women due to repression and denial surrounding the treatment of men in our collective past history.

On the political level, men and women now have the opportunity to investigate and reflect upon the abuses perpetrated by both sexes in our historical past. In this context, our culture needs to acknowledge this denial, work through our feelings about our collective family's abuse of power, transcend antagonistic polarization, and move onward to a more conscious rapprochement.[41]

The focus for the initiate in the Trial by Water, however, is not so much on history, but on how our images of history live within us. Sacred Marriage in the Age of Taurus[42] may have been enacted with the sacrifice of a human being or bull; in the Age of Aquarius, the Sacred Marriage reflects the growing psychological awareness of the injury and sacrifice that happens in a relationship. Through the act of metaphorical perception, historical images can be used as symbols to guide the inner psycho-spiritual evolution of the individual.

Each time we are in relationship to someone (male or female) and hopeful that our needs will be met, we may experience the myth of the Great Goddess and her son(daughter)/lover. When we don't get what we want we may feel a loss and a sense of being torn apart. We may feel like blaming our partner and calling it a slaughter, but if we remember we are undergoing an initiation into the Trial by Water, we may see how this suffering fertilizes the ground of our lives and enables psychological rebirth to take place.

Anyone who has "hunted" for another to share life with can identify with the intense pain of desire for our beloved. Nothing matters more than being with that person, and we lose ourselves to our worship of the Great Goddess embodied in our prospective mate. If our desire is fixated at a sexual level, we may become like Actaeon, the great hunter who saw Artemis naked in her bath and felt intense lust for her. She turned him into a stag, and he was then torn apart by his own hounds. When the initiate feels the frustration of sexual desire, he or she must focus on the deeper purpose in meeting with another. This sometimes requires sacrifice.

The word "sacrifice" comes from the Latin, meaning "to make whole or sacred." We have an opportunity to restore something sacred to the wider whole of which we are a part as we bleed from not having

143

what we want. We may then ask, "What is capable of growing as a result of this meeting with this other person?"

When our lovers withdraw their appreciation from us, we experience a dismemberment like Dionysus did when the Maenads first worshipped him and then tore him apart. Life and love teach us that romantic relationships don't give us the praise that we received from our mothers.

Though we may have difficulty accepting criticisms about our worth, such criticism initiates us into the archetypal pathway of Dionysus, who was prematurely torn out the womb of his mother, Semele, before birth and sewed into Zeus's thigh to be born. By going through the initiatory process of being torn away from our narcissistic need to be comforted by our mothers, we are reborn out of that virile leg that stands in the knowledge that, through rejection, we find the light of a more contained self.

Dionysus is a symbol for the positive and negative ways we can deal with emotional and physical dismemberment. He "went mad," and handled his pain through excessive use of drugs and alcohol; but he also became one of the twelve Olympians, and brought rites of ecstasy to the Greek people. His marriage to Ariadne teaches that the pain of life leads us to our inner labyrinth. "Dionysus comes out of the water and returns to it, he finds a place of refuge and a home in the watery depths."[43]

It is no wonder that in our culture, where the *de facto* god is money, men and women experience the wrenching feelings of rage about child-support payments and alimony. The rage around "economic forced bonding" for men may be traced back to a prehistoric, nomadic existence when males left their women and offspring after an average of four years. Perhaps the rage that so many women feel toward men comes from this ancient abandonment. Whether it is biological or psychological, freedom for men (or the archetypal male) and abandonment for women (or the archetypal female) seems to be at the core of relationships between the sexes. These feelings may be so intense that many otherwise law-abiding men will hide out for a lifetime to avoid what they perceive to be unjust alimony or child-support payments. For one person the path may lead to activating Mars, the God of War, and hiring an attorney to protest paying more than "what's fair." For another, it leads to transcending the war gods of the past and seeking out a mediator or couple's counselor and finding the scales of Libra in the process where the feelings of both people are acknowledged. In ancient Egypt there was a ritual performed after death: a person's heart was weighed on a scale against the feather of the Goddess Maat to determine whether he or she would be annihilated or achieve everlasting life.[44] We, too, can reflect upon how we would want to appear to the face of Death, and, perhaps, find a lightheartedness that will enable us to give to the wider whole of which we're a part.

Behind the feelings of economic dismemberment is the ancient act of sacrifice; for as we give our children a part of us dies to give support to the new king. Alimony payments to an ex-spouse are sacrificial offerings to the God of Love, requiring us to relinquish some of our loyalty to the God of Money. Sacrifices always hurt; but they bring us face to face with new archetypal deities within ourselves.

Like temporary the "year-kings," we learn the hard way that the Goddess of Love requires a sacrifice to something larger than ourselves. In place of the sacred ceremonies that honored ritual sacrifice, we have the sanction of the state forcing a sacrificial act. We may never know exactly how the ancient year-kings were prepared to die, but the bull-leaping fresco at the temple of Knossos serves as an eloquent symbol. Perhaps the rage at dismemberment in our culture stems from the lack of initiation into the rites of sacrifice and the lack of an initiatory tradition that teaches us how to leap through the bulls horns without being torn apart.

When Osiris was torn apart and his limbs were scattered throughout Egypt, it was the "dew" of Isis's tears that brought together his dismembered fragments. Sometimes it takes the tears of grief to wash away the pain of our suffering and bring us back together again when we experience the many forms of love's pain and sacrifice. If we only could remember these mythic stories, and that there is purpose at those moments when we feel torn apart in relationship. Instead we cry out, "I wish I could be with someone easier!"

Remember Rob (from Chapter 4), saying exactly these words at the beginning of couple's therapy? The intensity of Nancy's jealousy produced feelings of inadequacy and guilt over not being able to help her. He experienced pain in his back, neck, and shoulders making Rob a regular chiropractic patient. He described the pain in his neck as two disconnected wires—a psychological dismemberment with very real physical manifestations. Rob got in touch with the insecurities of his childhood for which he tried so desparately to compensate by caring for his sister. Rob was moved to tears as he came to the painful yet healing realization that it was his own "rescuing" behavior that led to the breakup of his first and second marriages. As Isis's tears mended Osiris's dismembered limbs, so do our tears mourn the losses of our past and begin to bring back the split-off subpersonalities from our childhood.

Though we may never be certain of the anthropological accuracy of the patriarchal subjugation of ancient Goddess-worshipping societies[45] or the historical accuracy of the ritual sacrifice of males in these societies, we can be certain that these images live as representations in the human psyche. Their appearance in scholarly literature and in the dreams of men and women shows us that there is a fear of dismemberment that each sex has of the other. From a psychomythological viewpoint this expresses a stage in the Trial by Water called dissolutio, where the initiate is tested to move through the experience of being ripped to pieces by relationship, die to the naivete of notions of peaceful merging, and use the ancient images in our collective psyche as an opportunity to fertilize the fields of psychological growth.

Flexibility

As the initiate moves into the realm of water, we must learn to flow with the changing tides of intimacy. Our desire for stability and consistency is continually challenged. One moment our lover is clear, the next moment his or her emotions are murky. We relax and enjoy the calm, only to have a storm follow.

> In Greek mythology, Proteus, old man of the sea, changed his form from a lion to a snake, and a leopard to a tree. When Menelaus needed information from him to find his way home, Menelaus disguised himself as a seal and waited with the rest of Proteus's flock until Proteus returned to his true form, and then he got the information he needed.

This story symbolizes our task with the water element. Sometimes we need to learn to wait patiently while our beloved goes through changes. Our partner may get as angry as a lion, try to wiggle out of a commitment like a snake, try to escape a painful issue and run up into the trees like a leopard or stand so fixed in an opinion that we might mistake them for a tree.

To deal with the old man in the sea inside our partners, the story tells us that we need to disguise ourselves and wait in the form of a seal. So disguised, we may find a balance between our observing self and our emotional self (the seal). Our observing self has the wisdom not to get lost in our partners' entry into the animal kingdom of instinctual re-actions, while our emotional self knows how to come into and out of the waters of emotional life with them. This psychological position will help us to swim side by side towards shore with our partners without drowning each other. On our voyage of seeing, experiencing and psychodramatizing the metaphors of nature contained in our partners' behavior we find the kingdom of nature inside ourselves. In the process we discover the form of our own emotional nature and find our way home.

Knowing Our Feelings

The initiate finds the way home by knowing what our feelings are. Finding our inner feeling is not an easy a task. It requires leaving the values of our parents, reclaiming ourselves, and finding our own way through life's pains. As Persphone left the orb of her protective mother Demeter so do we; and we get raped by the Hades' who are both darkness and light. We are abducted into these caves and initiated into a new home in the underworld.

Dr. Eugene Gendlin's Focusing[46] process is a useful method for knowing our feelings. Focusing involves a series of steps to help a person stay with a *felt sense* of a life problem as it manifests in the body, and to facilitate *felt meaning* to emerge. Whatever image, word, or sound comes, the person brings it back to the body sense until a *felt shift* happens inside from some new meaning discovered.

For example, a woman might feel an aching in her stomach if her boyfriend hasn't phoned her for a few days. She may feel lost or blocked regarding the feeling. At first she might deny that it's related to the issue of her boyfriend, "It's probably just something I ate." But as the aching is felt, an image arises from her felt sense, "I feel abandoned, like I've been left dangling over a cliff, and I'm waiting for the big fall." When this image and the resulting river of feelings emerges, something shifts inside, "Ah, that's what is going on." Finding the word or image that describes how we feel is like a jewel that crystallizes our awareness.

There is an old Gnostic tale called "The Hymn of the Pearl"[47].
It tells of a prince who is sent on a mission by his parents, the
king and queen. He needs to recover a pearl that has been
stolen by a dragon. This pearl holds the key to his kingdom

*and to his becoming king. He goes off to Egypt where the
dragon lives in a cave. Nearby is an inn where people know
the dragon's exact whereabouts.*

*While staying at the inn, the prince grows to like it and adopts
the ways of the people to "fit in." He wears their clothes instead of his princely garments. He drinks their drink and eats
their food and eventually forgets his purpose. Finally, one day,
despair and a sense of meaninglessness overcome him. In the
midst of his depression, his parents send him a message affixed
to an eagle to remind him of his mission to search for the pearl.
When he receives the message, the prince goes to the dragon's
cave, recaptures the pearl, and returns to his kingdom to
become king.*

From one point of view, we see a timeless story of one who has
lost the ability to crystallize something beautiful out of his emotions.
Perhaps the tale says that from the irritations of life, a beautiful gem
is produced that leads us to finding our kingdom. As did the prince,
many of us have lost sight of our purpose along the way. We have
dressed in the garment of another and assumed a false persona to adapt,
or for our partner's approval. What helps us refocus is a message from
a higher source which comes to the intuitive mind in the form of a
symbol, an image, or a story. Then we can continue the journey into
the cave of our own unconscious and liberate the pearl from the demon.
From this, we rediscover the beauty of the gems that our true feelings
are, and begin to explore them.

The aim of the water initiation is the dissolving of our old selves;
through the process of transformation we find our own lost feelings
again in a new way. In the story of "The Stream and the Sands," the
water of the stream is presented with a choice when confronted with
the sands—dissolve or turn into a quagmire. When the river chooses
to let go and dissolve its previous identity, a horrifying, yet transformative possibility arises. Perhaps in all intimate relationships, a fright-
ening time comes when we feel we are losing our very self. "I don't
know who I am anymore or what I feel." This may be because the ego
is taking on a larger encompassing framework, the other person. There
is confusion and our orientation to life is spinning as if in a whirlpool.

Anyone who has been caught in a whirlpool while river rafting
has learned not to fight the river; instead we need to dive down in
order to come up alive. Likewise, when we are spun around by the

148

overwhelming feelings in relationship, we must go down with the whirling current and ask the question, "Who am I now?" Otherwise at the end of a relationship we may say, "What hurts so much about the loss of the relationship is not so much it's absence, but how I abandoned my true self while I was in it."

The Secret Death We Seek

As we look back on the Trials by Water and the great pains involved, we might well ask, "Why would we choose something that would force us to dissolve the very structure that it has taken a lifetime to build?" The feeling of desiring our beloved more than life itself comes to many intoxicated lovers who have drunk from love's potion. Look at the number of crimes of passion where the lover risks his or her life in the service of love. This disregard for the suffering endured by lovers is universal.

What does the lover seek through his or her rash actions? In De Rougemont's analysis of *Love in the Western World*, he concludes that what the lover secretly seeks is death. He shows how the origins of love in the Western world—in the Cathars and Manichichaean sects of eleventh and twelfth century Europe—were meant as an initiation process.

> The chivalrous knight was not allowed to consummate the physical act with the woman of his desire. Only one kiss was allowed. The woman was meant to be an object of contemplation and mystic vision which led the initiate to a yearning for what lies beyond embodied forms. Although she was beautiful and desirable, it was her nature to vanish. The Eternal Feminine leads us away.[48]

In Arab mystical poetry, the connection between love and death is stated explicitly:

> . . . Death through love is life; I give thanks to my Beloved that she has held it out to me. Whoever does not die of his love is unable to live by it. . . . Death is but the Night of Illumination, the Soul's union with the Beloved is a communion with Absolute Being.[49]

There is a reason that we suffer the passion that common sense rejects. It is not the secret preference for unhappiness, nor the masochistic delight in the experience of impossible love. The reason we undergo this part of the Trial by Water is that we enter into self-awareness by testing ourselves with a pain and suffering that is like death. Suffering and understanding are deeply connected; death and self-awareness are in league.

The initiate of various initiatory traditions is taught that at the end of life that which was built dissolves. The ultimate goal of many initiation traditions is to maintain consciousness as we go through the death process. Esoteric mystical paths say that the ultimate achievement in self awareness is passing from one life to another and remembering the process.

Whether or not this is symbolically or literally true, the myth of Jonah and the Whale is one common metaphor for the process of going through the belly of something greater than ourselves and being reborn. Another example is the Polynesian hero Maui, who, according to myth, entered into the Great Lady of Night's (Hine mi-te po) body. He was able to make his way through it, but as he was emerging still half-way in her mouth, the birds accompanying him burst out laughing. Waking suddenly, the Great Lady of the Night clenched her teeth and cut the hero in half, killing him. It is because of this, the Maoris say, that we are mortal. If Maui had been able to escape the Lady of Night's body safely, we would have become immortal.[50]

There were actual practices in many initiatory traditions that gave the initiate an experience of passing through the door of death. In shamanic cultures various drugs were used to create a near-death experience for such a purpose.[51] Various authors believe that the sarcophagus in the king's Chamber of the Great Pyramid was a place where the initiate would pass through the kingdom of death and be reborn.[52] The Temple at Komumbo in Egypt[53] may have been a place where the initiate passed through a tunnel of water holding his or her breath to get to the other side—replicating the death process.

Now we have an answer as to why lovers the world over "seek suffering." Relationship gives us the opportunity to try out our prowess with regards to surviving the dissolving process. In meeting the other, the initiate gets immersed in something larger than himself or herself and, like the great demi-god Maui, attempts to emerge without being cut in half.

In love, inevitably some part of us is ravished by something greater than ourselves, and some part survives. We are immersed into the bowels of unconsciousness, and the consciousness that survives—the self-awareness that develops from the journey—grows stronger. Like the adepts of ancient temples, we become initiated into an understanding of a deeper aspect of life, having tasted death.

---

[1] Fehrenbacker, G. "Moose Courts Cows and Disaster." *Standard-Times*. New Bedford, MA. Jan 23, 1988.

[2] For an excellent review of the anthropological data, see Fisher, H. *The Anatomy of Love*. W. W. Norton, 1992.

[3] Liebowitz, M . *The Chemistry of Love*. Little Brown, 1983.

[4] op. cit.

[5] Sabelli, H.C. *Psychiatry*. 53:346-68, 1990.

[6] Johnson, R. *We*. Harper and Row, 1983, p. 45.

[7] Fisher, H. op. cit.

[8] "Sexual Secrets," *Kama Sutra*. Destiny Books, 1979, p. 105.

[9] Chia, M. *Taoist Secrets of Love*. Aurora Press, 1984.

[10] Fisher, H. op. cit.

[11] Jankowiak, W. & Fischer, E. "A Cross-Cultural Perspective on Romantic Love." *Ethnology*. 31 (no 2) p. 149-55, 1992.

[12] See Neumann, E. *The Origins and History of Consciousness*. Bollingen, 1954 for a thorough discussion of the development from participation mystique up through and beyond the development of rational consciousness. Also McKenna, T. *Food for the Gods*. Bantam Books, 1992 has a radical hypothesis regarding how psychedelic mushrooms may have played a part in helping early humanity achieve these altered states of consciousness.

[13] Wasson, G. *The Road to Eleusis*. Harcourt, Brace & Janovich, NY, 1978.

[14] The zodiac ages are measured by the processions of the equinoxes, a 25,868-year cycle. Each age is 2160 years, measured by where the spring equinox point moves in reverse through the zodiac. It is a matter of debate exactly when each processional era begins. The Piscean Age was affected by Jesus with his fishermen disciples bringing to the world a Piscean compassionate love, turning the cheek, etc. See Rudhyar, D. *Astrological Timing*. Harper and Row, 1969.

[15] Frazer. op cit., Graves, R. op cit., and Walker, B. op cit.

[16] Merlin Stone, in *When God was a Woman*. Harcourt, Brace and Jovanovich, 1976, discusses the history and implications of this change for relationships.

[17] "Secret Book of Artephius" in *The Lives of the Alchemystical Philosophers*. London: John M.Watkins, 1955, p.145-146. Quoted by Edinger *Solutio*. p. 65.

[18] Waters, F. *Book of the Hopi*. Ballantine Books, 1963, p. 11.

[19] Eliade, M. *Myth and Reality*. Harper and Row, 1963, p.83, quoting H. Maspero, *Journal Asiatique*. April 1937 p. 198. For more on embryonic breathing see Huang, Wen Shan. *Fundamentals of Tai Chi Chuan*. South Sky Books, 1973.

[20] This is a retelling of "The Three Feathers," originally from the Brothers Grimm. The story here comes from Von Franz, M.L. *Interpretation of Fairy Tales*. Spring Publications, 1982, p.71. This is an excellent source for a number of interpretations on this tale.

[21] Freeman, K. *Ancilla to the Pre-Socratic Philosophers*. Harvard University Press, Cambridge, MA, 1962, p. 27.

[22] Jung, C.G. *Mysterium Conjunctionis*. par. 15.

[23] Noble, Vicki. *Shakti Woman*. Harper & Row, San Francisco, 1991, p. 3.

[24] Baring, A., Cashford, J. *The Myth of the Goddess*. Viking Arkana 1991, p. 161. Also see Campbell, J. *Primitive Mythology*. Ibid. p. 384-460, and Stone, M. *When God was a Woman*. Harcourt, Brace and Jovanovich, 1976, p. 129.

[25] Baring, A., Cashford, J. op. cit., p. 162.

[26] Frazer, J. *The Golden Bough*, Macmillan & Co. 1950, takes much of his evidence from Mannhardt, M. *Wald-und Feldulte*, Berlin, 1875 reprinted 1963.

[27] Frazer, J. Lectures on the Early History of Kingship, London: 1905, p. 291-2 paraphrased from Houston, J. *The Hero and the Goddess*, Ballantine Books, 1992, p. 153.

[28] Frazer, J. *The Golden Bough*. Macmillan & Co., 1950.

[29] Frazer is not the only author to discuss sacrifice of the male. See Campbell, J. *Oriental Mythology*, and *Primitive Mythology*, Graves, R.

The Greek Myths I and II op. cit., Barring, A. *The Myth of the Goddess* op. cit., Burkert, W. *Greek Religion* op. cit. and even Gimbutas, M. *Goddesses and Gods*, p. 74, 199.

[30] Campbell, J. *Primitive Mythology.* p. 169.

[31] Campbell, J. *Primitive Mythology.* p. 166 quoting Barbosa, D., *Description of the Coast of East Africa and Malabar in the Beginning of the Sixteenth Century.*

[32] See Burkert, W. books including *Greek Religion, Structure and History in Greek Mythology and Ritual* and *Homo Necans*; Campbell, J. *Primitive Mythology*, Penguin Books; Baring, A. and Cashford, *The Myth of the Goddess*; Graves, R. *The Greek Myths I and II*; Walker, *The Women's Enclopedia of Myths and Secrets*, 1978; Froebenius, L. *The Childhood of Man*, Seeley. 1909; Frazer, J., Ibid.; Gimbutas, M. *Gods and Goddesess of Old Europe*, p. 74 and 199; and Stone, M. *When God Was a Woman.*

[33] See Frazer, J. *The Golden Bough* op. cit., Campbell, J. *The Masks of God – Oriental Mythology and Primitive Mythology*, Graves, R. *The Greek Myths I and II*, and Baring, A. *The Myth of the Goddess* op. cit. for a review of this literature.

[34] Burkert, W. *Greek Religion*, p. 155 and p. 37. Regarding the interpretation of the knife marks he says that full publication and further discussion must be awaited before confident judgement can be made about the possible limits of refinement and barbarism in Minoan religion.

[35] Burkert. Ibid. p. 59. Also see Graves, R. *The Greek Myths II*, p. 74 section 116 c for a discussion regarding how shipwrecked sailors were killed with a club, decapitated, and tossed into the sea from the precipice of Taurian Artemis.

[36] Graves, R. *The Greek Myths II*, p. 254-256.

[37] Also see Stone M. *When God Was a Woman*, Harcourt Brace and Jovanovich, 1976 for an important discussion of how the rise of patriarchy and monogomy grew from men wanting to know who their children were. The children that were born from the temple priestesses were without knowledge of the identity of their fathers and this contributed to the power of women during the era of matrilineal descent.

[38] See Gimbutas, M. *Goddesses and Gods of Old Europe*, preface p. 1, and Eisler, *The Chalice and the Blade.*

[39] See Daly, M. *Gyn-Ecology:The Meta ethics of Radical Feminism*, Beacon Press, 1978.

[40] See Gimbutas, M. *Goddesses and Gods of Old Europe*, Star Hawk, *The Spiral Dance*, and Eisler, *The Chalice and the Blade*.

[41] This would repeat Erich Neumann's understanding about the development of consciousness from an unconscious merging in the circular uroboric dragon phase, through a stage of separation and antagonism, and finally emerging as a coming together of the opposites into a conscious unity symbolized by a circle with a dot inside. See *The Origin and History of Consciousness*.

[42] The beginning date for each age is based on the processions of the equinoxes and is not exact. Some say the Piscean age began in 317 B.C. Since each age is approximatley 2160 years (one twelfth of a processional cycle of 25,868 years) the beginning of the Ariean age would be 1843 B.C. (around the Time of the Achean invasion in Greece) and the Taurean age would be 2160 years before this, to approximately 4000 B.C. See Rudhyar, D. *Astrological Timing*, Harper and Row, 1969 p. 107. The Age of Aquarius according to this schema would begin in approximately 1843.

[43] Otto, W. *Dionysus Myth and Cult*. University of Indiana Press, Indiana, 1965, p. 162.

[44] Budge, W. *The Gods of the Egyptians Vol. II*. Dover Books, 1969, p. 143.

[45] Though the research base of Gimbutas is respected, in a search of the literature on her book, many scholars critique some of the conclusions she arrives at. According to an article by Steinfels, P. in the New York Times, February 13, 1990, Bernard Wailes a professor of anthropology at the University of Pennsylvania say Gimbutas "is immensely knowledgeable but not very good in critical analysis...She amasses all the data and then leaps from it to conclusions without any intervening argument." Ruth Tringham, a professor of anthropology at UC Berkeley says, "No other archaeologist I know would express this certainty." David Anthony, an assistant professor of anthropology at Hartwick College says that contrary to Gimbutas's claims, the cultures of Old Europe built fortified sites that indicate the presence of warfare. Also there is evidence of weapons, human sacrifice, hierarchy, and social inequality. In other sources, such as *The New Republic*, August 2, 1992, Lefkowitz, M. critiques Gimbutas and Eisler as having "a utopian notion

of prehistorical religion…that emphasizes only those mythological 'data' that seem to support her contentions about the brutality of the patriarchal 'takeover.'" In her article, Lefkowitz questions the interpretation of "pregnant females and women giving birth…as representations of the Goddess of Life and Death [when they] may simply be votive offerings on behalf of pregnant or childbearing women."

47 Gendlin, E. *Focusing*. Bantam Books, 1978.

48 De Rougemont, Ibid. p. 64.

49 De Rougemont, Ibid. p. 105.

50 Eliade, M. *Rites and Symbols of Initiation*. Harper and Row, 1958, p. 61.

51 Some readings on this topic include Mircea Eliade's *Shamanism* and *Rites and Symbols of Initiation*; Carlos Castenada's books; Huxley's *Doors of Perception*; Wasson, G. *The Road to Eleusis*.

52 Hall, Manley. *The Secret Teaching of All Ages*. Philosophic Research Society, 1971, p. XLIV.

53 A student of mine, Judith Johnson, toured this Egyptian temple and was told that this was the purpose of the undergound passage there.

CHAPTER 8
TRIAL BY AIR

---

*... Let there be spaces in your together-
ness, and let the winds of the heavens
dance between you. Love one another, but
make not a bond of love: Let it rather be a
moving sea between the shores of your
souls. Fill each other's cup, but drink not
from one cup. Give one another of your
bread but eat not from the same loaf. Sing
and dance together and be joyous, but let
each one of you be alone, even as the
strings of a lute are alone, though they
quiver with the same music. Give your
hearts, but not into each other's keeping.
For only the hand of Life can contain your
hearts. And stand together, yet not too near
together: For the pillars of the temple stand
apart, And the oak tree and the cypress
grow not in each other's shadow.*

KAHLIL GIBRAN

e've climbed a long way up the evolutionary ladder from being biologically-based organisms rooted in the earth to the complex men and women of the space age. Homo sapiens have moved through many pivotal events that have affected human relationships. The movement from the forest to the savannahs and the loss of females' estrus deepened the sexes' connection to each other. Economic growth, in general, and women's ability to work in the marketplace, in particular, decreased the dependence men and women have on each other and made relationship less a matter of need and more a matter of choice. [1] Now we are on the verge of an equally significant leap.

If esoteric thought is correct we are entering a new age, an age represented by the sign Aquarius. Some think this age began with the Wright Brothers' flight and the importance of being an air power on the world stage rather than a sea power (the Age of Pisces). Aquarius (an air sign) rules knowledge, information, and air waves of life. Its ruling planet, Uranus, is a sky god who symbolizes the higher levels of communication. In his manifestation as Prometheus he rules technology, stealing fire from the gods. [2]

A key moment in the Aquarian "information age" will happen when picture phones can be purchased commonly. An individual will be able to "screen" prospective partners as if he or she is Eros looking down from the sky at humanity. Choice will be expanded to divine proportions. Connections will be made as easily as electricity flows (of course there will still be resistance in the wires of interconnectedness between us). A husband and wife will be able to stay connected through their picture phone system that they carry with them—for better or worse. Eros will reach his Aquarian goal of taking over the air waves, and of making an aspect of divine sight accessible to humans.

It's not just the change in itself (loss of estrus or gain of divine phone systems) that creates evolution. While we use these lines of communication, will we transcend our old beliefs and habit patterns, open to wider possibilities than our hearts have known, find the deeper meaning behind our own and our partner's ways, deal with the paradoxes of love, transcend "either/or" thinking, become our true selves, and learn to speak to each other in ways that expand our evolutionary potential? The task with which we are continually presented is to use high technology consciously. As Prometheus discovered at great cost, it's *how* we use the fire of the gods that will determine whether it will burn and destroy us or light our way and heal us.

Examining Our Beliefs

In alchemy, the air operation is called *sublimatio* and refers to the process in which a solid, when heated, passes into a gaseous state and ascends to the top of the alchemical vessel. The term "sublimation" derives from the Latin *sublimis* meaning "high"; so the sublimation process is an elevating process whereby a low substance is transformed into a higher one by an ascending movement.

We all have our own particular beliefs that have grown with us from childhood, and have developed from our life experience. It's no wonder then that we have a difficult time rising above our particular way of seeing the world. The first step in our Trial by Air involves re-examining these cherished beliefs, and like a bird, finding distance from them. This isn't easy. One person has been taught in their particular family that it's best not to talk about feelings—"No one else will understand," "No one else is interested," "I'll hurt another by my feelings," or "I'll be wrong." Another person learned it's best to get everything out—"Don't be a wimp, say what you're feeling; it doesn't matter what anyone else feels; what's life, anyway, if you don't have room to express yourself," "It's injurious to your body and yourself and others to hold in your feelings." Each of us can fill in the blanks with our own relationship. The point is that when two different people come together with different histories, it's easy to assume that our way is right. We forget that our beliefs are relative, are influenced by our early histories, and evolve as we meet another's. As the Plains Indians describe it, we move around the Wheel of Life by looking into the mirror of our conflicts and differences.

"Nasrudin and the Donkey"[3] is a classic Sufi tale about right and wrong:

> *"Reasonable people always see things in the same way," said the Khan of Samarkand to Nasrudin one day. "That is just the trouble with* reasonable people," *said Nasrudin, "they include at least some people who always see only one thing out of a potential two possibilities."*
>
> *Nasrudin then asked the king to gather his court of reasonable men together at sunrise. The next morning, Nasrudin rode before the assembled court on a donkey in such a way that his face was towards its tail and towards the rising sun. While riding by, he asked the king and his advisors what they saw. After whispering took place among them, a unanimous*

consensus was reached and the king replied, "We see a man riding backwards on a donkey."

"That is exactly my point," said Nasrudin. "Why did you not notice that perhaps it was me who was right, and the donkey facing away from the beautiful sunrise was facing the wrong way around. "

From Nasrudin's lesson, we can see that it's better to start a relationship assuming the other person is from another planet. On one planet perhaps, people merge together every day, on another planet, twice a week or less. It's important to wonder about another's planet instead of judging it by our "normal" standards. This hones the crucial skill of truly listening to another.

Transcending Either/Or Categories

A key to the air initiation is transcending our either/or categories. Our heritage identified the archetypal masculine with rites of strength, whereas the archetypal feminine was usually identified with the arts of softness. Although we are now experiencing a cultural revolution that defies all set roles, nonetheless relationship still provides an initiation into expanding our identities, whether it be masculine or feminine.

The Dance of Opposites:
Developing Our Contrasexual Side

If we have identified with either strength or softness we may be challenged in a relationship to become the opposite at our partner's dissatisfaction or request. Carl Jung spoke of this as a man meeting his *anima* (his feminine side) or a woman meeting her *animus* (her masculine side). Jung believed that a fundamental step in the individuation process was integrating the anima or animus into our personalities. Since our genetic makeup consists of a large number of predominant sex genes and also a number of contrasexual genes, Jung felt that for us to become whole, all of our genes need to be integrated.

In fact, this is one of the axes around which much of relationship revolves. A man or woman who has identified with his or her intellect is suddenly confronted by another who is emotional and irrational. In meeting our partners, we are forced to expand our emotional repertoires.

I remember Bob, a highly successful corporate executive. He was known for being able to rise above conflicts and maintain his composure under the worst of circumstances. In poker games "with the boys" after work he was able to present such a cool expression on his face that no one could read what he was feeling. Bob boasted that he was the best bluffer of all the players.

His wife, Darleen, a creative, yet struggling, artist was upset that he give her so little attention, and she never knew what he felt. Initially, they came to couple's therapy because Darleen attempted suicide several times. In couple's therapy, Darleen would describe a feeling and Bob would be expressionless. She would yell at him, crying hysterically—still no response. Finally, she would threaten to commit suicide and at the point when Bob felt it was possibile, his emotion would show on his face, he would express how much she meant to him, and tears would come to his eyes. In the course of this relationship, Bob met his inner feminine expressiveness in his partner and Darleen met her intellectually reserved inner masculine in her husband.

I have often noticed in my experience with couples that if one partner resists a certain lesson while in the relationship, often life brings the lesson later by an *enantiodromia*, a turning into the opposite. After this relationship dissolved, Darleen became successful in business. On the other hand, the first week after they parted, Bob was involved in a serious car accident and wrecked his car. A short time later, Bob enrolled in an emotional growth-oriented training program, something he had resisted during his marriage.

The myth of Teiresias, the blind seer, gives us rich metaphors to ponder regarding the difficult path of integrating our contrasexual side.[4]

> *Teiresias was a Theban seer. During his youth he came upon two snakes coupling on Mount Cithaeron, near Thebes or Mount Kyllene. He struck the female with his staff and killed her, and immediately found himself transformed into a woman. He remained a woman for seven years when he came upon two other snakes coupling. This time he killed the male snake, and suddenly he returned to his masculine form again.*
>
> *One day Zeus and Hera were having a dispute over Zeus's infidelities. They were quarreling about whether man or woman has greater pleasure in the act of sex, and they called*

> *Teiresias as arbitrator since he was the only man on earth who*
> *had knowledge of both sides of the issue. Zeus defended himself*
> *by arguing that when he did share his wife's bed, she had the*
> *better time because women derived more pleasure from the*
> *sexual act. Hera denied this, insisting that the truth was to*
> *the contrary, for why else would her husband be so flagrantly*
> *promiscuous. Teiresias gave his judgment:*

> *"If the parts of love-pleasure be counted as ten, thrice three*
> *go to women, one only to men." Teiresias's declaration that*
> *women enjoyed the act of love-making more so angered Hera*
> *that she struck Teiresias blind. But Zeus took pity on him and*
> *granted him inner sight and the ability to understand the lan-*
> *guage of the birds. He was given a life span of seven genera-*
> *tions and was permitted to keep his gift of insight even in the*
> *dark fields of the underworld.*

Mythology so beautifully creates images like this that capture the process of meeting differences in our partners. When we try to kill the
qualities that our partner possesses (the opposite-sexed snake), we are
destined to turn into that very thing ourselves. It can't be stated enough
that *whatever we resist in another is a mirror for that quality in ourselves.*
Often these qualities are different from what we identified with in early
childhood, so we have a difficult time admitting that we have them
within ourselves.

This was certainly true in the case of George, a wealthy man who
spent money freely. His wife Alice, was "the tight one" and it was difficult for her to admit that she also had a spendthrift side. Eventually
she developed the attitude. "If he is going to spend money, I may as
well, too." At first this was said angrily, reacting to George, but reflection led Alice to memories of withholding money as a child due to
guilt, and how she never felt free to spend, though as an adult she had
accumulated considerable resources. Though at first she wanted to slay
the snake she perceived George to be, he precipitated a journey to the
other side of herself. Alice's conscientiousness about spending money
also began to affect George and catalyzed his making socially conscious,
environmentally sensitive investments.

Like Teiresias, the intensity of our antagonistic feelings toward the
snake that we see in another makes us lose our ability to see clearly. Our
anger at our partner's spending literally blinds us but also gives us the
capacity to develop inner sight. Like Teiresias we develop the power of

this inner sight by going through the underworld of our own pain, and a great gift comes out of this journey. We develop a bird's perspective, for when we see the quality that we dislike in our partner as a part of our own inner circle, we then transcend the either-or attitude; like a bird hovering above both partners, we gain a perspective that sees both persons' legitimate places on earth.

Disidentification is another key aspect of what we learn in the air initiation. Some of us may disidentify from our habit patterns, such as being a "spender" or a "saver." Others may explore freeing ourselves from even more basic aspects of our identifications in life, such as our sexual roles. For instance, in Taoist and Tantric teachings, role reversals in mystical sexual practices led to the recognition that there is a female in every male and a male in every female.[5] In Greek mythology, Aphrodite, The Goddess of Love herself is pictured as being androgynous—in Hesiod the attribute to her *philommedes* means "to her belong male genitals."[6] In the ancient Greek festivals of Aphrodite at Argos, in the Hybristica celebrations, as well as in Athens, women appeared as men and men dressed as women, wearing veils.[7] In Japan, even to this day, the crowning of the emperor in the Shinto *daijosai* ceremony requires the crown prince to be transformed into a woman, and be impregnated by Shinto spirits. It is only through this ceremony that he can be reborn as emperor.[8]

To become an emperor in the Temple of Air, a man need not dress like a woman or become "effeminate," nor a woman dress like a man or become "aggressively masculine." Rather we all need to free our preconceptions about sexual roles and rigid patterns, and accept our "other sides" to enrich the realm of relationship.

Teiresias had seven years to explore this other side, but later returned to his original male form. We can imagine that his maleness would never be taken for granted again. The same is true in our life journey. We might identify with a particular quality at one point in our life (for instance, being an intellectual) and through our relationships assume the opposite stance (become more feeling-oriented). After a long period of time (seven years symbolically), we may find ourselves appreciating our original way of being or thinking and want to return to it. When we do, however, it is through new eyes. We are returning having experienced the opposite and therefore, will not take it for granted. Esoteric literature calls this "twice born."

The gospel according to Thomas is perhaps the quintessential description of the transcendent intention of the Trial by Air,

*When you make the two one, and when you make the inner
as the outer, and the outer as the inner, and the above as the
below, and when you make the male and female into a single
one, so that the male will not be male and the female not be
female. . .then shall you enter the kingdom.*

Cultivating Freshness of Perspective

The normal human state is to forget about the transcendent possibilities in every moment. Everyday life is taken for granted. The word *reification*, according to the Oxford English Dictionary, means "the mental conversion of a person or abstract concept into a thing." Before reification sets in, when children see a tree, they are filled with wonder. They feel its gnarled bark, or even chew on its leaves to taste the tree. Some children caress it, push it, and admire its strength. As they play with their new strong friend, it challenges them to the climb. Perhaps for awhile, they retreat in fear and a day later, the child takes the first step up. When eventually climbed, the tree has been "a relationship," an experience, a place to rest and lean against when the child needs support. It may even become a vital image to dream about.

Reification sets in after we have seen many trees. Then tree becomes a concept to be studied; the experiential dimension becomes "thingified." For awhile we may not even touch it while we study different kinds of trees: pines, oaks, and willows. Erich Neumann, in his book *The Origin and History of Consciousness*, writes that the process of initial unity with life's participation mystique can be symbolized by the circle of the *uroboric* dragon biting his own tail. There is no consciousness of, but rather, an unconscious identification with life. He believes that a separation must take place where we leave this unity. Finally, when we return to this unity, it is symbolized by a dot in a circle—a consciousness of the unity of life.[9]

From the perspective of the air initiation, breaking down reification and developing freshness of perspective is a key factor. Reification is the earth element gone awry; to have been with something so long that we no longer appreciate its place in the circle of all things. Air freshens dead reifications. It once again makes the world ensouled. The shaman and all those who had appreciation for the sacredness of the earth, would see nature and each part an aspect of the mysterious universe hidden within. It was here that herbal medicine began; for healing powers derive from this appreciation.

We begin our lives as male or female and establish habit patterns at an early age. Soon these are taken for granted as the process of reification sets in. By entering into the process of relationship and being introduced to our opposite, we can separate from the initial identification and gain a freshness, like the winds that move a seed to a new place. Later in life after finding distance from our origins, we can return to that earlier state and appreciate it anew. As T. S. Eliot said in the *Four Quartets*, "And the end of all our exploring will be to arrive where we started and know the place for the first time."

Developing Our Individual Selves

The separation from something with which we were once identified is another fundamental aspect of the Trial by Air. In alchemy it is called *separatio*, for which there are many chemical analogies. The extraction of a metal from its crude ore was done by heating, pulverizing, or by other chemical means. Many substances, when heated, will separate into a volatile part which vaporizes and an earthy residue which remains. Amalgams, for instance, when heated release their mercury as vapor and leave the nonvolatile metal.

In the water initiation we discussed the importance of merging in a relationship, for without letting go and becoming one with our partner an essential ingredient of love is missing. Here in the air initiation we must learn to separate from that unity and find our individual self again. Separation is a fundamental stage in all developing systems. In the Bible, God created heaven and earth as separate entities, and divided light and darkness. In Egyptian mythology, Shu formed the world by separating earth and sky.

According to Margaret Mahler's[10] research on the development of children, the separation individuation process is fundamental to the psychological birth of the human infant. She outlines the stages that a child goes through from an initial symbiosis with the mother to individuality.

Mahler believes that a key phase in the separation process begins at approximately sixteen months of age: the rapprochement crisis. This phase occurs after the child has begun to walk and has separated somewhat from the maternal orbit, due to the ability to stand. However during the rapprochement stage, the child has dual tendencies. On one hand, there is a desire to be separate and omnipotent while, on the other hand, there is a desire to cling to the mother. During this time, the toddler's belief in his or her omnipotence is severely threatened and the environment is coerced as he or she tries to restore the status quo. Temper tantrums, whining, sad moods, and intense separation reactions are at their height. Mahler believes that many psychological problems develop from this early stage of childhood development when the child is looking for "optimal distance" from the mother. Many psychologists believe that severe psychological disorders can be traced to this stage of development.

Masterson, for instance, believes that *borderline* patients suffer from an arrest occurring at the rapprochement subphase of the separation-individuation process.[11] He feels that the arrest in development may be due to the mother's withdrawal of her availability because of the child's efforts to separate and individuate. This may occur because the child's individuation constitutes a threat to the mother's need to cling to her infant and thus causes her to withdraw. The child, in response, experiences an abandonment depression, which leads him or her to cling to the mother and thereby fail to progress in separating from the mother.

We can see that many of the same issues that a child deals with during the rapprochement subphase exists in relationship. We feel like we can stand on our own two feet, yet at the same time, we may be afraid to stray too far from the orb of our relationship. Classical analysts, like the above mentioned authors, might explain difficulties that a couple has in separating from each other and finding *"optimal distance"* from each other in terms of their developmental history.

From the symbolic point of view, this childhood phase of development is the earliest example of the air (distance) initiation, a trial that occurs many times during our lives. But this trial cannot be reduced to a phase of childhood development. The rapprochement crisis is an archetypal issue about merging with or separating from another.

Life is an initiation journey where we need to find our way through archetypal issues and obstacles, not merely work out childhood traumas. Traumas are real and do present us with energy blockages which need to be worked out by facing these events. Often it is not a question of a single trauma, but a series of events that developed into a pattern of being. Behind these patterns and events lie the hidden trials of the human condition.

The story of Cronos wanting to swallow his children, for instance, captures the feeling that many parents have when their children stray too far from the parent's concept of reality. The hero's journey, where the child finds something while he or she is apart and brings it back to the parent is also archetypal.[12] If the discovered treasure is not accepted by parents, in childhood or later, something will be missing. Blocks about sharing may develop.

One person screams, another mourns. Regardless of who we are, we go through a process. We may develop understanding, compassion, or learn to let go. Most importantly, we become initiated into the human condition, and find our own mythic solutions.

Regardless if with our parents or our lovers, the issue of *bringing our discoveries back to the nest* emerges. One person attempts to solve this by being a warrior-like Mars, caught in the net of his aggressiveness[13] with an angry "Listen to me!" Another does it through sublimation, "I'll share with the world and show that my discoveries are worthwhile." Regardless of what choice is made a path begins. One person not able to share might retreat and sublimate their creativity into art, another may develop talent for music.

Balancing Separateness and Togetherness

The rapprochement issue of finding the balance between being separate and also needing another is well depicted in the story we discussed earlier of "The Stream and the Sands." At first the stream resisted merging with the sands and the air but then let go of its resistance and was able to experience an even deeper part of its identity—water vapor.

It has often been said that a relationship can't work if there is excessive merging. This is called *enmeshment;* where the partners lose themselves in each other. There is a need for both partners to honor themselves as individuals and, at the same time, honor the relationship. This is difficult and means that there are, in fact, three people in every relationship—the two individuals and the couple. In terms of the stream and the air sometimes the stream will separate from the air above. This is necessary for its own independent adventures. From a wider perspective, water and air always contain each other, just as each individual in a couple still has the other present within themselves. Even a partner's most different quality is a part of our own Medicine Wheels.

In the Trial by Air, the emphasis is on separation. After the merging of the water phase, the two people in the air phase of a relationship must find their separateness again. Without proper separation, we often experience our partner in terms of our own unconscious needs.

We don't separate our desires from the other person as a unique human being and are deprived of knowing another in the I-Thou sense.

Exploring Resistance

In the example earlier of Bill and Elaine from the Trial by Water, Elaine didn't have orgasms and Bill experienced this as a burden. After he was able to separate himself from his feelings, he grew to know Elaine in a deeper way. He learned what her withdrawals meant, and was able to listen to her family history. When he heard about her mother's heart condition in Elaine's youth, he developed compassion for Elaine and her fear of joy.

A key difference between the air and water realms is the difference between our feelings (water), and the space between two people (air). A man working on the Trial by Water who wants his wife to move wildly during sex might express his disappointment, while the air initiate might lightly mention that he notices that she doesn't like moving as much as he does, and from genuine inquisitiveness asks her why. This is called *exploring the resistance*. He might discover that she's afraid of her sexuality overwhelming a man, or that she isn't expressing what most excites her.

One of the problems in pop psychology is the overemphasis on the water element. It seems that the Water Temple, after being suppressed for so many years in our culture, has taken over the field of the psyche, at times leaving it waterlogged. Sometimes it is not appropriate to express feelings—we need to know when water will accelerate growth and when it will flood.

The adept of the Air Temple deals with our partner's emotional issues as Chang San Feng, the originator of Tai Chi, would hold a bird.[14] Folklore says that there was so little hardness in his hand that a bird could not fly away because there was nothing to push off of. Adepts of Tai Chi push-hands emulate this softness and work on developing a stickiness in their touch, adhering with no pressure. These metaphors give us a way to be with our partners when they are dealing with an emotionally charged issue. If they want to fly away and resist looking inward, instead of holding on tightly, we must find an open hand that gives them the chance to stay. The softness of touch comes from the empathy for the tenderness of our own issues and conveys "I'm ready to stick with you wherever your exploration goes." If they are open to exploring their resistance, then we can ask questions such as, "How long has this issue of yours existed?" "What do you think it's about?" "How is it for you to feel this way?" We can share our sexual difficulties so that our partner doesn't feel the issue is unipolar. We find a light touch. . . not being attached to our partner's staying with or leaving the issue.

Extracting Meaning: The Philosopher's Stone

One of the important things that comes from having the necessary distance in a relationship is conveyed by the alchemical term *extractio*,[15] extracting the essential part. Ancient alchemists tried to extract water, gold, or oil from a concrete substance, and Moses tapped on a stone in the desert to bring water to his people. The extractio process is one of the goals of the *opus*. It involves the extraction of meaning or psychological value from a particular object or situation.

The Philosopher's Stone symbolizes the quest for meaning in a concrete world. It represents the alchemical opus, turning lead into gold. Philosopher's Stone may sound like a misnomer. How can a lowly stone be linked with a lofty philosopher? But this is where the goal of the opus lies. When the most mundane things in life yield meaning, we know that indeed "we have arrived." As Malik Dinar learned to see treasures in everyday life, so does the initiate of this aspect of air initiation.

Consider the case of Fred and Karla who returned to therapy two years after our last work together. They said that their arguments had degenerated to the point of being intolerable. The first issue they raised was the ongoing fight about a bathtub drain. They said they were "passing each other in silence, and the air was as thick as molasses."

The first step in therapy was to use process for clearing negative feelings: expressing positive intention, making "I feel" statements and then asking for what we need. The emphasis is on one person listening and reflecting back their partner's feeling until the partner feels heard. Karla expressed feeling powerless and frustrated that Fred knew plumbing but hadn't worked on the drain in six months, and that if he didn't want to fix it himself, why not let her hire a plumber? When Fred finally heard Karla's feelings of impotence and frustration, he agreed to her request. Karla felt relieved and appreciative. This cleared the air somewhat; and they expressed that for the first time in months they had hope.

An even deeper treasure was discovered when Karla and Fred had a seemingly mundane discussion about how they didn't believe that the drain could ever be cleared due to the lack of slope under the bathroom. A silence filled the room when they realized that the faulty drain was a symbol of how so many negative feelings had built up in their relationship that they didn't believe they could ever be cleared— and that they needed to find the proper slope to allow the necessary drainage. Seeing the drain as a symbol crystallized the problem they'd been having better than any words could have; it became a messenger from their everyday reality.

Over the next weeks and months, the bathtub drain became a vehicle to explore what had created the blocked expression of their feelings. Both had passive-aggressive patterns of withdrawing from their families when they didn't feel their needs met. In time, humor returned to their relationship; they teased each other about the feelings that weren't going down the drain. The day the plumber discovered how to slope the drainpipe, Karla and Fred celebrated with champagne and dinner. The "Philosopher's Stone" hidden in the drain had been discovered.

What attracts us to another human being is itself a sacred symbol—a philosopher's stone to the inner eye. As our partner's uniqueness is a treasure and a mystery, so are the forces that attract us to another as great a mystery. Astrologers study this as chart synastry,[16] and examine how planets and zodiacal signs combine in two people's astrological charts. These symbols give lovers a language they can use to explore how the connection between them is governed. Are air people attracted to fire people to move stale air? Are water people attracted to earth people, like rivers, to give them direction? Whether scientifically valid or not, using metaphors allows a couple rising above the everydayness of life to explore their higher purpose.

Although people are tried by all the elements in their relationships, certain elements and trials by particular gods or goddesses enter into the foreground at one time or another. When a given relationship is characterized by symbiosis and merging, is the God of the Sea (Neptune) present in the synastry? When argument and adversity is present, what are the Mercury (God of Communication) and Mars (God of War) aspects? Even without a birthchart, we can analyze how the planets and the elements of nature play a part in our interactions and attractions.

Communication: The Path of Hermes

Communication is the foundation of making a relationship work, and the difficulties we have with it are part of the Trial by Air. Mythology contains many keys to becoming adepts of this temple. In Greek mythology, the God of Communication is Hermes/Mercury. Since Mercury rules the air sign Gemini, mythology tells us that it takes breathing space, an ability to disidentify, and perspective to communicate effectively.

Finding the right words often involves a balancing act. Thus the two poles in the glyph for Gemini (II) are connected by horizontal lines above and below. The symbol says that Hermes connects the opposites by having a spiritual yet grounded perspective.

The first symbol of Hermes was the *Herma*,[17] a stone heap that was placed along the roads to mark the way and to mark boundaries between villages, cities, and various other geographic regions. This search for the delicate balance between truth and untruth can be seen in how Hermes explains being caught stealing a herd of cattle from his brother Apollo.

When confronted with his deed by Apollo and Zeus, he didn't tell a lie nor did he tell the truth. He explained that he only stole two cattle from the herd and he divided them into twelve portions, for the "twelve gods." When asked by Apollo who the twelfth God was, because Apollo knew that there were only eleven gods, Hermes replied, "Your servant, sir."[18] Thus, although Hermes committed a crime, he included himself as one of the gods at the same time. He sacrificed what he stole to the higher powers of heaven and earth, unlike Prometheus who stole fire from the gods. Zeus punished Prometheus by binding him to a rock for eternity; whereas he simply laughed at Hermes's audacity.

Following the path of Hermes can involve skirting the boundary of truth. He is a trickster who rises to divine heights by cunning acts. Because he acts with a higher purpose, he wins a place in heaven and a golden triple-leafed staff with which he has the power to put to sleep or to "awaken the eyes of men."[19] The number three symbolizes that Hermes has found the way to transcend the opposites of true and false, yin and yang (he is hermaphroditic in nature), and all opposites. He is a master of balance between conflicting opposite principles on the wheel of life.

171

The Trial by Air involves finding the balance between complete honesty and withholding the truth when appropriate. The initiate in the Temple of Hermes looks at decisions with a willingness to sacrifice to the higher powers of heaven and earth. These divine principles require that we speak for the purpose of awakening others, not solely for our own egocentric needs.

Some Hermetic principles to keep in mind when communicating are listed in M. Scott Peck's book *The Road Less Traveled* :[20]

1. *Never speak falsehood.*

2. *Bear in mind that the act of withholding the truth is always potentially a lie, and that in each instance in which the truth is withheld, a significant moral decision is required.*

3. *The decision to withhold the truth should never be based on personal needs, such as a need for power, a need to be liked, or a need to protect one's map from challenge.*

4. *Conversely, the decision to withhold the truth must always be based entirely upon the needs of the person from whom the truth is being withheld.*

5. *The assessment of another's needs is an act of responsibility which is so complex that it can only be executed wisely when one operates with genuine love of the other.*

6. *The primary factor in the assessment of another's needs is the assessment of that person's capacity to utilize the truth for his or her own spiritual growth.*

7. *In assessing the capacity of another to utilize the truth for personal spiritual growth, it should be borne in mind that our tendency is generally to underestimate rather than overestimate this capacity.*

After love itself, the art of communication is perhaps the single most important factor in making a relationship work. Each act of communication requires a delicate balancing act between opposites. Sometimes our anger needs to be expressed with natural verbal force to cathart it; to do less would feel too "civilized," denying our integrity. At other times, blurting out anger serves no purpose because our partner can't hear us that way.

There are certain principles of communication involving constructive versus destructive modes of expressing anger. It is important to distinguish between attacking the person versus addressing their behavior; distinguishing between "I feel" statements and blame, framing the problem as one between two people rather than the other's fault, and each person clearly asking for what they want. (See Appendix.)

This kind of communication can't happen until inner work is done, that is, as long as shadow issues remain. For communication to work the staff of Hermes is needed. In earlier times the staff was the weapon that kept the attacker at the greatest distance, giving the most room to maneuver. When communicating with another, we need to possess the staff of Hermes which gives us the necessary room to explore one's inner workings, and "open the eyes of men." Communication doesn't work unless both partners are willing to enter their inner alchemical vessels. One of Hermes's powers is to "put the guards to sleep," for we can't communicate effectively if walls exist.

With the perplexing problems that come to us in relationship most of us would like to find a formula to follow. We'd like to read a book or take a workshop and learn how to express our anger and other emotions. The path of Hermes is a more difficult one; it stresses flexibility of response, being in the moment and letting the fluidity of the moment produce our words. This is why Hermes doesn't stand for absolute fixed truth; he finds flexible truth by skirting the opposites in a given moment existing on the boundaries between things. Hermetic speech might involve balancing our empathy for the other with our own need for catharsis, awareness of the limitation of how much the other can handle with the knowledge that growth comes from stretching our limits, being strong enough to express ourselves fully while being sensitive to another.

"Am I the best lover you've ever had?" asks a lover. Hermes might reply, "You're incredible, like no other," as he expands upon the beauty that he sees in the gem of this unique being. He uses his winged sandals to fly above the issue of comparison. If the comparison is pushed further, following the path of Hermes, we might help the other to explore their underworld and their issue with comparison, or explore our own issues about it.

The important point is that words and ideas send us on a journey that expands both people's perspectives. This has been called "the hermeneutic circle."[21] Any question or idea may trigger a journey to

173

the underworld to explore an issue emotionally or a flight to "heaven" to explore the issue philosophically. We may realize that both perspectives are valid and thus, a third way of seeing might emerge. Hermes's three-leafed staff helps us proceed on the path of life.

Paradox

The initiate in the Temple of Hermes learns through paradox. The paradoxical nature of psychological life, according to Carl Jung, is due to the fact that the psyche itself is built on a foundation of opposites. Any quality that we identify with inevitably has its opposite, and that opposite is present in our psyche. For instance, if we try to present ourselves as very intelligent, just at that moment a slip of the tongue may happen.

In relationships, we are continually confronted by paradoxes in order to free ourselves from one-sidedness. In this way our boundaries are broadened.

The Paradox of Surrender

When we let go of the way we want things to be, what we seek often comes to us. Dr. Susan Campbell gives the example in her book, *Beyond the Power Struggle*, "The more I tried to get my husband to *want* to make love with me, the more turned off he seemed to get. But when I accepted and appreciated the attention he did give me, instead of concentrating on what I wanted, he 'magically' became more loving."

The Paradox of Avoidance

The more we try to avoid a situation, the more it seems to recur in our lives. This seems to be particularly true of our emotions, and in fact, phobias are often due to "trying to avoid" a fear. Trying not to be anxious about the fear of going to public places increases the phobia. An effective treatment involves letting the person feel the primary fear while in a relaxed state and thereby "systematically desensitize" the fear of fear.[22]

The paradox involved in trying to avoid pain has been known at least since the time of the wedding of Peleus and the goddess Thetis, when one goddess was not invited—Eris, Goddess of Strife and Discord. She avenged herself by attending anyway and threw the

Golden Apple with the inscription "for the fairest" in the midst of all of the goddesses. Paris had to make the fateful decision as to who was the most beautiful.

Whatever we avoid does have a knack of haunting us. When our lover wants us to listen to feelings of depression and we refuse, the depression has a way of remaining stuck and creating disharmony. Often when we listen to our partner, the process of being heard helps ease the depression. Paradoxically however, sometimes it is better to avoid talking about an issue altogether. Delving into a problem area at the wrong time keeps us mired in the muck. One of Heracles's labors illustrates this issue.

> *Theseus, who was a great explorer of labyrinths, went down to the underworld and improperly and impudently asked Hades for his wife Persephone for his friend Peirithous. When Hades asked him to have a seat, he became stuck and could not rise without self-mutilation. He had to remain there for four years while coiled serpents hissed around him. He was lashed by the Furies, and mauled by Cerebus's teeth while Hades looked on smiling. It finally took the strength of Heracles to tear Theseus free from the chair, and even then a great part of his flesh was said to have remained on the rock.*[23]

We must know *when* to go into the underworld of issues in our relationship. There are times when it is not appropriate and we must develop discernment to know the difference.

The Paradox of Transcendence

Discussions are commonplace today of whether or not we can attain the spiritual wisdom to transcend the pain of life. Scott Peck[24] has a paradoxical answer to this question. On one hand the answer is "yes" because as we grow and accept the suffering in life, it ceases in a sense to be suffering. On the other hand, the answer is "no" because the more conscious we are, the more likely we are to suffer.

If, for example, two generals, one very conscious and sensitive and the other not so, must send ten thousand men into battle, the general who has blunted his awareness will probably suffer less. And, as we evolve spiritually, the likelihood is that we will be called upon to serve in ways more painful and more demanding. If our desire is to avoid pain and suffering, seeking higher levels of consciousness is not the way. The greater the pearl, the greater the irritation.

175

The Paradox of Responsibility

Each of us is responsible for our own mental state. Regardless of what our parents did or our partners do, we chose our responses to their actions. A common pitfall is blaming another for our own problems and reactions. We can't evolve while the blaming finger is pointing at another. On the other hand, anyone familiar with childhood psychology literature is aware that children are affected by the ways their parents rear them.[25] Likewise, we are affected by our partner's actions.

For a relationship to work the couple must have two hundred percent responsibility, that is, each person must take one hundred percent responsibility for working on their part of the pattern. Before the couple has passed through the double doors of air initiation, there is "either/or" thinking which involves an emotional (or physical) beating of the other person, or self-flagellation believing "it must be my fault." In the inner sanctum of the Temple of Air, we discover it is a "both/and" world we live in.

The Paradox of Truth

As the "Nasrudin and the Donkey" tale points out, truth cannot be one-sided. When we think we know the truth, inevitably our partner comes riding on a donkey and lets us see the world another way. As the initiate to the Temple of Hermes discovers, "Truth lies on the boundary line between two different points of view." We must embrace the paradox that each person is responsible for themselves while, at the same time, being sensitive to the other. For example, when someone feels moody it may not be enough to withdraw; this is one-sided responsibility. We can imagine the doorway to the Temple of Hermes as a swinging two-way door; it swings inward and outward, acknowledging self and other. A more effective way is to communicate that we feel moody or need distance so that our partner doesn't take it personally.

The two-way door of the Air Temple swings open just far enough so that we can take into account our partner's point of view, but not so far that we "rescue" them. If we decide not to be alone to save our partner from rejection, we deprive them of seeing their own neediness. When the door of our giving is too open, we fall into the Temple of Water (merging) when the Temple of Air is needed.

176

A fundamental problem in many relationships is exactly this: symbiosis is there instead of individuation which requires distance. Parents, as well as people in intimate relationships, often try to rescue their loved ones. They may try to protect them from the "harsh, cruel world" by doting on them. The result is that the person is deprived of an opportunity to grow and develop their own resources.

The Paradox of Aloneness

If one person sacrifices the need for solitude, both will suffer. Ironically, the more we acknowledge our aloneness and accept it, the closer we can be with another. Rilke says it well,

> A good marriage is that in which each appoints the other guardian of his solitude. Once the realization is accepted that between the closest human beings infinite distances continue to exist, a wonderful living side by side can grow. If they succeed in loving the distance between them, it makes it possible for each to see the other whole against a wide sky.

The Paradox of High Expectations

On the one hand, our discriminating function knows that there are differences between people so that not just anyone will do as our mate. But, as evidenced in "The Frog Princess" story, when we let go of our high expectations and jump into the water with another, we will find the one we love.

Robert Ardrey states the problem, "While we pursue the unattainable, we make impossible the realizable."[26] It does seem to be a basic law of human interaction that the more we try to change someone, the more they stay the same, and the more we try to grow the more we destroy that inner stillness from which growth occurs. The famous book of Chinese wisdom, the *Tao Te Ching*, states the *wu-wei* doctrine of non-pushing and non-trying:[27]

> Without stirring abroad, one can know the whole world; Without looking out of the window, one can see the way of heaven. The further one goes, the less one knows. Therefore, the sage knows without having to stir, identifies without having to see, and accomplishes without having to act.

All this is a very delicate matter because we know that the opposite is true as well. Having been raised in the Western tradition, we have experienced how pleasure and a sense of that achievement comes from the hero's quest and "dreaming the impossible dream." Perhaps Hermes stands behind us smiling as we struggle with all of the paradoxes, for he knows that the path itself is discovered when we find the boundary line between opposites.

We could forever find paradoxes in relationship. There is the *paradox of desires* as stated in the *Tao Te Ching*, "Rid yourself of desires to observe their secrets, but always allow yourself to have desires in order to observe their manifestations."[28] There is the *paradox of refusal:* if we allow ourselves the freedom to refuse to do something, that enables us to be more willing to do it. For instance, some of us experience our partner threatening us with the need for a commitment. When we allow ourselves the freedom to refuse, we soon find ourselves more willing to make the commitment.

In most situations, the opposites of the Temple of the Air initiation are present. Whether we call this Hermes's path or the way of the Tao is not as important as finding the path that emerges from the swinging door of this temple.

As in every temple, there are inherent dangers. There's the story about a man who came to a rabbi confused and befuddled because he learned that there were two sides to every issue and he could not find truth. In fact, he couldn't decide whether or not he had a nose because he read in a book on epistemology that our senses couldn't be trusted and that the world was illusion. The rabbi punched the man in the nose and cured him. He now knew he had a nose.

The Path Through Opposites

Finding the way through opposites is a Trial by Air. Jung said the solution was in "the transcendent function."[29] A rather tightly-held woman named Mary illustrates how the transcendent function is found through symbols, and enables us to find our way through irreconcilable opposites. Mary wanted an open-hearted relationship, but felt closed most of the time. She discovered the paradox through therapy that if she accepted her closed heart instead of forcing herself to be open, it would open wider. She saw the symbol of a castle with a drawbridge and realized that she needed to stand at the drawbridge and open and close it when appropriate. (Mary's idea parallels Taoist initiatory practices in which a person opens and closes the chakras through a series of sacred movements.)

Relationships not only open us to the other side of an issue, but to all sides of ourselves. This is why many people test a relationship at the beginning to see if the other will accept their anger, tardiness, sloppiness, or type of humor. We want to be totally ourselves with a partner, our dark side as well as the light.

Opening to Who We Are: In Love and Love-Making

The Trial by Air challenges us to become all things, and to let go and have distance from all things. In this way, like Hermes, we are challenged to play with creation. As in communication where we must find the appropriate balance between opposites, so do we in all aspects of relationship. Discovering our uniqueness requires finding our place between all opposites: strong and vulnerable, energetically expressive and sensitive, independent and enmeshed. Each moment gives us an opportunity to find our place in creation.

The ancient Taoist books apply this transcendent perspective to the realm of sexuality. They show, for instance how in the act of lovemaking, a man can embody various attributes of the natural world. Chinese authors also describe the love act with rich metaphors from the natural world such as galloping steeds, flying seagulls, late spring donkeys, and silkworms spinning a cocoon. Likewise, in the Greek tradition, we hear of Zeus sometimes taking the form of a bull (with Europa) while other times taking the form of a swan (with Leda). When making love today, the air initiate opens to what is needed to restore wholeness at a given moment—whether it is our hearts, lustful fantasies, electricity, or bathing in the light created by union with another.

The initiate of the Trial by Air opens to a wide range of possibilities and realizes that "the sky's the limit." It's natural for each partner to come into a relationship with certain ways of doing things, certain areas of life that have been identified with "who I am." Couples establish a relationship based on these patterns. One person works, the other takes care of the house; one person washes the dishes, and the other vacuums. If a role is split like this, we can explore switching roles to expand our repertoires and bring fresh air into our relationships.

Our boundaries are stretched in even deeper ways in relationship. As we mentioned earlier, we are bound to meet in our partner funda-

179

mental ways of being that "go against our grain." We may wonder if marriages are "made in heaven," and the gods and goddesses are looking down upon us from the lofty heights of Olympus, enjoying the dramas of human relationships.

A shy, withdrawn person lives with a partner who is socially active. A tidy, well-organized person finds a scattered, more fluid partner. The air initiation presents us the opportunity to effectively communicate differences, and to wonder about the magical forces that bring together two people to learn lessons that complement us so perfectly. After spending years in the Temple of Air, the qualities that we initially resisted in our partners may ultimately be seen as valid, and we find them in ourselves. The Kaivalya Upanishads summarizes the goal of the Temple of Air,

> *Seeing the Self in all Beings and all Beings in the Self, the Absolute is Obtained.*

To maintain appreciation for another and for the relationship is an opus indeed. Ancient rituals were meant to counter the human tendency to reify everyday life and forget its sacredness. Rituals that brought the initiate near the doorway to death served this purpose. Various psychedelic drugs were used to break down the relationship to the ordinary world and see it anew.[30] Fasting, still practiced today in traditional religions, gives us an experience of mini-death. After a fast, we eat with a renewed appreciation.

Living with Death

In relationships, death is always close at hand whether we choose to acknowledge it or not. Inevitably, our partner will die or the relationship will end. When we live with the consciousness that death is near, we live our life in a sacred way that makes every moment count, that makes every motion seem as if it was our final one. Sometimes we don't appreciate a relationship until it is over; then we realize how much we love that person. The image prevalent in our culture now due to many reports of "after-death experiences," is that at the end of our life, we may meet our partner and/or a beautiful white light on "the other side" of the tunnel. How sad it is if we don't arrive at the "other side" of life with our partners and share the deep appreciation for another while we're still alive.

The air initiation teaches us to carry this perspective of death in our everyday lives so that heavenly love may, in some measure, be experienced on earth. Our relationships fluctuate between the pains of everyday problems to ecstatic moments of heavenly love. *The Emerald Tablet of Hermes*, the bible of the ancient Egyptian mystery schools, says:[31]

> *It ascends from the earth to the heaven, and descends again*
> *to the earth, and receives the power of the above and the below.*
> *Thus you will have the glory of the whole world.*

Indeed at one moment our relationships seem heavenly, actualizing our dreams, filling us with divine ecstasy. At the next moment, we are confronted with the stark earthly realities, from taking out the garbage to working with what seems like emotional garbage. By seeing each event with our partners as an initiation to find our personal stance and develop our own mythic stories, each issue gives us a chance to formulate where we are in relationship to all those that have come before us and add our own solutions.

---

[1] An excellent discussion and review of the biological and economic dimension of the male-female bond is in Fisher, H. *The Anatomy of Love*. W.W. Norton, 1992. Dupaquier. *Marriage and Remarriage in Populations of the Past*. Academic Press, 1981, in particular has noted the correlation between economic dependence and low divorce rates.

[2] Liz Green and other astrologers feel that the myth of Prometheus best describes the qualities traditionally associated with Aquarius. See *The Astrology of Fate*. Samuel Weiser, York Beach, ME, 1984, p. 250.

[3] This story is retold in the author's words from Shah, I. *Caravan of Dreams*. Penguin Books, 1968, p. 30.

[4] Retold by the author from Tripp, E. *The Meridian Handbook of Classical Mythology*. New American Library, 1970; and Greene, L. op. cit.

[5] Douglas, Nik and Slinger, Penny. *Sexual Secrets: the Alchemy of Ecstasy*. Destiny Books, New York, 1979, p. 31.

[6] Burkert, W. *Greek Religion*. Harvard University Press, 1985, p. 155.

[7] Burkert, W. op. cit. p. 408, fn 2.7-5.

181

[8] Nov. 11, 1988, *The San Francisco Chronicle*. "Controversy over Next Japanese Emperor."

[9] Neumann, E. op. cit.

[10] Mahler, M. *The Psychological Birth of the Human Infant*. Basic Books, New York, 1975.

[11] Masterson, J. *Psychotherapy of the Borderline Adult*. Brunner/Mazel, New York, 1976.

[12] See Campbell, J. *Hero with a Thousand Faces*. Meridian Books, 1949, p. 194, and Eliade, M. *Myth of the Eternal Return*.

[13] In classical mythology Mars was trapped in a net when he had an affair with Hephastus's wife, Aphrodite.

[14] Jou, T.H. *The Tao of Tai Chi Chuan*. Charles Tuttle & Co, p. 9. Chang San Feng was born in A.D. 1247

[15] Edinger. op. cit.

[16] There are a number of books on Astrological Synastry, for instance, Michael Meyers. *The Astrology of Relationship*. Anchor Books, 1976, Liz Green's *Relating*, Weiser, 1983.

[17] Pedraza, R. *Hermes and His Children*. Spring Publications, 1977, p. 4. Also see Kerenyi, C. *The Gods of the Greeks*. Thames and Hudson, 1951, p. 171, where Kerenyi says that this symbol was derived from the early Mysteries of the Kabeiroi.

[18] Graves, R. *The Greek Myths*. Penguin Books, 1955, Vol. 1, p. 64.

[19] Kerenyi, K. *Hermes: Guide of Souls*. Spring Publication, 1976, p. 40.

[20] Peck, M.S. *The Road Less Travelled*. Touchstone, New York, 1978, p. 63.

[21] See Palmer, R. *Hermeneutics*. Northwestern University Press, 1969.

[22] Systematic Desensitization was developed by Joseph Wolpe. For evidence on the use of systematic desensitization's effectivenesss with agoraphobia, see Wilson, G.T. and O' Leary, K. D. *Principles of Behavior Therapy*, Prentice Hall, Englewood Cliffs, 1980.

[23] Graves, R. *The Greek Myths: I*. Penguin Books, 1955, p. 364.

[24] Peck, M.S. op. cit. p. 75.

[25] Miller, A. *Prisoners of Childhood*, 1981; *For Your Own Good*, 1983; and *Thou Shalt Not be Aware*. Farrar, Straus and Giroux, New York, 1984.

[26] Quoted in Watzlawick, P. *Change*. W.W. Norton and Co., New York, 1974, p. 47.

[27] Lau, D.C. *Lao Tzu: Tao Te Ching*. Penguin Books, 1963, p. 108.

[28] Ibid., p. 57.

[29] Jung, C.G. *The Structure and Dynamics of the Psyche*. Vol. 8 *of the Collected Works*: "The Transcendent Function," Princeton University Press, 1960, p. 67-91.

[30] See Fourths, P. *Flesh of the Gods; The Ritual Use of Hallucinogens*. George Allen & Unwin Pub., London, 1972 and Wasson, R.G. *The Road to Eleusis: Unveiling the Secret of the Mysteries*. Harcourt, Brace and Jovanovich, New York, 1978 which hypothesizes that psychedelics were used in the mysteries of Eleusis.

[31] Quoted in Edinger's *Sublimatio*. p. 73.

Section 3:

Finding Our

Own Personal

Myth

CHAPTER 9
CREATING OUR OWN STORIES
TO HEAL OUR RELATIONSHIPS:
THE MYTHIC JOURNEY PROCESS

*We have not even to risk the adventure
alone, for the heroes of all time have
gone before us; the labyrinth is
thoroughly known: we have only to
follow the thread of the hero path.
And where we had thought to find an
abomination, we shall find a god:
where we had thought to slay another,
we shall slay ourselves; where we had
thought to travel outward, we shall
come to the center of our own existence; and where we had thought to be
alone, we shall be with all the world.*[1]

JOSEPH CAMPBELL

Mythology: The Key to Our Psyche's Inner Door

Ancient myths are becoming new resources for the human venture. Joseph Campbell's written works and interviews are giving the study of world mythologies increasing respect. James Hillman, Sam Keen, Robert Bly, and a vast number of Jungian-oriented authors are showing the importance of ancient myths and storytelling to bring soul to modern culture.[2] It seems that we are in an age of mythological renaissance. It is a time when the mythic Sword of Excaliber can rise again . . . a time for reviving the gods and goddesses of Imagination to give meaning to modern life.

Throughout the ages, mythic stories have been passed down describing the deep inner transformations of the psyche. We've seen how these legends can show us oceans of possibilities within us and help us begin that odyssey that will transform our souls. Today, with the many different religious and mythic traditions, we are in a unique position. We are able to set sail and find our own myths on an even larger ocean. We can create our own mythic journeys from all past mythic literature and our imagination.

Our very lives are mythic journeys; and when we depart, it is not our bones that will be left; it is our stories. They are our link to immortality. Yet the importance of stories and myths have not been integrated as a formal part of our education.[3] We are told stories by our parents and teachers, but we are not trained in their deeper mysteries: their ability to soothe the soul, transform, awaken, and heal us. To understand the essence of the healing power of myth, we must first explore its primary ingredient—symbol. A symbol is to a story what a note is to a song. Edward Edinger[4] has pointed out that the early use of the Greek word "symbolon" referred to a stick which was used in a trading agreement. To mark the transfer of ownership of an object from one person to another, a stick was divided in half to symbolize the sale. Just as these sticks were reminders of a greater unity, symbols today help reconnect us with something larger than ourselves.

Everything is part of a greater whole. Just as a lung is part of a human body and its identity must be understood within that whole context, so human beings, in order to fully comprehend our identity, must connect ourselves to a wider whole. The secret of myth's healing power comes from creating a likeness between us and an aspect of the surrounding universe, with nature or the wider whole of which we are a part. This likeness is a particular use of symbol—a metaphor.

In the Mythic Journey Process, we create a likeness between our life situation and a person or situation of ancient times. We make room for the power of imagination to enter through this likeness.

Identifying and Overcoming Our Inner Demons

By facing the particular demons behind our psychological problems we can deal with suffering at its root. Picturing the form of the demon and how we will address it changes confrontation into adventure. The demon may turn out to be the monster of our fear. The giant may be our inertia or suppressed power. By directly facing and dealing with the demon, we can rediscover our lost selves and gain access to the treasure of our inherent nature.

Throughout time, myths recorded the numerous ways that heroes have confronted various demons. Whether it was by attacking, wrestling, or feeding them, each encounter offers us an approach to a present-day demon.

Petrifying Fear:
The Story of Perseus and Medusa

Hearing a story which contains a problem like ours helps us face our demons and feel less alone in our suffering. For example, imagine that our partner continually gets angry when we come home late from work. Perhaps we fear that the relationship is endangered because we need our freedom; or perhaps we feel smothered but are petrified to discuss it because our partner reacts so strongly.

A mythic analogy to this situation is the tale of Medusa. Her face was so horrifying that it had the power to petrify people into stone who looked at it. Reading this story, we can see that we are not dealing with our own personal neurosis, but a wider, universal issue—the petrifying fear of a powerful figure. Instead of feeling alone and isolated, we can feel a link with those ancient heroes who struggled with monstrous embodiments of the same forces with which we are now coping. What once felt like neurotic suffering becomes an adventure as we explore how our problems were dealt with in the mythic past.

We might look into the myth of Medusa and Perseus and wonder, "What in my life could function like *Perseus's shield?*" The shield was given by Athene, goddess of Wisdom, to help Perseus from being turned into stone by reflecting Medusa's image. By looking into the shield instead of looking directly at her face, Perseus was able to approach Medusa and behead her.

We can reflect on our situation through the distance of our own inner shield. Let's imagine that we realized that in the past, we felt petrified of hurting our mother or being rejected by her when she disapproved of and limited our behavior. We gave in to her demands as a child in order to survive. And perhaps we developed a pattern of constantly giving in to others' demands for fear of hurting them or being rejected by them. Metaphorically speaking, we may have turned to stone inside, acceding to the demand, but with a stiff upper lip, resenting the restriction. A pattern may have developed to withdraw in other ways in our relationships.

Seeing our partner's image in the mirrored shield, we might be able to understand. Perhaps our partner was feeling a loss of control in the relationship or wasn't feeling needed or cared about. Reflecting upon what caused the anger rather than reacting to it, we can "behead the monster."

Reflecting in such a way in the midst of seemingly monstrous emotions requires the proper implements. *Perseus was given an adamantine sickle and winged sandals by Hermes, and a helmet of invisibility by Pluto.* When we meet Medusa in our life we must decide what these implements mean. In the above example, perhaps the sword's parrying ability would be useful and its ability to point to the real issue, slice through the mire, and to find the truth of the underlying feelings.

Perseus's sickle was adamantine (made of the hardest stone). Today we know that the hardest stone is diamond; but any stone that is very hard has sustained years of pressure by the earth's forces. If it is a diamond it has become clarified. Perhaps the myth is telling us that we must be patient in regard to the difficult forces in our situation. There is a purpose behind the pressure. . .to create something that is clear and of great value.

The image of this sword tells us that we must combine the qualities of hardness (not being weak about "the hard truth") with the softness of a sickle's curve. On the one hand, we cannot passively cave into our partner's demands, and we must be strong in our assertion that there is more here than meets the eye. But the soft lunar curve must also be present in the discussion. . .reflecting on both partners' underlying issues. A straight-edged sword approach will not do. If we point our sword in a judgmental way, the mythic solution will not be found.

The imagery tells us that at a certain point in exploring our different points of view, *Hermes's winged sandals* might be useful to guide us into the underworld to see our own issues—our feelings of being smothered and our partner's difficulty with feelings of neediness.

Discussing these feelings can give us winged sandals that transport us to the upper regions, as Hermes's sandals transported Greek heroes to that place of compassionate perspective. This takes place only if we are able to keep our ego under the *cap of invisibility*. If we are enraged by our partner's neediness or withdraw in anger, movement will not occur.

In one version of the myth, after Medusa was beheaded, Pegasus emerged and as he ascended, he kicked a mountain top from which sprang one of the fountains of the Muses. Indeed, when two people work through issues such as these, a wellspring of creative energy is released. We may learn to humorously dramatize our issues or be awed by the insight it brings. Love may be reborn.

Remember that Perseus's quest was for Andromeda, his beloved, who was chained to a rocky cliff. Medusa's head and the weapons that he accumulated in his quest were used to free her from the dragon. Often it seems that our beloved is chained to a rocky cliff and that the relationship is tottering on the edge. Ultimately it requires a quest like Perseus's to rescue the feminine in us, that quality of inner reflection rather than the hard rock of rigidity.

Myths record the tests and trials of the human spirit. They are a key to the psyche's secrets, which are brought to life by our imagination. Just as it takes a combination of factors to create a rainbow (light, water, and a person at the proper angle), so do myths provide illumination when we see a story from a particular angle. There is not a correct angle to interpret a story; each angle produces its unique vision that is meaningful to us at a given time.

In the Mythic Journey Process, when we feel lost, we can create our own stories and use the symbols that arise from our inner vision to help us find the way into the cave of our unconscious. Here we can meet the demon, wrestle with it, and find the jewel of our own self.

Focusing and the Mythic Journey Process

The Mythic Journey Process is a way of harnessing the ancient power of myth to work through modern-day problems. It combines elements of the Focusing techinque with archetypal psychology.

Eugene Gendlin is a modern-day hero in the field of psychology who researched the factors in our finding guiding lights in the psychotherapeutic setting. In his study at the University of Chicago,[5]

Dr. Gendlin analyzed tapes of different therapies to discover what factors were present in successful therapy. The focusing process[6] was developed from this research. Gendlin proposed a way to develop our body's felt sense as a guide to new meanings and fresh perspectives on life's problems. The Mythic Journey Process adds to Focusing the richness of symbolic language.

The exercise consists of starting with our bodily felt sense of a chronic physical or psychological problem, and then telling a story about this problem, transposing it into ancient times as we did with Medusa. While the story is being told, we continually refer to the bodily felt sense, noticing how it changes along with the development of the story. We can reach a point where the story begins to tell itself and experience a felt shift and new meaning regarding our problem.

The Mythic Journey Process is a modern-day embodiment of the ancient mythic journey to the underworld. Just as the mythic Greek hero Theseus used Ariadne's thread to find his way into and out of the underworld labyrinth to free the captive children from the monstrous Minotaur, so do we use our bodily felt experience as a thread into and out of our psychological underworld to liberate the energies of our inner experience. The steps of the Focusing process become guideposts along our path.

In Focusing's first step, called "clearing a space," we find a friendly relationship to a life issue by saying, "Everyone has their stuff to deal with and here's mine. If I had a friend, I wouldn't be hard on him for having this to deal with." Since we are often harder on ourselves than we would be on a friend with the same problem, we need to find a relationship to ourselves that is like the relationship that we would have to a friend with a similar problem.

Dr. Gendlin also found that an important factor in successful therapy was a person's ability to use their body's felt sense to create movement in therapy. In the *Focusing* book, Gendlin gives an example of a traditional couple. A wife was home and cleaned the table. A man returned home after getting a job promotion and, in his excitement, knocked the milk onto the table that his wife had just cleaned. The woman became aware of her bodily feeling of anger and began the Focusing process. She *resonated* the word "anger" against the felt bodily sense of the issue surrounding her husband's promotion. She then stopped for a moment and said, "No, that's not quite right. I'm not sure what I felt, but it's not quite anger." For some people this can be a difficult moment, "I don't know what I am feeling."

In Gendlin's Focusing process, we learn to trust an unclear *felt sense* and wait for something to emerge. While staying in touch with the unclear feeling of "a hole in my stomach," the woman above realized, "It's not so much anger, but what's getting me the most is the void I feel about being left behind in my life." At this point she sighed and there was a *felt shift* in the way her body carried the problem.

In the Focusing technique, our bodily felt sense can be used as a guiding light. We can imagine that the woman might be guided to express her feelings to her husband and be comforted, or she might look for a way to develop her life further.

The healing role of the body has long been recognized in mythology. Modern-day students of mythology, however, often fail to give the body due respect. Body feeling and archetypal image are mutually interdependent systems, isomorphic translations of each other into another medium. Without the interweaving of body and myth, healing is not complete.

The insights gained from Gendlin's Focusing technique coupled with mythology can be an important next step in mythic voyages. Many of the subtle elements of the Focusing technique are integrated in the counseling setting; but to delve into these elements in depth goes beyond our scope here.[7]

Prelude to the Mythic Journey Process

The inner journey in the Mythic Journey Process parallels journeys to the underworld that have been spoken of by the earliest healers of the psyche.[8] Shamans and temple priests of the mystery schools have spoken of it as a journey into the body of the earth or into the dark caverns of the unconscious. Myths suggest ways to prevent our getting lost.

A modern person today can use Focusing, in combination with the Mythic Journey Process, one's experience, and felt sense as a thread through the psychological underworld, to liberate the energies of the natural child within.

The Mythic Journey Process starts with a grounding exercise that helps clear a space where we find our center, our inner pillar. Using a Taoist breathing technique, we can experience the Tan T'ien center below the navel. When the breathing meditation is done properly,[9] this center can become a pillar to return to when fear is encountered in one's inner labyrinth.

The Mythic Journey Process

The Mythic Journey Process begins with a breathing meditation combined with Focusing's "clearing a space" step, and an imagery exercise.

> *Notice your out-breath. . .the pause. . .and how the in-breath
> comes naturally from this pause. After a few cycles, notice
> how your body feels different and the way you have settled
> down to be in contact with the ground under you. Are you
> held off the ground in any way? Feel how being with your
> breathing cycle can help you let go to the ground under you,
> so that you're simply here.*

> *If there is any residual tension in your body, just notice it in
> a way that establishes a compassionate, friendly relationship
> to it. If a friend of yours had a similar tension, you'd find room
> to accept him, in spite of the issue. Find this relationship to
> any tension in your body, letting the natural breathing facilitate
> the friendly relationship. During the following process, when
> something arises that you want distance from, just breathe this
> way and return to the relaxed place, your inner pillar.*

> *One way to combine the breathing meditation with search-
> ing for an issue is to imagine that as you breathe out, it's like
> letting go of some of the tension in your body and lowering
> a bucket into the well of your self, deep beneath the surface
> that you may be carrying at this moment. The bucket is tied
> to a secure pillar at the top. As you breathe out and lower it,
> you come to a place where your breath pauses before taking
> in the next breath. As you pause, it's as though the bucket is
> waiting for something deep within to fill it, some issue that
> stands in the way of you feeling alright. As your breath comes
> in, the bucket rises. It may take quite a few out-breaths (low-
> ering of the bucket) until something from deep within you
> comes into your bucket.*

The first step of the Mythic Journey Process consists of the person finding an issue and an associated bodily felt sense of this issue, just
as in the Focusing technique. For some people the body sense comes
first, for others the issue emerges first. If the body sense comes first, do
you know what this body sense connects with in your life? If the issue

arises first, do you feel where this issue lies in your body? You might start by proclaiming, "Everything in my life is completely alright," and noticing what issue(s) arise to contradict this. With each issue that emerges, one establishes a compassionate, friendly relationship to it. Create enough distance so that you can say, "I recognize you're there but I'm not going to work on you right now, maybe I'll come back later." Imagining oneself somewhere else in the room feeling the way you do when you are with this issue is one way to clear a space here.

Give yourself time to notice, as issues pop up, how they affect that subtle barometer, your body. It's from your body's reaction that you'll know which one to choose to work with.

As you approach this "friend" you can get a felt sense[10] of the issue. For further aid in getting the felt sense, sometimes it helps to say, "I could feel completely fine about this whole thing." The voice inside which says, "No I couldn't feel fine about this," is the felt sense.[11] What's this sense all about?

Wait for something to come up from the felt sense. See if you can distinguish between trying to think about it, and just having something come up from the sense itself. It may be a word or an image or a sound . . . whatever comes for you. To get a *handle word/image* for this felt sense of the issue, just wait as if you're a fisherman by an ice hole. You can't rush a fish onto the hook. Just wait for what pops up from your body's sense of the issue as a whole.

What word or image seems to *resonate* with the sense of what this issue is all about? You'll know that you have something that resonates by the response that your body gives . . . the way its movement is facilitated when something gets to the crux of the matter.

What's the *worst thing about this issue* for you? At this point it helps to actually write down the issue on a piece of paper along with the bodily feeling you've noticed. Note bodily feelings in parenthesis:

Issue:

Body sense: ( )

Handle word/ image:

The worst of it:

Then the mythic dimension begins.

The Mythic Dimension

With your issue and the associated bodily felt sense, create a story about a character in ancient times who had the same problem. Begin by writing, "Once upon a time. . ."

First, describe the problem the person is facing in mythic terms, where he/she lives, terrain and surroundings, etc. How did this problem come about? Was it created in a relationship with a young prince or princess' mother and father, the king and queen? Use your own characters and imagery.

A key element is transposing the felt sense of your own obstacle in mythic terms. What created this problem in the character's life? Was a curse or spell put on you? For what reason? By whom? Give an actual face or name to the Demon. Naming or "facing" the specific demon is very important. For example, one client's issue was an intense criticizing that led to attacking his partners. The following story was written at a key point in his long-term therapy. He imaged his "Demon" to be a serrated sword.

> The serrated sword of criticism was given to my father's father many generations ago when he was down and out. He sat on a mountain top praying for power and the ability to support his family when a mountain demon came to him and gave him a serrated sword with a mountain emblazoned upon it. He said that the cuts made with it and the blood on it would proportionally increase the sword's power and would help him ascend the mountains of earthly life to be great, admired, powerful, and respected. He was told to make a family crest of it, and begin practicing with his own family.

> Indeed great power and admiration came to this family of swordsmen and women through the generations. Though wounds occurred and blood was let increasingly, the Sword's power was the key focus of the family. Applause was given at the family dinner table for the great sword-play of the day, whether it was against the bulls killed for dinner or the other swordsmen defeated. Even family wounds were respected if done in a skillful way.

Section Two of the Mythic Dimension describes how impossible it seems to defeat the Demon, and the problems it has caused. What

methods have you tried that haven't worked to defeat it? Transpose
these methods into mythic terms. For example:

> *Although a castle on a mountaintop and much power in the*
> *world came to our royal family through our fine discriminating*
> *cuts, the prince's life was not a happy one. As great a swords-*
> *man as he was, as admired as he was, he was alone most of*
> *the time.*
>
> *The problem was the sword, the very one that had given him*
> *such pleasure in his youth, the one for which he and his family*
> *had been admired for generations. When it was handed down*
> *to him, it went out of control. Each time it would become*
> *unsheathed, it would cut anything he looked at in a discrimi-*
> *nating way. It cut all of his lovers to bits. The prince tried to*
> *break the sword, but many generations of power made it un-*
> *breakable. He tried get rid of it, denounced it, and tried to*
> *bury it; but he felt impotent without it, and had trouble climb-*
> *ing the castle steps if the sword was not in his belt. (slumped*
> *chest, feeling of being defeated)*

Accentuating how impossible it seemed to defeat the demon
brings out the "soulful dimension"[12] and can help prevent Pollyannaish
solutions. Again check back on your body's felt sense and note it in
parentheses here.

Concluding Section Two, make a statement of "what is the specific nature of the impasse." What is the specific obstacle or demon the
character is dealing with? How, specifically, do you feel knowing that
nothing can be done to deal with it? This is "exploring the resistance"
mythically. For example, from the same person's story:

> *The prince felt that he could not give up the way of the sword*
> *for he was too good at it, and it was too much a part of his*
> *nature. Yet, at the same time, he could not live with it. There*
> *seemed to be no end to the loneliness and the guilt that the*
> *prince felt over cutting up his lovers. The Critical Sword*
> *seemed all-powerful.*
>
> *The prince used his discriminating insight to see where the*
> *power of the sword came from. He relaxed and sensed the*
> *presence of the old mountain demon above him. Above him*
> *and to the right he noticed a demon called "Smug-faced Pride."*

197

It added an electric glow to the the sword each time the prince said, "Look at what an adept swordsman I am." Upwards and to the left the prince was able to sense the presence of another demon, "Needy-faced Expectation." It added a desperate, angry, warlike hacking motion to the sword each time the prince said to others, "If you aren't the way I want you to be, I'll cut you up to fit into 'the right' mold."

Section Three begins with writing the words, "Then one day . . ." Then one day, what happened? Let some solution to the impasse come to you. Give it time. If nothing arises in you to break the impasse and no solution comes, then who could deal with this demon? Imagine some heroic figure, animal, or mythic creature and see what happens when it meets your demon. Use your creative story-writing capacity to let the story tell itself. Continuing the above person's story:

Then one day, while the prince was depressed and looking into a mountain lake, he began to reflect upon whether he wanted to be a swordsman if it meant having no love. (Something lets go in my chest area, a sense of openness comes there as I sigh.) At that moment a Maiden of the Lake[13] appeared with the golden sword Excalibur that had been thrown back into these waters many years ago.

Tears came to his eyes as he explained that he could not go on being a swordsman if there was no love in his life, and yet he could not give up his family's path either. He asked for her help.

With compassion the Maiden of the Lake taught him the one movement that the mountain demon had neglected to teach his forefather many years ago. She instructed him to feel with his heart before he was about to use the golden glowing sword, and caress it as if it was a beloved from whom he was asking guidance. Then he was to look at the polished mirror that the sword's metal became, reflect as he was doing in the lake when he met her, and ask for guidance on how to use the sword in the service of love and truth.

As the prince followed her instructions, he noticed that as he held this sword in front of him, a ray of light came from his heart and bounced off the sword. Further, it could be directed by his eyes—only when they were reflecting inward with clear intent. This light, the Maiden of the Lake said, had the ancient power to transform anything that he wanted to heal.

The Maiden said that this was the true power of the sword that had been lost through the ages. She explained that before the sword was used for fighting, it was used for directing energy to points on the body that were in need of healing. She told him stories of how her teachers of the Golden Age used this sword in daytime to bring the healing power of the sun, and at night to bring the powers of the stars to earth. All this was done with the same meditation that she had just given him— through the powers of reflection and the power of the heart's glow.

With the Maiden of the Lake before him, the prince felt his heart's desire to be a healer, and reflected upon the mountain demon above him. A light went to the demon and transformed him into a beneficent mountain spirit whose purpose was to help others to climb to their own heights.

As he reflected on the electric light around "Smug-faced Pride" this conceited demon changed to a healing ally. The smug expression changed to a smile like the Buddha's as he realized that "skill" is not one's own, but is borrowed from the powers of the universe, the stars, the sun, the earth.

As the prince reflected upon "Needy-faced Expectation," he realized that much of the world's and his own suffering came from this demon's misplaced needs. . .for power over others, for false security, ego recognition, and worldly success. With the sword's light on this demon, a new power came to the sword—a compassionate understanding of human foibles. A new form of sword dancing came from this transformed demon which gave the prince's movements a heartfelt, gentle, slicing motion, as when a person cuts a flower for a loved one, and in the cutting wants the flower to suffer as little as possible. As when the sword-masters of ancient times had cut a field of wheat with deep appreciation for the forces of nature that went into producing the growth of the plant, so would the prince try to appreciate that which went into the growth of all that he was to use his sword upon. The prince vowed to make *it his new practice to have tenderness when he used his sword to point out the places that became uncentered in his own and other's everyday life.*

When the prince returned home, he created a new family crest with the Golden Glowing Sword of the Heart over the Critical Serrated Sword. The Maiden of the Lake's sword had the power to stir the prince's compassion. In the future, when the Critical Sword came out, the Maiden's sword was there to help remind the prince that its sharp power was to be put to a healing rather than a destructive use. This was not easy work, but at least now the prince knew what the work of his kingdom was. When the old sword arose, his work was to reflect on it with the heart meditation that he had learned, and thereby bring love and compassionate understanding to the kingdom. (Open-hearted glowing feeling in my chest, and hope through my whole being—a feeling like I've found what my life work is.)

Your story does not have to have a happily-ever-after ending. Simply note your actual sense of the issue and transpose it into mythic terms. Sometimes "time" is an important force to integrate into the story. Remember it took Moses forty years in the desert to complete his destiny. What is the destiny, the purpose for which your character is going through his/her trials and tribulations? Sometimes this dimension of meaning and purpose can contribute to a felt shift.

After you reach a place in the story where it feels complete for the moment, notice your body's felt sense and note it in parentheses at the end of the story.

Bring the adventure of this character back into your own life now. Reflecting on his/her quest, what can you learn form the character's adventure? How does your own path feel different now?

Reflection on the Mythic Journey Process

Many people experience new meaning emerging from their story and note that, at a certain point in writing, they find the story writing itself. Some report that it is as if something was overtaking their writing and giving them a solution. It is unimportant whether one calls this, in ancient Greek terms, a muse, or the person's higher self, right brain function, or intuition. The felt shift that happens and the new meaning and perspective born on a blocked life issue are healing regardless of what one calls the source of healing.

The Desperately-Grabbing Parrot

The significance and healing attributes of a mythic name can be seen with Mary, a woman in her mid-twenties who had therapy for the guilt and desperation she felt "hanging out places" looking for the man of her dreams. She described her disappointments going home each night without a man. She realized that the rejection she felt was similar to what she felt from her single mother who would often abandon her to go out on dates when Mary was young.

In doing her Mythic Journey Process, Mary took her "needy" felt sense and imagined being a huntress in ancient times. Her demon was a "Desperately-Grabbing Parrot" who would try to hold onto desired objects with its weak claws. The grasping claws though, would frighten its prey away. It would chatter, parroting back clichés that it had learned in order to impress, but all the chatter only frightened away all the beautiful, wild creatures of the forest.

> The young princess was originally given the parrot as a present by her mother, the queen, as she abandoned her to go off for greater adventures than could be had with a young child.

(Mary's single mother actually did go out on dates quite often in Mary's formative years, and Mary traced her first memories of this sense of neediness to these times in her early life. She learned to talk incessantly whenever her mother was there, to fill up the silence. She would try to say all the right things, parroting what her mother might like to hear so that her mother might stay there more.)

The curse was that the parrot would emerge out of her needy stomach each time Mary went hunting for someone to love. The parrot drove everyone away. The healing intervention came for her "one day" in her Mythic Journey process in the form of the Greek goddess of the hunt, Artemis, whom she had come across earlier in her reading of mythology.

> One day, when the princess was depressed in the forest because she had not caught anything, Artemis appeared and offered to teach her the secrets of hunting. . .how in primordial times the Master Huntress knew that love was something that came from our connection to the whole world.

As if it was out of classical mythic literature, Mary was describing anima mundi, soulful love of the world. She was expressing, in her own terms, the classical idea that at a certain point in our evolution,

201

we as human beings transposed this anima mundi into anima personalis, a love for one human being, hopeful that this one person could contain her love for the world and universe. A large task indeed!

> *Artemis taught the maiden how to hunt by enjoying all that was around her. If no deer came to her, she could still feel love for all surrounding life, the way light bounced over the meadow, the colors at sunset, and her relaxed position against the tree while she waited. Artemis told her that it was only in modern times, when the cult of true hunting decayed, that hunters would be devastated if they returned home without a deer. In primordial times, through the quality of waiting, the Priestesses of the Temple of Hunting always returned home with something of value. Upon hearing this, the princess' stomach opened and relaxed, and her pet parrot was stilled as never before. (A melting sensation in my stomach.)*

A few months later, Mary related how she sat watching the interesting variation of light shine on the table plants at her favorite local bar. She described a new sense of "life as practice." Though feelings of loneliness still arose, she said that her "hunting" now had a felt sense of adventure to it. A new context emerged, one of practicing the ancient art of "true hunting." She became more aware of her desperate needy chatter and began to practicing being a "Stilled Parrot Who Enjoys the World While Waiting," her new symbolic name.

Many people who do the Mythic Journey Process find a new name for themselves. As it did in ancient initiatory rituals, it offers a new identity for the person. It defines a new path and a new practice in one's life.[14] The new name is much like a Native American's new name in that it is a power which links him or her to a transpersonal purpose, a path to a sacred life and a destiny worth pursuing.

The Mythic Journey Process is a way of responding to those who might ask, "Where are our heroes today? Where are those mythic adventurers who were able to deal with the archetypal demons of their age and open a path for fellow sufferers?"

Perhaps, if we follow Ariadne's thread into our own underworlds, our stories, like hers will be placed in the night sky; they will be like the crown of Ariadne (the Corona Borealis constellation) that Dionysus put there to immortalize her as a guiding light for lost souls to find their way. By opening our mythic imaginations, each of our life stories can become a guiding light for humanity. For who are we but stars in the making, hoping to shed light on the darkness of space and thereby give new life to ourselves, our planet, and to fellow travelers everywhere.

> *The minute I heard my first love story,*
> *I started looking for you,*
> *not knowing how blind that was.*
> *Lovers don't finally meet somewhere*
> *They're in each other all along.*
>
> Rumi

Hear, O Humankind, the prayer of my heart

For are we not one, have we not one desire

to heal our Mother Earth and bind her wounds

to hear again from dark forests and flashing rivers

the varied ever-changing Song of Creation?

O Humankind, are we not all brothers and sisters,

are we not the grandchildren of the Great Mystery?

Do we not all want to love and be loved, to work

and to play, to sing and dance together?

But we live with fear. Fear that is hate,

fear that is mistrust, envy, greed, vanity,

fear that is ambition, competition, aggression,

fear that is loneliness, anger, bitterness, cruelty...

and yet, fear is only twisted love, love turned back on itself,

love that was denied, love that was rejected...

and love...

Love is life—creation, seed and leaf

and blossom and fruit and seed, love is growth

and search and reach and touch and dance.

Love is nurture and succor and feed and pleasure,

love is pleasuring ourselves pleasuring each other,

love is life believing in itself.

And life…

Life is the Sacred Mystery singing to itself,

dancing to its drum, telling tales, improvising, playing,

And we are all that Spirit, our stories all

but one cosmic story that we are love indeed,

that perfect love in me seeks the love in you,

and if our eyes could ever meet without fear

we would recognize each other and rejoice,

for love is life believing in itself.

Manitongquat[15]

---

[1] From the frontpiece to the Association for Transpersonal Psychology's Second East Coast Conference, November 1984.

[2] See Hillman, J. *Revisioning Psychology.* Harper and Row, 1975; Bly, R. *A Little Book on the Human Shadow.* Harper and Row, 1975; Gimbutas, M. *The Goddesses and Gods of Old Europe.* University of California Press, 1982; Von Franz, M.L. *Individuation in Fairytales.* Spring Publications 1982; Salant, N.S. *The Boderline Personality: Vision and Healing.* Chiron Publications, 1989; Krippner, S. & Feinstein, D. *Personal Mythology.* Tarcher Pub., 1988.

[3] For an excellent discussion of "story" to enhance self-awareness see Keen, S. *Telling Your Story.* New American Library, 1973.

4 Edinger, E. *Ego and Archetype*. Putnam, 1972.

5 Gendlin, E. *Focusing Ability in Psychotherapy, Personality and Creativity*. Research in Psychotherapy, Vol. 3, 1968.

6 Gendlin, E. *Focusing*. Bantam Books, 1978.

7 For a more complete discussion of the Focusing process, see Gendlin, E. op. cit.

8 Several references to the journey to the underworld are: Harner, M. *The Way of the Shaman*. Harper and Row, 1980; Eliade, M. *Shamanism*. Princeton University Press, 1972; Halifax, J. *Shaman: The Wounded Healer*. Crossroad Pub., 1982; Meier, C.A. *Ancient Incubation and Modern Psychotherapy*. Northwestern University Press, 1967; Campbell, J. *The Mysteries*. Princeton University Press, 1978.

9 For a more complete understanding of this type of breathing meditation see Huang, W.S. *Fundamentals of Tai Chi Chuan*. American Academy of Chinese Culture, 1973; Yu, L.K. *The Secrets of Chinese Meditation*. Samuel Weiser, 1972; Jou, T.H. *The Tao of Tai Chi Chuan*. Charles Tuttle Pub., 1980.

10 See Gendlin's *Focusing* for a discussion of the distinction between a feeling and "the felt sense." A feeling is clear and well defined whereas the felt sense is an unclear edge around the feeling that contains its wider felt meaning, i.e. what it's "all about." Gendlin gives an example of a woman whose husband spilt some milk after a job promotion. The feeling she had was anger; when she tuned into the felt sense she discovered that she was afraid of being left behind in life. So the felt sense contains the felt meaning, the crux of what life issue is contained within.

11 I learned this particular way of getting in touch with the felt sense from Ann Weiser, one of the district coordinators of Focusing in San Francisco.

12 See Hillman, J. op. cit.

13 The person here was referring to the Maiden of the Lake in the story of King Arthur who helped repair the sword that Arthur broke when he angrily struck Lancelot. She appeared after Arthur repented and lamented that he did not deserve the sword for his violent use of it against such a pure knight.

[14] For more on the healing power of "the name," see Mayer, Michael, Ph. D. *The Mystery of Personal Identity*. ACS Publications, San Diego, 1985.

[15] From Roberts, E. and Amidon, E. *Earth Prayers From Around the World*. Harper San Francisco, 1991.

———————

No one can escape the initiation into the Trials of the Heart.

To become "an adept" is our life's work.

And there is no greater fool than one who proclaims to be Master of
The Realm of Love, for Love is the Master of us all.

Michael Mayer, Ph.D.
The Woodlands of Orinda, 1993

———————

APPENDIX

The Four Step Process for Constructive Expression of Negative Feelings

1. *Express your intent* in communicating your anger. "There's something I want to clear up with you because it's really affecting my feelings about our relationship and I want to clear it up because I care about you." (Fire—raises the intentionality to a higher level, like fire ascending.)

2. A key to the positive intentionality stage of communication is to *distinguish between the whole person and the behavior you don't like.* "I want to make it clear that I love you and care about you deeply, but the mess you leave in front of the closet is really getting to me." (Air—clearly distinguishes between the whole and the parts.)

3. *Express your feelings* as "I feel" statements. "Dealing with this mess is really making me angry. I notice myself walking around feeling resentful for hours after coming into the room and I don't like being this way." In the water stage it's important to distinguish between your feelings and blame ("You are..." statements) or name calling. (Water—expresses the hot and cold of you inner river of experience.)

   A way to get in touch with and deepen "the river of your communication" comes through getting in touch with our body's felt sense. Wait to find what emerges to the question, "What gets me the most about this?" "What gets me the most about the mess there, is that it makes me feel out of control. It makes me feel scattered, like the way I am when I'm messy. And just like I'm impatient with my own scatteredness I get that way with yours. I guess I have to admit that I have a hard time with not having my own way, and it scares me to reflect upon whether I'll ever be able to make it long term in a relationship because of my issues with this kind of thing."

4. *Ask for what you want.* Frame the issue as a problem that the two of you have. "I wonder how we can work this whole thing out. I'd like us to be able to find a solution to this together because I'm at the point of tearing my hair out. Are you willing to try to find a way that we can work this issue out together?" This is the bargaining phase. (Earth—finding practical solutions to the problem.)

INDEX

A

"After-death experiences," 180
Abandonment depression, 166
Abusive behavior, 76, 142-43
    setting boundaries on, in intimate
      relationships, 45-47
Actaeon and Artemis, myth of, 143
Acupuncture/acupressure,
  66, 114, 115
Aesculapius, 71, 72, 114, 115
Agamemnon, 141
AIDS, 4
    and cosmic synchronicity, 9-10
Air, as element of soul, 27, 66
Air, Temple of, 66. *See also* Perspective
Air, Trial by, 158-81
Alchemical concepts, 73-74, 75, 133, 165
    calcinatio process, 73
    coagulatio process, 73
    extractio process, 84, 169
    golden ball of light, 109, 111
    mortificatio process, 138
    separatio process, 165
    solutio process, 73, 133, 138
    sublimatio process, 73, 159
    trial of fire, 95-96
Alimony payments, 144-45
Aloneness, paradox of, 177
Anatomy of Love, The (Fisher), 101
Androgeny, 163
Androgyne, Plato's image of, 53-54
Anger
    containing, 73, 172
    expressing, 172, 173, 210
    four step process for constructive expression
      of, 210
Anima, 110
    integration of, by men, 160-64
Anima mundi, 201-2
Anima personalis, 202
Animus, integration of, by women, 160-64
Anti Co-dependency Temple, 20, 91

Aphrodite, 21, 30, 35-36, 163
Apollo, 171
Apuleius, 32
Aquarian Age, 158
Arab mystical poetry, 149
Archetypal forces, and relationships, 131-32
Archetypal psychology, and Focusing technique,
    in Mythic Journey Process, 191-93
Ardrey, Robert, 177
Ariadne, role of, 59, 202
Ariadne's thread, myth of, 54-55, 56
Aries, 38, 76
Artemis, 21
Ashes, as symbol, 82-83
Astrological signs, 9, 38, 170
Astrology, 131-32
    chart synasty in, 170
    metaphors of, 116
    and relationships, 8-11
    and synchronicity, 9
    zodiacal ages, 38
    zodiacal signs of relationship, 9
Athene, 189
Avoidance, paradox of, 174-75
"Awakened heart," developing, 80-81

B

Back to the Future (film), 55-56
Balancing of opposites, 171-79
    catharsis and empathy, 172, 173
    love and power, 77-78
    merging and separation, 138, 167-68
    truth and untruth, 171-74
Barring, Anne, 139-40
Batten, Mary, 128
Being in the moment, 73
Beyond the Power Struggle (Campbell), 174
Blame/blaming, 56-58, 176
    externalizing through scapegoating, 57
    in intimate relationships, 56-58
    parallel processing, in therapy, 57-58
Bly, Robert, 77, 82-83, 108, 116, 119, 120, 188

Cronos, myth of, 20, 166-67. *See also* Boundaries

Cross-cultural metaphors, 52-60

Crystals, symbolism of, 41

Culture, materialistic, and relationships 102

Cybele and Attis, myth of, 141

D

Dark side of self, hiding, 33-34. *See also* Demons, inner; Underworld *headings*

Death, 9
  initiatory rites and, 150
  living with consciousness of, 180-81
  and love, connection between, 138-39, 149-51
  and suffering, 150

Deception, acquiring love through, 87

Deification, connection with universal meaning through, 18

Deimos, 36

Deities
  creating own, method of, 19

Demeter, 11, 12, 27, 147

Demons, inner, 85, 189. *See also* Underworld *headings*

Desires, paradox of, 178

Destinies, sculpting own, 21, 89-90, 104, 107

Dionysus, 22, 144

Disidentification, 163, 171

Dismemberment, 139-46
  economic, 144-45
  psychological, 145-46

Dissolution
  alchemists on, 133
  of ego boundaries, in love, 128, 131, 148
  of personality structure, spiritual quest for, 133

Distance, psychological, 179
  and individuation, 177

Divorce rate, 4, 6
  peak, time of, 103

Dream incubation, 80, 107-8

Dreams, 80

Drugs, psychedelic, 180

Dumuzi, 141

E

Eagle
  perspective of, 10, 40-41, 53, 163
  symbolism of, 40-41

Earth, as element, 27, 66

Earth, Temple of, 66

Earth, Trial by, 100-22
  Iron Hans story as symbolic of, 110

Earth initiation
  aim of, 100
  importance of, to child's relationships, 118
  tale of Malik Dinar and, 106-7

Earthly Desires, Temple of, 18, 19

Edinger, Edward, 188

Egalitarian relationship between sexes, 113

Ego boundaries
  expanded, in relationships, 148, 174, 179-80
  dissolution of, in love, 128, 131, 148

Egyptians
  initiation rites of, 67, 150
  mystery school, 181

Eisler, R., 113

"Either/or" attitude, 176
  transcending, 160-64

Elemental osmosis, 66

Elements
  symbolic meanings of, 66
  trial by, 66-67
  understanding of, in healing practices, 66

Eliade, Mircea, 11-12, 18, 75

Eliot, T. S., 165

Emerald Tablet of Hermes, The, 181

Empathy, 47-48, 58
  versus catharsis, balancing needs for, 172, 173

Empowerment, male, 110

Enantiodromia, 161

Ending relationships, considerations in, 79-80

Endorphins, 101

Energy of life, 73-75. *See also* Chi
  finding key to, 111
  love and, 73
  tale of golden ball of, 108-16
Enmeshment, 167
Entitlement, feeling of, 84
Epimetheus, 89
Equinox
  fall, 9, 12
  spring, 12
Eris, 21, 174-75
Eros. *See also* Eros and Psyche, myth of
  image of, 31
  origin of, 30
  powers of, 31-32
Eros and Psyche, myth of, 31-45
  ant symbolism in, 38
  Psyche's first task, 36
  Psyche's second task, 36, 38-40
  Psyche's third task, 36-37, 40-42
  Psyche's fourth task, 37, 42-45
  seed and grain metaphor in, 37
Erotic love, 30. *See also* Eros
  Aphrodite and, 35-36
  defined, 30
  and fire, 70
  myth of origin of, 30
  nature of, 31
Everyday life, hidden treasures of, 107
Evolution, 158
  emotional, 60
Excesses, cleansing of, 88
Expectations
  high, paradox of, 177-78
  unrealistic, 17
Experience, learning by, 106
Exploring the resistance, 168-69
Extractio process, 84, 169
Extraction of meaning, 169-70

F

Fairy tales, 16, 46. *See also* Iron Hans, tale of
Fall equinox, 9, 12

Family mythology, 107
Fantasies, getting caught in, 71-73
Farmer archetype, 103
Fasting, 180
Father-principle. *See* Senex
Father-son relationship, 119-20
  and industrialization, 77, 110
Fears, own, reflection of in myths, 189-191
Feelings
  communication of, 176
  empathizing with, 47-48
  own, finding, 147-49
  relating, 92
  sharing, 59, 60
  resistance to exploring, 168-69
Felt sense. *See* Bodily felt sense
Felt shift, 73, 147
  and new meaning and perspective, 192, 193
Fire, 27, 66
  and love, 70
  as metaphor, 75-76
Fire, Temple of, 66, 78
Fire, Trial by, 70-96
Fisher, Helen, 101, 103-4
Flexibility, 146-47
Focusing, 73, 147
  and Mythic Journey Process, 191-93
Focusing (Gendlin), 192
Four Quartets (Eliot), 165
Frazer, James, 140
Froebenius, 140
Frog King, tale of, 109
Frog Princess, story of, 177
  fear of merging expressed in, 135-36
Future, altering, 56
Future Shock (Toffler), 6

G

Gemini, 171
Gendlin, Eugene, 73, 147, 191-93
Genes, contrasexual, 160

initiation of, into womanhood, 36
Temple of, 26, 27
Psyche (soul), 26. *See also* Soul
moth/butterfly as symbol of, 26-27
Psyche, Temple of, 26, 27
Psychotherapists, 42-43, 59, 79
Psychotherapy
couple's therapy, 46, 57-60, 134-35
re-activation of past in, 56
successful, factors in, 192
Puer aeternus. *See* Youth, eternal

R

Rapprochement crisis, 165-66
Rebirth
Jonah and Whale as metaphor for, 150
in relationships, 83
setting boundaries and, 55
Reflection, 26, 169
Epimetheus as symbolic of, 89
mythology as tool in, 190, 191
self-, 90, 120
Refusal, paradox of, 178
Regression to earlier stage of personality
development, 87, 133-35
Reification, 164-64
countering of, through ritual, 180
Relationships, intimate
abusive behavior in, 45-47
and astrological synchronicity, 9-10
blaming in, 56-58
changing patterns of, 5-8
compassion in, 45
conceptualizing, in terms of different temples,
18-23
in culture of today, 4-8
emotional support in, 38
ending, considerations in, 79-80
entering, 82
healing, 113-15
and humbleness, 38
as initiation rite, 4-13
and quest for Grail as symbol for object of,
16-18
lack of permanence in, 6

as learning process, 23
meeting dark forces in, 43-44, 46-47
movement of planets in relation to, 8-11
negativity in, 47-48
over-choice in, 6
pain in, 33-34
personal choice in, 6, 7-8
priorities in, 37
purposes served by, 17-18, 26
quest for, 80-81
questioning purpose served by, 16-18
as reflection of socio-cultural environment,
5-8
regression to earlier stage of personality
development in, 133-35
Scorpio and, 9
suffering in, 4-5
symbolic importance of small details in, 37
timing in, 39
toxic, 79
unconscious beliefs in, 44
underworld emotions in, 40
variety and forms of, 8
wounding in, 45-48
Repression, cultural, 122
Resacralizing life, through resacralizing language,
18
Rescuing pattern, 88, 95, 177
Resistance
exploring, 168
to falling in love, 132
Responsibility for own mental state, paradox of,
176
Rhea, 20
Rituals. *See also* Initiation rites
in love-making, 94
purpose of, 180
Ritual sacrifice, 139-42
lack of, and rage at dismemberment, 145
of males, 141-43
Road Less Traveled, The (Peck), 172
Role reversals, 163
Romantic love, 29-30. *See also* Love;
Relationships, intimate
beginning of, 129
and fire, 70